SEASONS
OF SUN & RAIN

Seasons of Sun & Rain

Marjorie Dorner

MILKWEED EDITIONS

© 1999, Text by Marjorie Dorner
(800) 520-6455 / www.milkweed.org / www.worldashome.org

Cloth edition published 1999 by Milkweed Editions
Printed in the United States of America
Cover design by redletterdesign.com
Cover photo by Jay Steinke
Interior design by Donna Burch
The text of this book is set in New Baskerville
00 01 02 03 04   5 4 3 2 1
First Paperback Edition

Lyrics from the following songs are reprinted with permission in *Seasons of Sun and Rain:*
"Hot Fun in the Summertime" by Sylvester Stewart. Copyright © 1969 (renewed) by Mijac Music and Stone Flower Music. All rights administered by Warner-Tamerlane Publishing Corp. All rights reserved. Used by permission. Warner Bros. Publications U.S. Inc., Miami, Florida 33014. "Puff (The Magic Dragon)" by Peter Yarrow and Leonard Lipton. Copyright © 1963 by Pepamar Music Corp. Copyright renewed, assigned to Silver Dawn Music and Honalee Melodies. All rights reserved. Used by permission. Warner Bros. Publications U.S. Inc., Miami, Florida 33014.

Milkweed Editions, a nonprofit publisher, gratefully acknowledges support from the Elmer L. and Eleanor J. Andersen Foundation; James Ford Bell Foundation; Bush Foundation; General Mills Foundation; Honeywell Foundation; Jerome Foundation; McKnight Foundation; Minnesota State Arts Board through an appropriation by the Minnesota State Legislature; Norwest Foundation on behalf of Norwest Bank Minnesota; Lawrence and Elizabeth Ann O'Shaughnessy Charitable Income Trust in honor of Lawrence M. O'Shaughnessy; Oswald Family Foundation; Ritz Foundation on behalf of Mr. and Mrs. E. J. Phelps Jr.; John and Beverly Rollwagen Fund of the Minneapolis Foundation; St. Paul Companies, Inc.; Star Tribune Foundation; Target Foundation on behalf of Dayton's, Mervyn's California and Target Stores; U.S. Bancorp Piper Jaffray Foundation on behalf of U.S. Bancorp Piper Jaffray; and generous individuals.

Library of Congress Cataloging-in-Publication Data
Dorner, Marjorie.
    Seasons of sun and rain / Marjorie Dorner. — 1st ed.
      p. cm.
    ISBN 1-57131-027-4 (cloth), 1-57131-033-9 (paperback)
    I. Title.
PS3554.0677S4 1999
813'.54—dc21   98-50092
                                                                                          CIP

This book is printed on acid-free paper.

For the women of Camp M,
especially Judy Wochos Leiterman,
whose gallantry inspires us all.

For information about North Shore places and backgrounds, I am indebted to Shawn Perich's *The North Shore: A Four-Season Guide to Minnesota's Favorite Destination* (Pfeifer-Hamilton, 1992). For information about the Witch Tree and the Anishinabe legends about it, I am indebted to *Witch Tree: A Collaboration* by Joanne Hart and Hazel Belvo (Holy Cow! Press, 1992).

Thanks to Ginny, Pat, Alexi, Marilyn, Judy J., Barbara, Sarah, and Mary who gave me more inspiration for this project than they can know. And to Scott and Mary for putting up with us all.

SEASONS
OF SUN & RAIN

Prologue

The notes marched in a jagged line across the vanity mirror, cream-colored rectangles stuck to the glass at about eye level. At the top of each one, dark lettering proclaimed, "From the Desk of Professor Shaw." She still thought that was rather pretentious—she would have chosen "From the Desk of Micky Shaw"—but the children had given her the notepads one Mother's Day, so she felt attached to them, determined to use them up even though she no longer worked for the university.

Standing between the bed and the mirror, she turned back and forth from the notes to the stacks of folded clothes arranged along the edges of the thick comforter: "jeans and sweatshirts, in case of cold" one of the notes said, and there were the stacks near the pillows; "nightgowns—one warm" a second note said, and there was the flannel gown with the violets on it underneath two sleeveless, light cotton gowns. Did she need three nightgowns for a six-day vacation? Would everything fit into the two cases that yawned open in the center of the big bed?

"Need any help?" The voice from the doorway behind her made her jump a little. Before she turned around, she consciously erased the frown of concentration she knew must be creasing her forehead, replaced the expression with a smile.

"No, I've got it pretty much under control, I think," she answered.

Her husband's lean body was draped against the door frame in a pose he must have meant to seem casual, but she could see the tension in his shoulders.

"Have you got bug spray?" he asked, his gaze not quite meeting hers. "You know the mosquitoes up there are the size of hummingbirds."

When had he got so gray? Wasn't it just yesterday that his wonderful, thick hair was almost black? Maybe it was true that you could go gray overnight from shock or trauma.

She turned back to the bed with a flicker of irritation threatening to erase her smile.

"Yes, I've got the bug spray," she told him. "And the rain gear and the—" Her eyes flicked to the row of notes—"the hiking boots."

"Okay," he said, and she could hear the slightly wounded tone. "I'll get out of your way."

"No," she said quickly, turning back to him. "I want you to stay." It wasn't a fib. These days, she wanted him near her all the time, in the same room where she could raise her eyes and find him whenever she felt the first tremor of panic. But sometimes—like just now—he distracted her when she needed to focus on what she was doing.

He looked straight at her finally and came into the room, stopping near her side.

"It'll be fun for you," he said, almost as if he were answering some objection she had made. "Seeing them all again. And this year Lindy's coming too. You haven't seen her since Jan's birthday party. Lots of catching up to do."

"I know," she said, and she could hear the peevish tone in her own voice. "I'm looking forward to it. I told you that this morning."

She could tell from his expression that it hadn't been this morning; the muscles around his eyes tightened up slightly whenever she made any little mistake like that. She glanced away from his face, looked again at the clothes, the row of notes. She would have to start over.

"It takes so long," she murmured, a little surprised that she'd said it out loud.

"What does?" he asked.

"The trip," she lied. "It's a long way to Grand Marais."

He took her by the shoulders, turned her back to him.

"Listen to me, Micky," he said. "You don't have to go if you don't want to. It's not too late to change your mind, you know."

"Of course I know that," she said, irritation boiling up again. "I don't *have* to do anything."

This was new, too, this "Listen to me" stuff, making her look at him when he spoke, the intent lowering of his face to hers, as if there were no other way to guarantee that she would pay attention to him. Once they had communicated in an efficient semaphore, quick flashes of words spoken on the run, sometimes only a glance, each of them confident that the other was picking up and decoding the signals that made their busy lives run smoothly.

"You listen to me, Peter," she said, more kindly now. "I *do* want to go on this trip. And I'll be fine. You know I will."

"Okay," he said with a little smile. "I hope *I'll* be fine for a whole week without you."

"Don't be silly," she said, reaching her slim hands out to his sides. "Matthew will come home while I'm gone, and you two can get in some male bonding, take in a Twins' game, rent some movies where heavily armed men with crew cuts blast aliens back into space."

"That doesn't have nearly as much charm as we men

would like you to think," he said, chuckling softly. "We only enjoy that stuff when you women are around to object. When you're out of town, we sneak off to the opera and go shopping at Crate and Barrel."

"That's something I'd like to see," she said, sliding her arms around his waist. "Come on, good-looking. Let's just throw all this stuff into suitcases, so we can use this great big bed for something else besides a shelf."

"Why, Mrs. Shaw," he murmured against her left ear. "I do believe you're trying to seduce me."

"What a clever fellow you are, Dr. Shaw," she whispered, her lips fluttering against the soft skin of his throat. "I think you should have something nice to think about while I'm gone."

When she pulled back to look up into his face, she recognized the familiar expression: the softening of his mouth, the flicker of desire in his eyes. Yes, this was much better; this was the face she wanted to remember on cool nights in Grand Marais.

1 / Linda

Wild lupine and evening primrose leaned out of the woods toward the strip of sunlight made possible by the narrow road, their purple and yellow blossoms almost touching the two cars, which were bumping slowly downhill after leaving the paved surface of the Gunflint Trail. The graveled road was pocked by small pools of standing water, the ravages of a wet spring and a still-wetter early summer.

The three women in the lead car had been silent for a while when one of them, Peg Brunner, finally spoke, her voice a little too loud with the forced cheerfulness that women use to signal a new beginning after an incident of social awkwardness.

"This year we have to go up to Hat Point to see the Witch Tree," she said. "We keep saying we're going to do it, but we never do."

"You're right. It's time we did." This from Jan Werden who spoke without taking her eyes off the road, her hands gripping the wheel. The grim set of her jaw seemed to signal that further conversation would have to wait until she'd led the two-car parade to safety at the bottom of the hill.

Alone in the backseat, Linda Tourneau held her peace for a few more seconds and then addressed the inevitable question to Peg.

"What's the Witch Tree?"

Peg turned in the shoulder harness, treating Linda to one of her dimpled smiles. Her eyes signaled her relief at this return to normal conversation.

"It's a cedar tree that clings to the rocks right at the edge of Lake Superior," she explained. "The local Indians think of it as sacred or magic, I guess. Anyway, it's become quite a tourist attraction."

"Oh," Linda said, bracing herself against the bags that filled the rest of the backseat as the car lurched around another pothole. The cases contained her own camera equipment, which wouldn't fit into the trunk once the suitcases had been loaded inside. Linda sighed and glanced out the back window at the Mazda bouncing along behind them. She could expect a lot of exchanges like the one about the tree, she supposed. The others would talk about places, objects, and events they had shared in this location, and she would be shut out unless she was constantly asking for explanations. She was the only first-timer among the six of them.

Last summer, the other five women had managed to sort out the complications of their lives enough to bring off a weeklong get together. Leaving behind husbands, children, and jobs, they had filled all the rooms of the Sawtooth Bed and Breakfast. Only Linda had been unable to make it, explaining that her fall exhibition in New York made it necessary for her to work straight through the summer. So she would inevitably feel on the outside whenever anyone said, "Remember last year when . . ."

That might have been enough by itself to make Linda feel "out of it," but now, it seemed, she had caused a sort of incident by speaking her mind, had brought on that earlier silence in the car. She felt sore, wounded about it because she'd had no intention of producing such an effect—had spoken in the old confidence that these were people before whom she would need no pretense, no tailoring of her opinions to please or appease.

They had been discussing Micky's condition ever since the brief stop in Two Harbors, where Micky had said she would ride the rest of the way in Sharon's Mazda, and Jan had switched places with her and volunteered to drive Peg's Lumina. It was the first time since leaving her Chicago home that Linda had had the chance to talk to Jan outside Micky's hearing, to question the one person among them who had the most information. Last night they had all rendezvoused at Jan and Mike's house on the St. Croix River, but the customary euphoria of reunion, eating and drinking, deciding where everyone would bed down for the night, had precluded serious conversation. And they were all keenly aware of what Jan had written to them in the note she'd sent just a week ago to confirm last-minute details: "Micky knows that all of you know. She knows you love and support her. But while we're in Grand Marais, she doesn't want to talk about it."

As the miles slipped away from Two Harbors to Silver Bay to Little Marais, Jan talked in a strangely detached voice about symptoms and prognosis. Peg cried softly almost from the first words, but Linda had felt a diffused sort of anger, the outrage she always experienced in the presence of injustice or waste, aching for a concrete target against which she might vent her frustration. If only there were somebody to punch out! But all she could do was listen in silence as the words fell like blows. She watched the passing shoreline, noticing how the sunlight played across the choppy water, glanced off the pale hulls of sport boats cutting along near the beach. Finally the awful details came to an end, and there was a moment of silence. Even Peg's weeping stilled.

"If it were me, I'd kill myself," Linda said at last. "I would save up whatever pills I could lay my hands on, and then I'd write a few notes and swallow the lot."

"Oh, Lindy," Peg breathed, swiveling in her seat. "Don't say such things. Micky wouldn't do something like that."

"I'm just saying what I'd do," Linda said. "And if I couldn't manage it on my own, I hope my friends would help me."

"You say that so easily," Jan said, her tone suddenly harsh. "But you don't know what the hell you're talking about." Her voice vibrated with anger.

And then the silence had fallen. To Linda, Jan's reaction had seemed inappropriate, too much for the provocation. In fact, Linda didn't think her remarks had been at all provoking. And it wasn't like Jan to flare like that; she was ordinarily the mediator, the calmest one among them.

The car rounded a sharp curve and the road leveled. A clearing in the woods opened before them, revealing a graveled lot flanked on all sides by the pine and birch trees that typified this northern forest. Linda leaned forward to look. The building at the far edge of the clearing was a two-story lodge with natural pine siding; to its right, open decks at the ground level and second floors were connected by rustic stairs. To the left, the wide front door looked out toward a picnic table and low, rough-hewn benches. Shadows of the birch trees fell across the shallow lawn, reached fingers up toward the second story. As the two cars pulled into the spaces next to a dusty red Trooper, an Airedale of impressive size came bounding around the house, his barking sharp and urgent.

"Here we are," Jan said, switching off the ignition. "Welcome to Camp Men-O-Pause, Lindy." She didn't turn around as she spoke, but Linda could hear the apologetic tone, the intent to lighten the mood.

"It looks like a wonderful place," Linda offered, eager to

make peace, smiling a little as she heard again this name her friends had created last year for their retreat into the woods.

"It is," Jan said, turning now with her old smile. "I know you're going to love it the way we all do. Don't worry about the dog. He's a pussycat."

They threw open the doors and stepped out into a slight breeze; Linda could feel at once that the temperature was much cooler than it had been that morning on the St. Croix. Lake Superior was a huge natural air conditioner and they were near enough to it even now, some five miles up the Gunflint Trail from the shore, to enjoy its effects. The first person out of the Mazda next to them was Sharon Kazmerinski.

"Jesus!" she exclaimed, lifting her hands at the road they had just descended. "That's no better than a cow path. At least the stuff in the potholes is water instead of cow piss." Then she flashed a grin in their direction. "Maybe it's moose piss. Would moose piss take the finish off my car? What do you think?" Before anyone could answer, Sharon bent to the Airedale, which had run straight up to her. "Well, hello there, Duncan," she cried, offering her hands for the big dog to sniff. "I think you're even bigger than last year. What the hell are they feeding you?"

Whenever she saw Sharon, it struck Linda anew that Sharon had undergone the least physical change since they had all graduated from St. Augustine College in 1968. Tall, angular, and rawboned, she still moved with the headlong energy that had propelled her through the corridors of Boyce Hall. Her pale skin was still drawn tight over raked cheekbones, and her short, fluffy hair was still the same shade of blond-gone-brown it had been when they were in college. Linda suspected that Sharon didn't have to resort to the potions she herself applied to cover the gray patches that were fast becoming gray thickets.

The Mazda's second occupant emerged from the back seat. This short, plump woman with the gray streaks in her ponytail had had so many names over the years that Linda always had to pause a second to think before she addressed her. In college she had been Mimi Cavallo, a tiny sylph of a girl with a musical voice and a perpetual twinkle in her dark eyes. But she seemed to change her name every time she made any other change in her life. Now she was just plain Mary Morgan, but Linda was relieved to note that the twinkle remained the same.

Micky was the last to get out of the car. Linda caught herself looking away—she'd been doing that a lot since last evening whenever Micky was near her. Now with a guilty twitch, she forced herself to refocus on the woman standing slowly up into the bright afternoon sunshine. Michelle Marie Jaeger Shaw had never been called anything except Micky—not that anyone could remember anyway. A slim, natural blonde, she had missed being a genuine great beauty by only the half inch of her overbite. Even so, Micky Jaeger's power owed little to her looks. "There's something about Micky," people always said when they were trying to explain why they would have followed her into tempest or fire.

Linda couldn't help thinking that she looked smaller somehow. Her once shoulder-length hair was cropped close to her head and so looked more light brown than blond. Everything about her body seemed to have gone just a little slack; she didn't look frail, just not "fit" anymore. Once, after hugging her in greeting last night, Linda had looked straight into her face and had felt a tremor of shock. The once-familiar features seemed to have shifted slightly; the flesh around the eyes had flattened, dragging outer corners downward. Linda had the creepy feeling that she was looking not at Micky, but at some less alert, coarser-featured twin or clone.

Later, when she was trying to sleep on the futon bed she was sharing with Mary in Jan and Mike's family room, Linda could not stop herself from remembering in detail the visit Jan had paid to her in October. Jan had called her from the Palmer House where she was attending a conference for clinical psychologists and had asked if she could just drop by for a while. "I have something I need to tell you in person," she'd said cryptically.

"I'm afraid I don't bring good news from Minnesota," she said over a glass of wine in Linda's sprawling living room. "It's about Micky."

Linda could feel a frisson of alarm. "Cancer?" she breathed, producing at once the terror that headed the list for women their age.

"No," Jan said softly, staring down into her glass. "Worse."

"What could be worse?"

"Alzheimer's. She has early-onset Alzheimer's."

Linda sat listening to the word, repeated twice, but she could not connect it somehow with anything. Of course, she knew the word, knew what it meant, but the context seemed to make it impossibly inappropriate. Jan might have been announcing the name of some newly imported beer that Micky had decided to try. Then Linda's mind turned over, made the link.

"No," she said, her voice sharp, dismissive. "That can't be true."

"I'm afraid it is," Jan said. "The neurologists at Mayo are ninety-nine percent certain. Apparently she's had it for a long time, longer than she let on to us, but they only had the MRI and other tests done last month. Peter made her go, finally."

"Oh, shit," Linda kept saying softly all the while Jan was speaking. "Shit, shit, shit." Finally when Jan fell silent, she said, "She just turned fifty."

"Alzheimer's is rare in somebody this young," Jan said, nodding. "And even then, you have to factor in that she's been covering the symptoms for years now. They might have begun in her mid-forties. And what's so strange is that there's no other case of it on either side of her family. You remember how she used to talk about her grandparents. They lived into their eighties and were pretty sharp until the end. Peter says the doctors are just baffled as to a cause."

Linda was still too numb from shock to keep up with Jan's stream of words. "Covering symptoms for years?" she echoed. "What do you mean by that? I talked with her for a long time at your birthday party, and she seemed just fine." That party the previous June had been Linda's last in-person contact with Micky.

"Sure she seemed fine. That's what I mean by 'covering.' She was in denial. You must have noticed something in the round-robin letter. Her entries have been getting shorter and more disorganized in the past few years. Her handwriting doesn't even look the same anymore."

"I suppose," Linda murmured. "But I thought that was because she was so busy with her program. And she never was very organized, was she? Are you saying you knew, or guessed, from that?"

"No, but I was worried about other things. She'd already begun with the Post-it notes by then." In answer to Linda's blank stare, Jan went on, "She stuck Post-it notes up all over her house and office just to keep herself on track, and sometimes she'd forget to take them down and would do things twice. She tried to joke about it, said she was becoming the national poster child for absentminded professors. When Peter expressed concern, she just snapped at him."

"But Peter's a doctor," Linda exclaimed. "Why didn't he insist on some tests?" She couldn't shake her outrage, couldn't abandon the irrational conviction that if only something had been done in time, Micky wouldn't have this disease.

"Well, he's not that kind of doctor," Jan sighed. "And you know what it's like trying to insist on anything with Micky. But then she took that unpaid leave last year—to do research, she said—but he could see that she wasn't doing any research at all. And there were lots more Post-its by then. This summer, he went around the kitchen and read them. They were lists of what was *in* each cupboard."

"Oh, God," Linda moaned. "Oh, my God." She knew that Micky and Peter had lived in that house for over twelve years, ever since Peter had gone to work at the Mayo Clinic, and Micky had taken on the directorship of the social-work program at a nearby state university.

"Of course, Peter made her go in then," Jan went on. "The tests took four days. She fought the diagnosis for two weeks, Peter said—just refused to discuss it. Then one morning, she came down for breakfast and asked if there were any research programs into Alzheimer's at the clinic. When he said yes, she said, 'Tell them they have a new guinea pig.'"

For the first time, Linda could feel tears stinging her eyes. That was vintage Micky.

"And then she wrote a letter of resignation to her university so they could appoint a new director before the school year got under way."

By this time, Linda had buried her face in her hands, palms against her mouth to stifle her sobs. Now in this cool, sunny clearing, she watched as Micky approached the big dog, a smile on her face, her slim hands already reaching out before her in greeting.

"Here's Steve," Peg said, and Linda turned toward the house. The front door was standing ajar and a tall, lean man was walking toward them. As he got closer, Linda noted that he was far from what she had been expecting. She'd stayed at B&Bs many times and had noted that the owners of such establishments tended to be retired couples indulging long-held fantasies of owning a "grand" house, but able to afford such a move only by renting out rooms on a regular basis. This man was young—in his thirties, she guessed—and looked more like a cowboy than an innkeeper. He had a thatch of curly brown hair and a long Scandinavian face. His muscular arms were deeply suntanned, and his weathered jeans hugged a narrow waist and hips.

Sharon leaned close to Linda and said, "You know, half of these friends of ours think he's a real stud muffin."

Linda watched as a quick blush spread up Peg's round face. "Oh, for heaven's sake, Sharon," she giggled.

"What about you, Sharon," Linda said. "Are you guilty of such unseemly thoughts?"

"I plead no contest," Sharon smirked and turned to watch the man, who was smiling as Jan stepped forward to shake his hand.

Linda ducked her head back inside the Lumina and began lifting her camera cases off the backseat. Eventually somebody would remember that she was the only one who needed an introduction to their host, but there was no point in just standing around waiting for it. There was plenty of unloading to do.

2 / Peg

B y the time Peg came downstairs for breakfast the next
morning, all the others were already seated around the
big dining-room table. She didn't normally sleep in. In fact,
lately, she'd been having a lot of trouble sleeping. Night
sweats had joined forces with worry to keep prodding her
awake even now that school had been out for several weeks.
But she had quite deliberately shut a door in her mind,
determined to spend this week focused on Micky, on enjoying her time with an old friend she knew was going away.
Family troubles would have to wait. Besides, there was something about the air up here and the deep quiet of the woods
that seemed to render her almost comatose; she had noticed
that last year.

"Well, Sleepyhead," Jan said. "You've missed Kim. She had
to leave for town to set up her stand."

"Oh, that's too bad," Peg exclaimed softly. "And she got
home last night after we'd all zonked out. But I'll see her
tonight, I guess."

Peg felt genuine regret at not being among the group to
greet Kim, Steve's wife. She liked this young couple, was
impressed with their work ethic. The B&B, she knew, had
been Steve's idea. He was an incurable outdoorsman whose
efforts at a few "regular jobs," as he called them, had left him
frustrated and longing for the forest. This business gave him

the chance to spend his afternoons as a guide over the system of trails he had carved out of the Sawtooth Range—hiking and biking in the summer, cross-country skiing in the winter. He was also an expert canoe guide. Kim had gone along with his plans, partly, Peg supposed, from a desire to accommodate her husband, partly from her own love of the North Shore. She was an avid runner, one of those wiry, intense women who filled Peg with a kind of awe. But she was also a gifted artist; she designed and made jewelry that she sold from a sidewalk stand in the summer. And she worked several nights a week as a waitress at Pierre's, a pizza place in Grand Marais. Peg suspected they needed the extra money and wondered if that was why they didn't have any children. Young couples had a harder time of it these days.

Peg sat down in the one remaining chair and surveyed the room with renewed satisfaction. There were a few new touches—a long buffet table topped by trays for the afternoon tea and coffee things Steve would leave for them—but the room looked pretty much as she remembered it. The two outside walls were mostly windows. No curtains, no interference with the view. The long eastern wall looked out over a gap in the birches beyond which, shimmering in the distance, the great expanse of Lake Superior faded away toward the horizon. The door to the deck was ajar, letting in the fragrant morning air. Behind Peg was the alcove where a love seat and two upholstered chairs surrounded a Franklin stove. This part of the house was for guests only. Behind a swinging door to Peg's right was the kitchen and, beyond that, the Olsons' private apartment.

Peg reached for one of the insulated coffeepots resting next to an informal bouquet of wildflowers in the center of the table.

"That one's leaded," Sharon said quickly. "Aren't you unleaded?"

Peg grinned at her old friend. How like Sharon it was to remember, even after a whole year, which of them were now off caffeine. There was a time, Peg reflected, when they had consumed gallons of strong coffee late into the night when they were studying for exams, and later, too, during the frequent get-togethers they had arranged when they were raising small children and juggling jobs.

"The white ones are unleaded," Sharon prompted. "The gray one is for those of us who still need a jump start in the mornings."

Somebody had already brought out the first course, small individual bowls of fresh fruit, and Peg took up her spoon as soon as she'd poured herself a cup of coffee. She glanced across the table at Micky who was smiling in a vague, distracted way but not making eye contact with anyone. Through the window behind Micky's head, Peg could see a ruby-throated hummingbird hovering over a narrow feeder, its wings blurred in that fierce motion necessary to achieve such delicate suspension. Motion and calm in one tiny enigma. Peg never saw a hummingbird without wondering over its energy, its seeming fragility. What powerful muscles it must take to sustain that blinding whir of wings, what heat must be generated by that tiny, fast-beating heart. If you could touch those bright feathers on its throat, would they be red hot?

"What's the plan for today?" Mary was saying to no one in particular. "What's the first adventure going to be?"

The year before, they had fallen into a pattern of scheduling one "adventure" per day, an activity all participated in, and allowing the rest of the time to be largely unstructured with subgroups forming spontaneously to go on a spur-of-the-moment hike or play cards or drive into town to see a play or go to a gallery. The beauty of Grand Marais in the summer was that there was something for almost any taste, and having the entire B&B to themselves meant they didn't have to give place to strangers—even staying "at home" was a possible choice.

"I suppose you athletic types are going to drag us couch potatoes on some mad excursion into the Boundary Waters," Sharon grumbled. Peg had always been amazed that Sharon stayed so trim when she professed such a deep antipathy for vigorous exercise. It was all genetic, Peg supposed. Not fair.

"I think that's pretty much out, isn't it?" Mary said. "We'd have to drive for a few hours just to get to the Boundary Waters. We can canoe around here if we want to, can't we? What do you think, Jan?"

Jan, seated at one end of the table, came to attention as if from a long way off. "Oh, whatever you guys say," she murmured.

"Since when did you give up the role of social director?" Mary asked. There was no malice in the question, just a sort of good-natured ribbing that was so much a part of their usual exchanges. For years they had teased Jan about her tendency to "manage" things.

"Oh, didn't I tell you?" Jan answered with a wan smile. "I'm working on curbing my eldest-child bossiness."

"I swear," Sharon cackled. "Since you got that last degree, you're analyzing yourself into catatonia. It was bad enough when we were at St. Augustine and nobody could mention a dream without being told every gruesome detail of the sexual hang-ups we were inadvertently revealing."

Jan had been a psychology major who displayed all the fervor of a recent convert to a new belief system.

"Don't you know that Freudianism has been debunked?"

Jan said now, a trace of her usual good humor lighting her pale eyes. "And about damn time too. Our therapies today aren't based on the stereotypes of the nineteenth century. What did you used to call them, Mary? 'Patriarchal, Euro-centered, adolescent fantasies.'"

Now it was Mary's turn to bear the brunt of the common laughter.

"Hey, listen," she cried above the din, "when I'm right, I'm right."

Peg had been watching Micky. She laughed when they laughed, tipping her perfectly shaped head upward, but Peg could see that she wasn't really following the conversation. By the fourth exchange, she was no longer even looking at the speaker. Was she distracted by her own thoughts, far away in more serious concerns? God knew she had reason to be distracted. Or could she no longer keep up with rapid-fire conversation involving more than two people?

Peg was having trouble getting used to how Micky looked now. Maybe it was the haircut. Micky had always had gorgeous hair, had taken such trouble to keep it stylish over the years. Probably this boy cut was the only style she could care for on her own now, requiring no more attention than a shower and a quick combing. Her crown was exactly centered and the cropped hair fanned away from it gracefully; it would probably look neat even without combing. Still the sight of Micky's head made a wave of tenderness sweep over Peg, made her want to stroke Micky's hair the way she had petted her own child's hair when she was a baby.

Maybe it wouldn't be so bad looking after someone like Micky. She would just go backward through the stages of maturation. First it would be like taking care of an adolescent, somebody who acted on impulse and needed firm guidance. Then she would be like a child, needing help dressing herself and crossing the street. Finally, she would be like an infant who needed to be fed and held. It was hard for Peg to imagine that Micky could be unappealing at any of these stages.

"So we have to decide what's on the agenda for today," Mary was saying, "and Jan abdicates her role as mother of us all."

"I think we should go up to see the Witch Tree," Peg threw in. "Sometime while we're here. Not necessarily today."

"That's a good one," Sharon exclaimed. "And since we have to go up to Grand Portage for that, we could combine it with a few hours of gambling at the casino. Maybe Friday?"

"There's one day," Mary said. "For today, I vote for an expedition into town. We have to show Lindy the Ben Franklin, or she'll never believe what we've been telling her about it."

The mention of Linda's name made everyone look at her. She had been silent so far, sitting at the other end of the table from Jan. Even in T-shirt and shorts, she still managed, as she had always done, to look different from the rest of them. Her shirt was tie-dyed, a combination of oranges and yellows, and its front was almost covered by the ropes of bright beads suspended from her long neck. Her dark hair was swept up behind her head, its thick folds fastened casually by beaded combs. No makeup was necessary to highlight her immense, dark-lashed eyes. If any stranger had been asked to identify the artist in the group, he would have no hesitation in identifying Lindy Tourneau.

"I still think it's mainly fiction," Linda said now. "You make the place sound like Bloomingdales."

"Oh, it's better than that," Peg responded. "Bloomies makes you change floors if you want to go from shoes to microwave kits for drying flowers. This place has everything you'd ever want to buy all on one floor—if you can find it."

"Okay," Mary said, lifting her small hands to command attention. "Who votes for going into town? Come on, Sharon. You should be up for this. Shopping isn't athletic."

"Speak for yourself," Sharon crowed, thrusting her hand into the air. "I get some of my best exercise running from store to store."

They were just making the vote unanimous when the door to the kitchen swung toward them and Steve Olson came in carrying two plates. When he set them down in front of Jan and Sharon, the sight of the frittata squares flanked by huge, crusty muffins elicited a chorus of oohs and ahs. When everyone was served, Steve lingered for a few minutes to listen, somewhat sheepishly, to their admiring exclamations. Peg wondered, as she had last year, how much innuendo Steve detected in the remarks her friends often made in his presence. When Sharon said, "And the food here is always enhanced by the lovely presentation," she meant her remark to include both the way the frittata looked on the plate and the way Steve's jeans cupped his lean backside as he bent to set the plates down. And Sharon didn't need to wink or nudge to ensure that the other women recognized her double meaning. They knew Sharon.

"Well, Steve," Jan said finally. "You're now in the presence of fifteen percent of the females who graduated from St. Augustine College in 1968."

"And four percent of the whole class," Mary added. "The most prestigious four percent, of course."

"I take it you've done the math before this very moment," Steve said, grinning at them. Peg liked his smile; he really was a nice boy.

"It's one of our oldest calculations," Jan admitted. "But the math isn't very tough. There were forty women in the class and one hundred and ten men. At least at the end. A few more when we started, of course."

"I suppose it's easy for everybody to be close in such a small school," he said, lifting one of the coffeepots to check whether it needed refilling.

The women exchanged knowing smiles.

"Well, not everybody," Mary said quietly. "Some people are drawn together more naturally than others, I guess."

They decided to leave it at that. Steve was only making polite conversation, after all, not really fascinated over what had brought them together in the first place or held them together for thirty years since. Peg had been thinking about those old days on her way across Wisconsin from Menominee, Michigan, where she and Jerry had been living since 1983. Passing above Green Bay, where St. Augustine was located, had inevitably reminded her of the place where she'd met her husband and her best friends.

In the mid-sixties, St. Augustine College was emphatically out of America's mainstream, a sheltered, conservative institution where the wealthy Catholics of Milwaukee and Chicago sent the sons who weren't quite bright enough to get into Notre Dame or Loyola and the daughters they hoped would major in elementary education or music while pursuing the main goal—marriages to good Catholic boys who would end up in the professions. But St. Augustine also gave out a handful of scholarships to students who compensated for being poor by having finished in the top two percent of their high school graduating classes. The college went even further, establishing in 1962 an honors program designed to provide high-powered and accelerated courses to those students who distinguished themselves academically during their freshman year. It was therefore no accident that the honors program was made up largely of students whose family income and social inferiority kept them out of the sororities and fraternities that dominated the social scene and invariably produced the homecoming and military ball royalty.

In 1965, the honors program recruited eight women and seven men from the sophomore class. Six of the women and four of the men were scholarship students. And so the bond was formed, made up of almost equal parts common interests and common enemies. Six young women, who were too smart, too poor, or too "arty" to be accepted by the regular student body, who found them either "weird" (mostly the girls) or threatening (mostly the boys), were drawn to each other in rigorous intellectual pursuits and rebellious fun.

After they graduated, it was Peg who started the round-robin, the second New Year's they had been apart. She wrote to Mary, who was in Pennsylvania then, urging her to add her own news and send the blended letter on to Micky, at Columbia by that time; then Micky could send it on to Linda in Chicago, and so on. The growing composition could make as many rounds as they had energy for, ending up with her, Peg. But, she said, every January she would start a new one. At first the letter made as many as four rounds in one year, its December postage shockingly high. They were so eager then, she remembered, to keep each other posted about the exciting and exasperating developments in their lives. Inevitably, the demands of jobs and children made the frequency fall to one round a year. And there was a period of six years, in the late seventies and early eighties, when there had been no round-robin. Peg had begun one several times, but it had sputtered before making even half the round.

Then Mary's divorce and return to Wisconsin in 1983 had

begun a series of visits and reunions that reminded them of how important the regular contact had been, so Peg had succeeded in getting the letter circulating again. She had kept all the letters, storing them in a metal box where her own grandmother had once kept loosely packaged spices sealed for freshness. The aroma of cinnamon and cloves and mace perfumed the paper and became associated inextricably in her mind with her friends, tying them to memories of family and childhood. She wished now, sitting here in this airy dining room, that she had brought the letters along; maybe the other women might enjoy reading those records of their shared history.

Glancing around the table, Peg couldn't help but wonder how Micky's illness would affect their circle. The years had established certain habits, certain assumptions about the roles each of them took in relation to the others. Would the ground under their feet shift, first subtly in barely perceptible tremors, and then shake and roll in some terrifying and cataclysmic upheaval? Would the circle be able to hold?

They lingered over the breakfast, draining cup after cup of coffee as they chattered. Micky joined in from time to time when somebody asked her a direct question. But Peg couldn't help noticing that Jan didn't seem like herself. Her usual energy and what she herself called her "sassiness" were muted. Was it just the burden of Micky's illness weighing on her? Or was it something else, something more? When Steve had cleared the last plate, he came back into the dining room carrying a large package wrapped in brown paper and bound with twine.

"I'm supposed to read this to you before you open the package," he said, fishing a piece of paper out of his shirt pocket after setting the package on the nearby buffet table.

"What the heck is this?" Sharon asked. "Are you giving us presents now?"

"It came by UPS last week," Steve explained. "Here's the message that goes with it." And he opened the paper and began to read. "For the six people who taught us the most about what it means to be grown-up women. May your celebration of this new stage in your lives be full of joy and crazy goings-on. Your loving daughters, Elizabeth Brunner Clark and Angela Schneider Powell."

Liz was Peg's daughter, recently married and living in the same Milwaukee neighborhood as Mary's older daughter, Angela. Liz and Angela, born only five months apart, had gone to UW-Madison together, establishing a second generation of the bond first formed by their mothers.

"I swear I didn't know a thing about this," Peg exclaimed in answer to the inquiring looks from the other women. But her eyes had immediately filled with tears of pride while Steve was reading.

"Me either," Mary insisted. "They concoct plots without checking in with their parents these days."

"Well, you two should open the package, I guess," Sharon said, and Steve set it down between them.

Peg pulled at one end and Mary tugged the twine off the other. After the crackle of paper had subsided, the opened package revealed six cream-colored T-shirts rolled into tight cylinders. Peg lifted one and shook it out. The shrieks of laughter were instantaneous. The shirt had a design in bright green on the left breast: a stylized pine tree had the words *Camp Men-O-Pause* emblazoned in a semicircle above its tip. Under the tree were small letters saying *Est. 1996*. Two more lines of type under this said *Sawtooth Bed and Breakfast, Grand Marais* and listed the dates they would be in residence this summer.

"Photo Op! Photo Op!" Sharon shouted. "Linda, get that fancy camera equipment of yours while we put these on."

"Oh, Linda doesn't take pictures of people," Peg said. "Get your own cameras, everybody, and we'll impose on Steve to take pictures of us once we've figured out which sizes the girls think are appropriate for each of us. Mine, of course, will have to be XXL and Liz knows that."

While they were sorting out the shirts, Peg caught sight of Linda's face. Her hawk's wing eyebrows were pulled into a little frown, her full lips pinched shut. Did she feel embarrassed about the shirts? Reluctant to proclaim so openly that the once-taboo word applied to her? Last summer, they had talked about this, how their own mothers had treated the word *menopause* as if it were some form of obscenity, not to be pronounced. Among themselves, their mothers had spoken in hushed tones of "the change," never to be discussed in mixed company and regarded as a reason to solicit and give condolences. It was Micky who had declared, "To hell with that! We should celebrate it, make a national holiday called Menopause Day to balance Mother's Day." But of course, Linda hadn't been here then, so they didn't know how she felt about it. She was, after all, the only one of them who had never married and maybe she wasn't ready to think of this transition the way the rest of them did. But whatever she might be feeling, she was pulling the shirt over her head.

When the others had struggled into the shirts, putting them on over their clothes, they went out onto the deck where Steve patiently took one snapshot after another, asking directions each time he picked up a new camera. They crowded together, leaning in on each other the way they once had when some classmate or boyfriend would call out, "Let's get the Sextet from Mensa to pose for posterity."

"Don't we look grand!" Micky said, her voice high and

excited. Peg looked over to where she stood with one arm draped over Jan's shoulders and the other clasped around Linda's waist. She was wearing the first wholly sincere smile Peg had seen on her face since she had arrived at Jan's house on Sunday night.

3 / Mary

The crowded aisles of the Ben Franklin seemed to Mary
even more claustrophobic than she remembered. Could
there be more stock than there had been last year? Was that
possible? Stuffed racks of adult sweatshirts, two tiers high,
were only a few feet from towering stacks of shoe boxes; the
tiny area for trying on shoes was crowded up against the rows
of jackets and men's trousers.

This store really was a phenomenon scarcely to be
believed. What was, in other towns, a sundries store where
people could pick up a magazine, aspirin, and eyeshadow
had once been Grand Marais's only general store—indeed,
the only general store for fifty miles in any direction. It had
encountered competition in recent years from small, upscale
boutiques and, especially, from the Lake Superior Trading
Post built directly on the shore. But "the Ben," as locals
called it, could hardly be topped for variety and bargains.
You could find Pendleton wool suits, the best hiking boots
currently manufactured, place settings for eight, yarn,
Battenburg lace doilies, bras that went up to size 48 DD,
Tinkertoys, camp stoves—all jumbled together on one floor.
And you could buy a lot without wilting your credit card.

Mary was paging through a rack of children's T-shirts, her
back almost against the ladies' sundresses. The little shirts
were all so adorable—chipmunks on one, a cartoon moose

on another—that Mary was having trouble choosing. Of
course, she knew this was only the beginning; before Sunday
sent her back to Kenosha, she would have a pile of presents
for her grandson. Austin was fourteen months old, and Mary
still couldn't get used to the pure joy that filled her when she
saw him, held him. She carried a whole pack of baby pictures, flashed them whenever she could find an excuse to
do so. She took a quiet satisfaction in being the only grandmother among these friends of hers.

She selected the cartoon moose, reasoning that *moose* was
a word Austin could pronounce, and turned to check on the
whereabouts of her friends. Linda had gone off to explore
on her own almost as soon as they'd come into the store.
Typical. The others had bunched up to examine the mer-
chandise, exclaiming to each other over every item. At the
end of the tunnel formed by the childrens' clothes, Jan and
Micky and Peg were within a few feet of each other. Jan was
not so much shopping as supervising Micky's shopping, hovering near her as she had done since they came into the
store. Mary felt a painful sense of loss just looking at Micky,
whose shaved-head, hollow-eyed appearance reminded her
uncomfortably of films she'd seen of Holocaust survivors.

But it must be worse for Jan. She and Micky had always
seemed more like sisters than friends. They had settled down
near each other in Minnesota, and their bond had never
been interrupted by distance or silence. As Mary watched
them, Micky turned to speak to Jan, who smiled and said
something Mary couldn't hear. But as soon as Micky looked
away, Jan's face lapsed again into the lines of worried strain.
She was still as whippet-thin as she'd been in college, her
small-breasted torso a stylish frame for her silk blouse, her
long neck making possible the chandelier-type earrings that
were something of a trademark for her. She wore her hair

Kaz, as he was invariably called, and learned to her surprise—
the years without contact had intervened—that Sharon was
now his partner in the business. In the years since then, Mary
had been to weekend get-togethers—in St. Paul and in Green
Bay—weekends that included Sharon and Kaz. She liked Kaz.
They all liked Kaz. He was good-natured, generous, clearly
adored Sharon. But it was hard to know what to talk about
with Kaz. The couple had no children—Sharon had never
discussed this with any of them—so even the everyday experiences shared by all parents seemed inappropriate. Only Mike
Werden, Jan's husband, seemed to find some common
ground in discussions of tools and woodworking.

Mary left Sharon to her decision about the dress and wandered over to a shelf displaying tiny birdhouses. She picked
up a red one, turning it in her hands and checking for labels.
This was a set habit of hers whenever she saw any merchan-
dise she might consider stocking in her own shop. When she
had come back from Pennsylvania to Wisconsin with her two
daughters and her pathetically small divorce settlement, she
had kept her terror about the future buried beneath her
anger and her newly acquired feminist sensibility. After a few
months spent living first with her father and then with one
of her brothers in Milwaukee, she had drawn a deep breath
and plunged into business. Her settlement and a huge bank
loan made it possible to lease and stock a small storefront
in Kenosha. Her specialty was Victorian and country-style
decorative items for the home—picture frames, lace and cro-
cheted window coverings, kitchen canisters, painted geese
to perch on mantles and countertops. Against the advice of
her then-smart-mouthed older daughter, she had named the
shop Warm Hearth. "It sounds like a bakery," Angela had
observed. In three years, she moved to a bigger shop, and in
seven years, she was able to buy the building. Now she had

three employees and could finally bring herself to take vacations without the nagging fear that it would all evaporate into air if she looked away from it. Not bad for a philosophy major, she would sometimes tell herself.

She felt a hand on her shoulder now and lifted her gaze to find Jan's panicky face above her.

"Have you seen Micky?" Jan said in an urgent half-whisper. "I looked away from her for a second, and she was just gone. Peg didn't notice where she went either."

"I haven't seen her recently," Mary answered. "You don't think she'd wander out of the store, do you?"

"I don't know. I have to admit I just don't know what she might do."

"Calm down," Mary said soothingly. "She's probably still in here somewhere. Surely five of us can track down one shopper. Even if she's outside, how lost can anybody get in Grand Marais?"

"She might not even remember that she's in Grand Marais," Jan said, her tone irritated now. "She's always worse when she gets confused or scared."

"There's no reason to get so excited," Mary said, trying to laugh. "Go out on the street so you can watch the exits. I'll get the others to help me search in here. Relax, Jan. She'll be all right. We're not going to lose her."

4 / Micky

She stretched the sleeves of the sweatshirt out to arm's length, frowning down at the embroidered cardinal whose bright red wingspan splashed against the white background. There was something about shirts. Something recent. And it had reminded her of Samantha, of her daughter. What was it? Was she supposed to buy Sam a shirt? Sam was a grown-up now, of course. She knew that. Matthew too. They weren't little kids anymore. Still, she could buy things for them, wait for them to tear through the bright paper, see the joy shining in their eyes if it was something they really wanted. Would Sam like a sweatshirt with this radiant bird caught in midflight over a snowy field?

They loved the winter, Matt poised on skis at the edge of the bunny hill with his wind-chapped cheeks glowing, his pale hair peeking out from under the knit cap. She had tried to keep smiling, to look nonchalant, but wasn't this hill too much for him? He could be hurt if he started going too fast. He was too young for this, just a baby really.

She shook her head, dropped the sleeve. But of course Matt wasn't a baby at all. She knew that perfectly well. He was in medical school now, was going to be a doctor like his daddy. Brilliant. Maybe someday, the "Clinic," the Mayo. Just like his daddy. Those long halls, that echoing sound footsteps made, the smell—all hospitals had the same smell. They had to strap your head to keep it perfectly still as you went into the tunnel, the ceiling just above your nose. If you moved at all, they couldn't get a perfect picture of your—. She caught herself, just in time, veered away from the word, from the knowledge.

When she raised her head, there was only a wall of shirts, nobody she knew. She turned in place, feeling sleeves brushing against her face, her ear. Behind her, a rack of jeans pushed forward into her waist when she took a backward step. A tall woman with dark glasses came toward her and then crowded past—a stranger. She could feel her breathing beginning to quicken. Where was she? What was this place? She hurried to the end of the narrow aisle, looked around a stack of boxes. Another woman with a little girl at her side was peering nearsightedly at a price tag—a pale, lumpy woman with frizzy hair. Another stranger.

She could feel the beginnings of nausea—that sick, falling sensation in her stomach and bowels—and she knew that it always came just before the other thing, the thing that was worse than any nausea, so she fought against it, made herself move. She would find Peter. He would explain this place, tell her why the cry of gulls was floating above the hubbub of busy shoppers. He must be in here somewhere. She scurried down a long aisle, glancing quickly from side to side into the openings that branched away, some of them like dark caves of jackets and trousers. Now she found herself among kitchen utensils and a whole crowd of shoppers. She searched the faces, stooping a little to bring her own face closer. An old woman flinched away, the wrinkled skin around her eyes stretching into a startled look. All strangers.

This was the wrong place to look for Peter. He would never buy cookie cutters or paring knives. Maybe he wasn't in this store at all. But then where could he have gone? She had to find him. If he stood right next to her, even if he didn't say anything or touch her, she would be all right. She could feel the warmth of his body even across eight or ten inches and know that she could reach out any time and touch him, the way she sometimes did in bed when he was asleep and she was lying there awake—just touch him softly with the ends of her fingers, not enough to wake him. Then she could keep the horror away, could stop herself from wailing aloud in the dark.

Where had she last seen him? If she could recall a familiar scene with Peter in it, maybe she could trace forward to this strange place, this jungle of clothes and gadgets that was threatening to close in on her, to strangle her in jacket sleeves. There had been a long car trip; she was sure of that much. But recalling was such hard work. Bringing back a place or a conversation, stitching the moments together into hours where "before" and "after" lined up into clear rows, was exhausting. How long had she been fighting to remember? How many years now since the numbers in the check register had refused to organize themselves into sense? Sometimes she would shake her head, hard, as if she could make herself wake up again into a world where street signs had a logic, where the name of her dentist would come off her tongue easily, popping out like a pea dislodged from its pod by a thumbnail. But the shaking only made her slightly dizzy.

That trip to the dentist had been one of the first bad nightmares. When was that? This year? Last? Last year, it must have been, because she had just quit working. She'd always had such strong teeth, hard and straight. Trips to the dentist weren't scary for her. Only some cleaning and scraping, a pleasant taste of mint as the spinning brush made its soothing buzz. She had started out early on a bright morning, leaving the house even before she'd planned because there had been a few times already when she'd got a little lost on the way to the grocery store and to her hairdresser. But she'd said the route out loud six times, starting just after her shower: Lexington to Sarnia; right on Sarnia to Elmwood, where there was a big supermarket on the corner; left at the super-market and then a half-block to a low gray building. Easy.

But she stopped the car to put on her sunglasses—the glare off the other cars was almost blinding. And then the street didn't seem familiar anymore. Had she taken a wrong turn? She didn't remember making a turn at all, but surely those lilac hedges weren't on any street she knew; their puffy blossoms seemed almost menacing, pushing out at her across the sunny sidewalk. She looked for a street sign, but this was the middle of a block; she would have to get to an intersec-tion. She watched for traffic and then, when she saw that the street was clear, tried to swing the car around. It wouldn't move. The engine was running, and she was pushing on the gas, but the car wouldn't budge. She could feel the rising panic, like waves threatening to pull her under. Lost in a strange neighborhood and now the car had broken down. How had she wound up here? Where was she supposed to be going? Peter would know. She had to get to him somehow. Her knuckles on the steering wheel were starting to turn white, and the roaring of the engine was making the panic flood even faster.

There was a phone in the car. Yes, right there. A phone. It had a special name, but she couldn't conjure it up. When she reached for the phone, the engine stopped making that awful noise, and she realized it was because she'd taken her foot off the accelerator. What was the number, Peter's num-ber at the hospital? She knew this number, had called it so many times. But it was gone, evaporated into air. Tears were beginning to fall onto her shaking fingers now, and she fi-nally pushed the only numbers she could remember: 911.

The police officer was young, and his uniform looked very clean. When she got her voice under control enough to say, "I'm lost and the car won't work," he frowned a little and said, "It's running. Engine sounds all right." She choked back her irritation and smashed her foot down on the accelerator. "But it won't move," she exclaimed and even she could recognize the near-hysteria in her voice. He ducked his head briefly into her window and said, "It's in park, Ma'am. Won't move unless it's in gear." She stared helplessly at the *P* in the semicircle behind the steering wheel; her head felt as if someone had poured freezing water on it.

The cop was silent for a minute, and then he said, "May I see your license and registration, Ma'am?" His voice didn't sound so polite anymore.

She thrust her purse at him. "It's in there," she muttered.

"Would you take it out for me, Ma'am?" he said, his voice even more cold.

She didn't look at him, just bit down on the insides of her cheeks. "It's in there," she repeated through her teeth. "I don't know where."

It took a few more seconds for the young policeman to take the purse and then such a long time of silence while he looked for what he wanted that she finally glanced up at his smooth, hairless face. He was holding a plastic card close to his eyes. Once, she could have spoken in a silky voice, tilted her head just so, and he would have melted, caved in, offered to serve her, to take care of her. But now when he looked down at her, he was wearing an expression she had begun to notice on people's faces lately, a combination of bafflement and contempt.

"Lady," he said slowly. "You're only three blocks from your house."

After that, Peter took away her driver's license and gave her car to Matthew permanently. And he got her one of those bracelets with the staff and snakes on it. He said she had to wear it all the time, no matter what other jewelry she was wearing. She could see it there, dangling from her wrist right now. But Peter was still nowhere in sight.

She was almost running by this time, her purse bouncing against her bare calves. Faces lifted toward her, some of them annoyed, some just blank. But it was all a sea of strangers. Her shoulder brushed a cardboard display rack, sending its plastic-sheathed cigarette lighters sprawling onto the countertop, but she didn't even pause. The terrible sinking sensation was pulling at her innards, twisting into a panic. And she couldn't keep it away anymore, couldn't fight off the horror that always came on her like a scream, like a voice inside her head—always the same words: "My brain is dying! This is happening because my brain is dying."

A short, round woman was in her path, wasn't moving to one side to let her by. This woman had dark hair, streaked with gray, and there was something about her face that was teasingly familiar. Micky made herself stop, swallow the nausea, focus hard.

"Mimi!" she exclaimed, sudden joy ringing in her voice. "Mimi Cavallo. What are you doing here?"

"Looking for you," the little woman said, grinning in the easy way that Micky remembered now.

"Well, you found me, I guess," she said, covering fast. Because now she remembered, of course. This was the Ben Franklin in Grand Marais and Mimi was just plain Mary now and there was nothing to panic about and she must not let them see how scared she'd been. If people she knew saw too much, they got that look, and sometimes they even cried. And she was having none of that. None of that, at all.

5 / Sharon

They were walking along the shore, grouped into pairs now with Jan and Linda out front, Peg and Mary straggling behind, toting their packages. Sharon was glad to have this chance to talk one-on-one with Micky. She'd noticed, at Jan's house and again at breakfast this morning, that Micky's eyes glazed over whenever the conversation became noisy and rapid-fire. And where on earth was there a group of women more noisy and rapid-fire than this one? Too many high IQs trying to impress each other. How could they expect Micky to keep up now? Honestly, sometimes she just wanted to smack them all. They must be in denial or something, just plain ignoring the loss that was so obvious.

Yet, as they dawdled along in this quiet place, Micky could easily carry on a simple conversation: "What's Samantha doing now?" elicited the immediate response that she was "wasting her expensive education waiting tables." Sharon knew that Sam had followed her boyfriend to Dallas after college. And "I hear Matt's doing well in school" brought a bright smile to Micky's face and the quick answer, "He's just like his dad that way. He loves it too."

Losing Micky at the store had been scary for a few minutes, but getting her away from that crowd had settled her right down; she'd even been a little irritated with Jan for looking so worried. "Maybe you were the one who was lost," she'd said, something of her old spirit coming out. Now here she was, chatting normally about her children, strolling in the sunshine that was beginning to make Sharon regret the sweatshirt and envy the short sleeves of her friends. In some ways, Sharon found it easier to walk and talk alone with Micky like this than she would have in the old days. Not that she ever had many such opportunities when they were in college, or even later on those occasional get-together weekends. Micky was always surrounded by people, always dazzlingly social. And, in truth, Sharon had often felt daunted by Micky's quick wit. It wasn't that she was ever mean or nasty—not to her friends, at least—but she was what Sharon's own mother would have called "sharp." It was hard to keep up with her in conversation, impossible to surpass her, so Sharon had early on fallen into the role of "the earthy one," having discovered that a capacity to shock was a serviceable alternative for a capacity to impress.

But Sharon knew quite well that her place in this group had been secured by Michelle Jaeger and no one else. A farm girl who lived with her parents, who was unable to take part in the normal social life of the campus because she spent every evening twenty-seven miles away helping with the chores, would otherwise have been firmly on the outside. Peg and Mimi lived at home, too, but in Green Bay, a short bus ride from campus, and they had nighttime access to their families' cars, a perk that was bound to endear them to the dorm-bound girls when they wanted to get around town. Sharon had no such prizes to offer, so it had always filled her with amazement when Micky would say about some event at school, "You'll stay over, Sharon, won't you? We'll fix it with the Dragon Lady." This was their name for Hilda Sweetly, the dean of women who presided over the only women's dorm. Micky's joke was that Miss Sweetly's chief function at the college was to keep IT from happening on campus. "It's okay if IT happens in a motel in Appleton," Micky would say, "but not on campus. She'd lose her job."

Sharon had never figured out what Micky saw in her, just accepted gratefully that Micky's interest had seemed genuine—no condescension in it. But it was like Micky to recruit people that others wouldn't look at twice. Lindy had been one of Micky's recruits too, Sharon reminded herself as she looked ahead at Linda's swinging gait.

Linda had first appeared on their horizon when the honors program sponsored a sophomore seminar on comparative religion—daring subject matter at St. Augustine. After a few weeks, Micky had decided that Linda was a pagan and therefore somebody they should know better. "Maybe artists—especially visual artists—have to be pagans," she'd said musingly. "They're so intimately involved with material reality that they have to glorify matter. Maybe even deify matter."

Sharon had thought at the time that "pagan" was an odd label to put on the reclusive girl who sat always at the edge of the discussion circle. Sharon would not herself have made much of an effort to befriend Linda; she always felt rebuffed somehow in the presence of quiet people. But she was willing—as were the others—to accept anyone Micky found interesting. And, really, she wouldn't have called Linda standoffish. No. That word suggested a deliberate withdrawal based on some illusion of superiority. Lindy wasn't a snob, and she wasn't a cold fish. What then? She had always kept a space around herself, emotionally, and she looked across it with curiosity, a nonjudgmental attention. There was nothing "needy" about Lindy. She made no demands. And she made no promises either. Yet Micky had crossed that space of Linda's, deliberately and stubbornly, and had yanked her in.

In time, Micky's label of "pagan" seemed prophetic,

for Linda had been the first among them to abandon Catholicism, announcing calmly at a senior-year beer party that Christianity, in general, was "life-denying and soul-crippling." Most of them had felt profoundly shocked, but Micky had laughed at them. "Get that capital *C* off *catholic*," she said. "Aren't we committed to a bigger picture of the universe?" Micky's sponsorship of Linda was no longer necessary by that time; the rest of them had accepted her and had even begun to notice that Linda was the only one among them who didn't automatically defer to Micky. Sharon wondered now if this distance hadn't been exactly what Micky liked and admired about Lindy Tourneau.

"You think Sam's going to marry that guy?" Sharon asked now, shortening her own long stride to keep pace with Micky.

"Oh, you know what kids are like these days," Micky sighed. "They don't think it's necessary to marry the ones they're living with."

"Well, considering the divorce rate these days, maybe they're right. Screwing is better than suing. There's no hurry, is there? How old is Sam now?"

The long silence next to her made Sharon glance sharply at Micky's face. A little frown between her shapely eyebrows made it clear that she was trying to respond. Either she couldn't remember Sam's age or she couldn't make sense of the question.

"She must be about twenty-four, right?" Sharon said quickly. "She's got plenty of time to think about marriage."

"I guess," Micky said quietly, not looking at her. "But I'd like to be a grandmother. And pretty soon too." She took three more steps before finishing her thought. "While I still know what that means." She said it almost matter-of-factly.

Sharon felt her breath rushing out of her as if she'd been punched. She turned her face away so that Micky couldn't see her expression. Oh, God! Dear God. To not be able to remember your own child's age! And to *know* what was happening to you. They walked on in silence for a moment, Sharon's view of the harbor blurred by the moisture in her eyes. She wanted to respond, to put her arm around Micky's shoulders, but she was uncertain how such a gesture would be received. Jan or Peg could do that sort of thing easily; people expected them to do it and responded in kind. But Sharon felt awkward about emotional displays, and her awkwardness was sometimes contagious; she knew that from experience.

So now she just focused on Lake Superior, noticing how it still looked slate gray, even in the sunshine, how it seemed to rise uphill away from the harbor, swelling in its immensity toward the faraway horizon. The lighthouse looked tiny, even ineffectual, with that ponderous expanse behind it. People who hadn't actually seen Lake Superior couldn't really appreciate its size. You had to drive along its shoreline for hours and hours, stand on some high outcropping like the one at Split Rock, in order to realize that it wasn't a lake at all, but a huge inland sea. You could plunk West Virginia down in the middle of it and still have room left over for a few of those little bitty eastern states like Connecticut or Rhode Island.

"Should we get a coffee?" Micky said suddenly. "I'd like some coffee."

"Me too," Sharon said, grateful for this new tack. "There's that little cappuccino place on the beach next to the Trading Post. Would you like a cappuccino?"

"Yes, I would," Micky said with one of her sweetest smiles. "I think they have decaf for our sissy friends, don't they?" This last was said with a conspiratorial wink, the old claim that the two of them were somehow more daring than the others. It was suddenly almost impossible for Sharon to believe that this woman could get lost in a store, could blank on her daughter's age.

They had dragged two benches into a V-shape, open end toward the shore, and were half-facing each other as they cradled their steaming cups. Sharon sat directly across from Mary, noticing that the other woman's small feet dangled beneath the bench. How Sharon had once envied Mary's tiny size, her exotic prettiness. There had been no malice in the envy—it was impossible to dislike Mary—just an aching wish to look like that. And in a wholly predictable pairing, Mimi Cavallo had begun dating David Schneider during their sophomore year— handsome, brilliant, funny David Schneider. It was not that Sharon had any secret crush on David. She didn't. What she longed for was *someone like* David. It was the whole Mimi-and-David, David-and-Mimi phenomenon that she had a crush on. They looked, she always thought, like the dolls on the top of a wedding cake. But, of course, that marriage had turned sour. And now, Sharon thought with a little rush of satisfaction, Mimi Cavallo was chubby. And gray-haired. She felt almost immediately guilty for the satisfaction. Why couldn't she just admire Mary for her accomplishments, value her for her good humor and her kindness? Why, even now after all these years, did she need to focus on looks?

They were talking about their kids, catching each other up on the latest developments in the lives of that busy generation. As usual, they were affecting that tone of long-suffering tolerance that parents seemed to think was a required mask for their pride; it was almost as if they believed a direct boast would trigger some vengeful harpy hovering always overhead, ready to heap misfortune and shame onto any child whose mother had the temerity to say, "My kid grew up just fine." But Sharon could see that Micky had tuned out again, was staring out over the harbor, her coffee cup balanced on her right knee; she seemed almost to have forgotten that she had coffee, hadn't taken a sip in several minutes now. What was she thinking about? What was going on in that faltering brain? She looked serene, but deeply sad, and distant—far away. Sharon couldn't bear the feeling that Micky had already left them.

"Jan," Sharon said suddenly, more loudly than she'd intended. "Why don't you tell that story about when Adam was born? I love that story."

The others fell silent, turned to look at her.

"Oh, I'm sure everyone's heard that tale," Jan said, and she was blushing slightly.

Sharon looked at Micky, dragging the collective attention in that direction.

"You'd like to hear it again, wouldn't you, Mick?" Sharon asked.

"Hear what?" Micky said, her voice muffled.

"Jan's story about when Adam was born," Sharon replied, watching focus come back into her friend's eyes, seeing a spark of interest, a slight smile.

"I've never heard this story at all," Linda chimed in. "This must be good. Come on, give."

Jan took another sip of her café mocha, and when she looked up, Sharon could see that she understood.

"Well, let's see," she said slowly. "You knew, of course, that I had the first two the old-fashioned way—just let them knock me out with painkillers. But in the mid-seventies I was going through my Earth Mother phase. Wearing granny dresses and baking whole-wheat bread. The whole nine yards."

The other women laughed, remembering the recipes Jan had sent them, the increasing references in her letters to organic gardening and the vital importance of breast-feeding infants. Jan's famous "enthusiasms" had been entertaining them ever since their days in college when she had tried to persuade them that the greatest novel in the history of the world was *Kristin Lavransdatter* and that its author, Sigrid Undset, rivaled Shakespeare—all of Shakespeare.

"When I found out I was expecting Adam," she went on now, "it was a big surprise to me. We'd actually bought into the whole rhythm method nonsense, taking my temperature daily, keeping elaborate charts. Well, Mother Nature was having the last laugh, as usual. But I was determined to get into it, to do this pregnancy better than any pregnancy ever. I wouldn't take so much as an aspirin when I had a headache. I dragged Mike off to Lamaze classes, even tried to find a midwife who would do that underwater delivery that was just becoming trendy then. Thank God Mike had sense enough to put his foot down about that. I could have a midwife, but the delivery would take place in a hospital."

Sharon could see that Micky was leaning forward, her face alert, a smile playing over her features. Every now and then, she would take a sip of coffee, but she never took her eyes off Jan's face. Whatever fog had settled on her brain inside that store had been blown away, had left the old sunshine on Micky's face.

"Well, when my labor started, I was *ready*. Or so I thought. I was puffing like a locomotive through every contraction. But I gotta tell you, it hurt like hell, and I was beginning to think longingly of drugs. But Mike was there. It was his first time in the labor room, and I didn't want to look bad in front of him. Especially after all my big talk. Then Adam did something we later came to think of as typical for him—he presented himself to the world ass-first."

The women made soft, clucking sounds, that universal empathy of women whenever childbirth is the topic of conversation. It would make no difference how often they heard Jan tell this story. The sounds came automatically at this juncture. Sharon found herself joining in the chorus, she who had never had a child. She glanced at Linda, the other childless woman among them. But Linda was silent. Attentive, alert, absorbing the details with her usual interest in other people's experience. But not joining in.

"Well, as soon as they knew for sure they couldn't turn him, they whisked me into surgery, chased Michael out, and did a cesarean. It all went so fast that they didn't even give me very much anesthetic. I was almost awake when they wheeled me back to my room. Awake and feeling like there was a fire on and in my gut."

"I remember that feeling," Peg murmured. "After my hysterectomy. You feel like all your insides are going to burst out and fall on the floor if you move even a little bit."

"Exactly," Jan said. "And then these two orderlies were going to hoist me off the gurney onto my bed. I saw them coming at me and glommed onto the frame of the gurney with both hands. 'No, no,' I told them. 'I'm staying here.' I could hear that I sounded drunk, could see it on Mike's face. So the orderlies started that 'Now, now, Mrs. Werden. You'll sleep better in a bed' stuff. But I wouldn't let go. 'Let me alone,' I said. 'I'll sleep right here.' Then one of them said, 'But we need the gurney, Mrs. Werden.' And—I don't know where this came from—I shouted, 'I'll buy the goddamned gurney! I have money. Get my checkbook, Mike. It's in my purse. I'll write this idiot a check.' Mike looked like he was going to sink through the floor. But the orderlies just laughed."

The other women were chuckling now, and Linda was doubled over. "You didn't!" she kept saying between bursts of laughter.

"Yes, she did," Micky put in now. "You should hear Mike's version of this. These big guys are trying to pry her fingers loose, but she's hanging on so tight they can't budge her. So finally a nurse has to give her a shot, just knock her out again, so they can get her off the gurney. So much for natural childbirth."

They were causing quite a scene now, Sharon thought— six middle-aged women yukking it up on the shore. Tourists ambling by were turning their heads, and the gulls, normally bold in their quest for handouts, were skittering away in alarm. Micky's face was flushed; her eyes were leaking tears from her laughter. She looked like a girl again.

6 / Jan

They were walking again, heading downtown to consider the possibility of some light lunch, chatting cheerfully. Odd, Jan was thinking, that it should have been Sharon who hit on the way to snap them out of the combination of anxiety and denial that had been triggered by the incident in the Ben Franklin. But maybe not so odd. Jan had noticed on several occasions over the years that Sharon was really very good at spotting distress, at "tuning in," as they had once phrased it. And she had always admired the way Sharon dealt with children and old people. She never condescended to either, never spoke to children in that teasing, ironic way that some adults used, largely to entertain the other adults who were listening in. Sharon talked "straight" to children, took them seriously, entered with respect into their level of interest and awareness. In fact, it was really a pity that Sharon had never had children.

Jan remembered a conversation she had once overheard between Ryan, her own youngest son, and Sharon when the Shaws, the Werdens, and the Kazmerinskis had gone canoeing and picnicking on the St. Croix. Ryan was about eight at that time, fascinated by everything to do with space travel. After the meal, Jan noticed that he and Sharon were huddled in a quiet conversation near the campfire.

"When I grow up," he was telling Sharon solemnly, "I'm

going to be a mechanic and an astronaut, and I'm going to Mars, and I'm going to marry Sally Ride."

No shadow of a smirk passed over Sharon's face.

"Those are all good things to want," she said seriously. "I think it would be very interesting to travel in space. Dangerous but exciting. And I'll bet Sally Ride is a nice person, too, not just a good astronaut."

Any other woman, even the kindest, would have felt it necessary, however gently, to point out that Sally Ride was already married, that she was too old for him, anyway.

So it was no wonder, really, that Sharon had intuited what she, Jan, had reason to know for sure—that Micky could "join in" only when the subject was familiar, when the stories were ones she already knew. In the past ten months, Jan had taken a crash course in Alzheimer's disease, reading stacks of books and articles. The short-term memory went first, while the long-term memory remained surprisingly intact. Someone in the early-to-moderate stages wouldn't be able to recall what he'd had for breakfast, but could recount in detail things that happened thirty years before.

Jan knew that she should have been more sensitive to Micky's inability to follow conversations. What was the matter with her? she wondered irritably as they passed a row of tiny gift shops along Grand Marais's main street. Why was she feeling so anxious and helpless on this vacation, when she should be the one with the best coping skills? If a licensed psychologist with a shiny new Ph.D. was going to fall apart because a confused friend wandered two aisles away in a store, what good was she to anybody else? And she had spent more time with Micky since the diagnosis than any of the other women, had seen first hand that Alzheimers didn't move in a straight line, that there were good days and bad days.

She could tell as soon as they got up this morning that

Micky was about to have a bad day. They had slept together in the king-sized bed in the largest of the four bedrooms at the Sawtooth B&B. When Jan had finished her shower, she came back into the room to find Micky sitting on the edge of the unmade bed, still in her underwear and holding a sock in each hand. She had a dazed look, her eyes unfocused as if she were drunk or stoned.

"What's up?" Jan had said, trying to keep her voice light.

Micky brought the socks up to either side of her face, turned first to the right and then to the left to look at each one. When she glanced up at Jan, the dazed look had been replaced by a pleading expression.

"They go on your feet," Jan said, aware that her smile must look ghastly, fake. "One on each foot. Then the shoes." But then she caught herself, considering carefully before picking up Micky's sneakers. The order in which she put on her own clothes was something she never thought about at all. "Wait. You'd better put your jeans on first." The activity of selecting and sequencing Micky's clothes made it unnecessary to keep looking at her face.

But this shouldn't be such a surprise, such a painful shock, Jan told herself now. Any big change of scene, especially to a place that was new or only marginally familiar, could trigger a bad day. People with this condition did best with stability, habit, familiar surroundings. All the books said so. As soon as Micky relaxed, she would bounce back, have a really good time up here with her oldest friends. Jan knew that, objectively, but she also knew that it was almost impossible for her to be objective about this particular patient. This was, after all, Micky.

Jan watched her now from behind, walking between Peg and Sharon, bending her cropped head to listen to what the other women were saying, following with her gaze when they pointed to skirts or jewelry or molded candles displayed in shop windows. And Jan felt again the stab of pain, of outrage, that this horror was taking the light away from one of the most vibrant, shining personalities she had ever known. And now she had to admit something else to herself. Back in the Ben Franklin, when she had looked up from a cap she was thinking of buying for Mike to discover that Micky had vanished, the first rush of panic had been underscored by irritation. And by the time Mary had found her among the housewares, Jan had felt furiously angry with Micky, the way she had sometimes felt when one of the boys would pull a childish prank like playing with firecrackers behind the house, or conning Ryan into jumping off the garage roof.

Of course her anger had been completely out of proportion. She was not solely responsible for Micky, after all, and the danger had been minimal. Insignificant, really. Why, then, had she overreacted? The habit of quizzing herself about her own emotions and reactions had formed only slowly during her clinical training. Her former life had worked against such self-analysis. When she was a young mother and part-time school counselor, she'd had no time for such "nonsense," so in the first year of her Ph.D. program, she'd reacted with barely concealed amusement to the self-absorbed navel-gazing of her much younger fellow students. At forty-four, she'd become the classic "nontraditional student," that PC shorthand for "older woman going back to school after raising her children." But gradually she'd come to realize that she would be a poor therapist for troubled clients if she ignored or denied her own hidden agenda, that analyzing her own feelings was good practice.

Why was she so mad at Micky? And guilty, of course, for being angry? Walking along in the gradually warming midday air of Grand Marais, reassured by Micky's delighted participation in the story of Adam's birth, she was beginning to come clean with herself. She had been upbeat about her own new career, eager to affirm the second half of her life. She had urged the summer getaway in the first place so that her oldest friends could share in, and reinforce, this affirmation. Last year they had turned fifty, one after the other: Sharon in February, Micky in March, Peg and Mary in April, she herself in June. Mike had given her a big party, inviting old friends and new. They had reserved a dance club, had worn clothes that Ryan said made them look "like old hippies." Only Linda had a late summer birthday and so had not yet reached the new plateau by the date of that party. Fiftieth birthdays, she knew, were traditionally greeted with ribbing, bad jokes about sexual dysfunction of various kinds, cakes edged in black frosting. But she had insisted on having a sock hop.

Because, on the inside, she didn't feel any different than she had at thirty-five. Menopause should be celebrated, she thought, as the transition into a productive and energetic new stage. But now Micky's diagnosis had introduced—no, insisted on—the themes of disintegration, decline, inevitable death. Since learning about Micky's condition, Jan had begun to monitor her own mental acuity with growing anxiety; every memory lapse—however small or short-lived—filled her with terror. She knew that her anger at Micky was a mask for her own fear: if this could happen to Micky, to her virtual twin, then it could happen to her.

And, of course, there was the other thing, the additional burden that the others had been spared, the special pressure for which Micky had selected her.

"Let's go to Leng's," Mary called from behind her. "I'm getting hungry, and my feet hurt."

"What's Leng's?" Linda asked, her necklaces making a faint clicking sound as she turned to look back at them.

"Leng's Soda Fountain and Grill!" Several of them said it in unison.

"Wait till you see this place," Peg gushed, taking Linda's arm for emphasis. "Straight out of the fifties. It even *smells* like an old-fashioned soda fountain."

They arrived just enough past the usual lunch hour to allow them to sit across from each other, in two groups of three each, at the horseshoe-shaped counters that bowed out from the wall of gleaming soda-fountain equipment. Jan had always loved the place. Leng's was not some tacky recreation, but the genuine article, had been here since 1938. The only concession to modernity was a rack of video rentals at the back. The floor, a huge checkerboard of black and white linoleum, was old and worn. The signs for Meadow Gold Ice Cream and Rochester Root Beer were certainly original, and the dusty, faded appearance of a large Marilyn Monroe poster suggested that it had been on the wall since 1960. A bulky Seeburg Select-o-matic jukebox was filled with old 45s: "Book of Love" by the Monotones, "Walk Like a Man" by the Four Seasons. And the food was as authentic as the setting: burgers and sandwiches served with heaps of greasy potato chips and real honest-to-God ice-cream sodas, frothy and noisy in their tall glasses.

Mary was helping Micky to order, discussing the menu items in her low, rich voice. Sharon sat on the other side of Micky, almost as if they had tacitly agreed to flank her from now on, whenever they were in public. On a good day, Jan knew, Micky would know what they were doing and resent it. But now she was listening to their advice about the menu with childlike openness. Maybe, Jan thought, her heart lifting, maybe Micky would never again remember what she had said in the long conversation they'd had at Christmas.

They had been together, just the two couples, at Jan and Mike's house for four days between Christmas and New Year's, after spending Christmas itself with their respective children. On the third morning, Mike and Peter had set out early to go cross-country skiing—"As long as we have all this sunshine," Mike had said. Micky was alert, almost her old self, but she firmly declined the men's invitation to join them, even though skiing had always been one of her enthusiasms. "We girls need a good old gossip session," she'd said brightly. "And you know we can't have one with you guys around, expecting us to pay attention to you."

Over a third cup of coffee, the women sat silent for a few minutes, staring out the wide windows of the great room at the rows of winter bird feeders Mike had installed just beyond the deck. Tough little sparrows pecked aggressively at the seed balls while a cold breeze lifted the thick feathers along their backs.

"I need to talk to you about something very serious and important," Micky said at last, both the words and the tone uncharacteristically formal.

Jan cringed inwardly, by this time dreading any direct discussion of Micky's illness, but she put on a brave smile and said, "Okay. Shoot."

Micky turned her whole upper body toward Jan, squaring her shoulders in a purposeful set, her blue eyes squinting a little with intensity. It took her a minute to begin, but once she had, Jan could tell that the hesitation had not been due to any groping for words. Micky had clearly thought through the words pretty carefully.

"I've decided what to do," she began in the firm,

no-nonsense voice she must surely have used in the class-room to impress her students. "This thing that's got hold of me is going to drag me down a long, long road, and I plan to dig in my heels and fight the leash for as long as I can. But eventually I'll be pulled along. We all know it's true, so don't raise your eyebrows at me like that. But I don't intend to stay on the road till the end. I plan to get off while there's still some bit of me left."

Jan sucked in her breath in a small gasp. "You don't mean that you're going to—" she began and then stopped herself before she could voice the fear, suddenly gripped by the atavis-tic notion that speaking a thing might cause it to happen.

"You've got to let me say all of this without interrupting," Micky said. "Promise? My thoughts get derailed pretty easily when I'm interrupted." She paused, waiting for the expected promise, her face pushed forward in the urgent way she'd used in their college days when exacting a pledge to keep a secret or to sign up for the same courses so they could help each other study.

"All right," Jan said quietly. "I promise."

"I know you've been reading all about Alzheimer's," Micky went on. "So you know the last stages are pretty grim. And they're the hardest on the family—all that lingering when the poor zonked-out patient doesn't even recognize them any-more." Here she paused and took a deep breath, as if saying that out loud had proved harder than she'd anticipated. Finally, she swallowed and rushed on. "That's why I plan to head for the ditch before it gets me that far along the road."

"Stop that right now," Jan said, panic making her voice stri-dent. "You are not going to kill yourself."

"Well, not right now," Micky said calmly, sliding a shapely finger around the edge of the coffee mug, "and not for a while either. The trick is going to be to find the right time. No, not find it. The trick will be to recognize the right time. Because I won't be able to do it on a bad day—I won't remember how I planned to do it—and on a good day, I might not think it's necessary to do it yet. So I'm going to need help."

"Oh, no," Jan breathed. "Don't you dare!"

"You're interrupting again," Micky said, but she didn't sound peevish, only a little sad. "You know it's out of the question to ask Peter or either of the kids to help me. They would never agree."

"But you think I will?" Jan was feeling outraged now, more angry than horrified.

"Yes, I do," Micky said simply. "They can't help me because, by the time I'm ready to go, they will already have wished it. So, of course, they would feel too guilty to help me after that. You won't be with me enough to wish for release. It'll be easier for you."

"The hell it will!" Jan shouted.

"I need your help, and I've always counted on you when I needed help. You work in that clinic now, and you can get pills. No, no"—and she lifted a finger to forestall the speech Jan was about to make—"don't deny it. I know you can't pre-scribe medication, but there's a psychiatrist on staff and that means there are drugs around. You could manage it. You for-get that we social-worker types are making referrals to outfits like yours all the time, so I know what I'm talking about. I've read the suicide book, and it lists the best cocktail of drugs to ease somebody like me out. I won't be physically sick, so I'll be able to swallow, and I won't throw up."

Jan felt as if the top of her head was going to fly off. How could Micky sit there on a nice, clear, winter morning—just a few days after Christmas, for God's sake!—and speak such horrors in the sort of voice she might have used if she'd been asking for Jan's recipe for Indian lamb stew?

"I will do no such thing," Jan said coldly. "You have no right to ask me such a thing."

"Sure I do," Micky said, and she smiled a little. "I'd do it for you."

For that, Jan had no reply.

"And I need you to help me take the pills too," Micky went on relentlessly. "To stand by to make sure they work. We'll have to fix it so we're alone at the time."

"I won't do it," Jan said. "Just forget all about this nonsense because I won't do it."

"If you mean that," Micky said softly, "I'll just have to do it myself. Of course, that means I'll have to do it sooner while I'm still pretty alert. And if I can't get pills, I'll have to use something less certain and maybe more painful."

"That is the worst kind of emotional blackmail," Jan shouted, her outrage finally boiling over.

"I know," Micky said with something of the wicked gleam she would sometimes get in the old days when she was trying to persuade Jan to let her wear some new sweater or skirt. "Dreadful, manipulative behavior on my part. But I'm a desperate woman. And I mean what I say. Every word."

Jan sat silent for a moment, casting about for an answering argument. Well, two could play at this guilt-trip game.

"What about Peter, then?" she said. "He's bound to find out what you died from. And he'll know where you got the pills. It won't take him more than ten minutes to figure out that I helped you. And then he'll hate me. He'll never forgive me and neither will Sam and Matt. You'll be gone, and we'll have lost each other behind you, just when we most need each other."

Micky took a slow sip of her coffee, looked out the window for a minute. "I've thought about that," she said finally. "Peter will be very angry with you at first, but he'll come around. You know how sensible he is. And how fair. He'll see that I was right and that I had a right to decide this for myself. The kids too. In the long run, when they think it all through, they'll even be relieved—for me, of course, that I was spared the worst." Then she took another sip of coffee before she finished the thought: "And a little bit for themselves too."

Again, Jan found herself unable to think of anything to say. Micky reached into the breast pocket of her flannel shirt and fished out a small key, which she placed onto the oak tabletop and pushed toward Jan with her right index finger.

"I've written letters to each of them," she said. "To some other people too. You and Mike, for instance. But long letters to Peter and to Sam and Matt. I've explained it all so they'll understand. I hope."

Jan stared down at the key and then lifted her gaze to Micky's solemn face.

"It's one of two keys to a safety deposit box," Micky said. "I rented it at Thanksgiving. Peter doesn't know about it. Nobody does except you and me. The letters are in there and some other little things. After—afterward you can get them and play mailman for me as a last favor."

"I'm not taking this," Jan said, feeling at once that touching the key would commit her to the whole crazy scheme.

"It's all right," Micky chuckled, seeming to read Jan's mind. "You can think of it as a precaution. You know, I could wander away from home and get hit by a bus next week. By accident. A *real* accident, I mean. Somebody should know about the letters. I worked damned hard on them."

"I can't believe you've done all this already," Jan said, shaking her head. "How long have you been thinking about this?"

"On and off since I first heard the diagnosis," Micky answered. "Or I should say, since I *believed* the diagnosis. It took me about five good days in October to get the letters written. And they weren't five days in a row either."

"But you said you don't want to do this now," Jan responded. "Or even for the foreseeable future. Why write the letters now?"

"Because, dear Jan," Micky said softly, "in a year from now, I won't be able to write coherently anymore. Even on a good day. And in a year after that, I won't be able to read anymore."

For the first time in this surreal conversation, Jan could feel tears stinging the corners of her eyes. Michelle Jaeger Shaw had been, all her life, a voracious reader, had delighted in everything from fluffy romances to serious treatises on the behavior of baboons. Television sets and radios could be blaring while Micky sat curled in a chair, her pale head bent over an open book, one hand playing idly with a strand of her fine hair.

"Take the key." Micky was almost whispering. "You don't have to give me your answer now. Think about it. And remember that I count on you to think clearly in spite of all the emotion involved. You don't even have to volunteer an answer until I bring up the subject again. And who knows? Maybe I'll just forget all about it. You know what my memory is getting to be." And she smiled a sweet, sad smile.

Jan glanced down at the key, lying there between them on the smooth, polished surface of the dining-room table, but she didn't take her hands out of her lap where she had been clutching them together, almost as if in prayer.

"What makes you think I won't take this key straight to Peter and tell him all about this conversation?" she asked at last.

Micky eyed her coolly for a moment, her delicate eyebrows

lifting speculatively. "No, you won't," she said, her Cupid's bow mouth turning up smugly. "You might decide you can't help me. But you'll never squeal on me. I know that."

And Jan knew it too. In thirty-three years, she had never betrayed any secret Micky had asked her to keep.

"You promise me you won't do anything about this plan of yours until we talk again?" she asked, watching Micky's face carefully for any hint of evasion or deceit.

"I promise," Micky said. And Jan believed her. Had to believe her. She pried her own hands apart and reached out to take the key, finding to her surprise that it was rather warm. She had expected a metallic chill.

The key was back at her home now, in a corner of a tray inside her jewelry box. Jan had seen the Shaws five times since that winter day, and each time she had watched Micky with a wary glance, almost as if her old friend were some formerly docile pet that had shown recent evidence it might bite at any moment. But Micky had never raised the terrifying subject of assisted suicide again. Once or twice, Jan had seen in the familiar eyes a knowing light, always followed by a secret smile, as if she were saying, "Not yet. Not yet. Don't look so scared." And, of course, Jan had told no one about the conversation.

Now she watched Micky lifting potato chips to her mouth, her dazed glance drifting from the picture of Marilyn Monroe to the gleaming rows of soda spouts. And Jan wondered suddenly why she hadn't said on that winter morning, "Please don't think about leaving us. We all want you to stay. We'll light the road, so it won't be so dark for you. We'll walk along with you, so it doesn't have to be so scary." She wanted to say it now, to reach across the battered countertop and take her friend's hand. But, of course, there were strangers around, and one didn't make such speeches in public. But perhaps she hadn't said it then and wouldn't now because in some sense she knew that no one could really go very far along that road with Micky—that was only brave talk—and no light could keep the last darkness at bay.

7 / Linda

Linda stifled a yawn and stretched her bare feet out a little farther onto the low wooden table that fronted the loveseat. Her opened book was resting on the cold surface of the Franklin stove, which Kim Olson had surrounded with big pots of wildflowers, but she didn't feel much like reading, and despite the yawn, she wasn't ready for bed. In truth, she was enjoying the sense of relief she felt flood over her the moment Jan and Micky had gone upstairs to turn in early. They had returned to the B&B about seven-thirty, and by nine-thirty Micky was beginning to look exhausted. Jan, apparently guessing that Micky didn't want to be alone up-stairs, had claimed weariness herself, and the two of them had gone off before 10:00. Peg and Sharon were playing gin rummy at the dining-room table, and Mary had gone out onto the deck to have a cigarette; she was the last of them to be struggling with the habit. Peg had never smoked, but all the rest of them had been hooked at one time or another. Mary claimed to be down to "three or four a day."

Linda wasn't proud of her relief over Micky's departure. She knew it was one of her flaws that she found illness of any kind hard to deal with. She felt panicky and trapped when-ever anyone was suffering in ways she knew couldn't be immediately relieved or cured. If she felt that such a person was looking to her for answers or solutions, she wanted to run away, to summon professional caregivers and then leave the afflicted person to clinical, objective ministrations. And if she couldn't flee, she soon began to feel a simmering resentment that threatened to poison any other feelings she might have for the sick person. Even the thought of caring for an invalid over a long period of time made her begin to hyperventilate with anxiety.

She knew the roots of this horror, of course, but life had taught her the painful truth that knowing the cause of a problem doesn't necessarily make the problem go away. Her childhood and adolescence had been scarred by her mother's chronic depression. She never got used to the long silences, the projected demands, the need to tiptoe around the house, darkened at midday by drawn drapes because "Mom's resting." Her father had worn out his life trying to make up to his wife for her incurable sadness—anything short of getting her the help she needed, that is; anything to avoid the stigma he associated with mental illness. And he had inexorably drawn Linda, the only child, into the secrecy, the hiding of "Mom's nerves"—the kind, gentle voice that pressed on her more insistently than shouts or blows would have. She could never have friends over to the house, never cheer at the televised touchdowns the Packers scored on Sunday afternoons. And she must—always, always—be nice to Mom, be cheerful, be helpful. Only, of course, none of it ever helped, and there was no answering cheerfulness.

So Linda had fled to college with the relief of an escapee from a maximum security prison. She was already twenty-five and living in Chicago when her father died—just dropped onto his face on the sidewalk while shoveling snow one late January morning. She had come home for the funeral, had sat there in the perfumed quiet looking at the kind, serious face frozen in death, and the only thing she could feel was a dull anger that he had left her, had sneaked off at last to some place where there was loud music and dancing and nobody who needed cheering up. For a week after the funeral, she had alternately watched her mother's catatonic face and the blank whiteness of the snow-covered Wisconsin hills, certain that her presence could not thaw either landscape. And then she had packed up again and run away to Chicago.

She supposed now that it was a miracle her mother hadn't died, too, either from suicide or from slow starvation. Marie, her mother's younger sister, had taken over when it became apparent that Linda wasn't going to be the dutiful daughter the relatives expected her to be. It was Aunt Marie who finally got the afflicted woman into the care of a good psychiatrist. Today, Eunice Tourneau lived a quiet life in a retirement community near Wausau, Wisconsin, her moods elevated, usually, with the help of modern chemistry. Linda visited her for brief stays at Christmas and Easter, but the relationship was not warm. Objectively, Linda had "forgiven" her mother, understood how the illness had imprisoned both of them for all those years, understood that it was nobody's fault. But she couldn't seem to translate that understanding into feelings. Distance, both emotional and geographic, had been the most effective drug for her childhood pain, and she couldn't seem to cure herself of the habit—any more than Mary could give up the cigs.

Mary came back inside now, muttering, "Damn bugs," and rubbing her elbow where a ravenous mosquito had apparently helped itself to a late snack. "You're not reading," she said as she pulled one of the upholstered chairs closer to the low table so that she, too, could rest her feet on its surface.

"No," Linda sighed. "Just relaxing. I've been trying to get into mystery fiction, but this isn't a very good one."

"I can recommend some good ones if you'd like," Mary said, stretching her short legs. "I became a fanatic mystery fan when we lived in Pennsylvania."

"How'd that happen? You used to disdain popular fiction, as I remember."

"Oh, it's one of those sad stories," Mary sighed, making a wry face. "When the girls were babies and I was a neglected housewife, I could almost feel my IQ points slipping away. No adult conversations for twelve hours at a stretch, the constant interruptions that small children inflict on their caregivers. You find it hard after a while to even remember that you used to read Plato and Descartes for pleasure."

"So you descended to mysteries?"

"Oh, the descent was much farther than that. One day, I realized that I had become addicted to no less than four of the soaps. I had actually begun to care whether Dr. Marlena Brady would escape from Stefano's island fortress or sink further into her amnesia. When I confessed my shame to one of the other faculty wives, she lent me a copy of Dorothy L. Sayers's *Gaudy Night,* and I discovered there was something about midway between "Days of Our Lives" and Plato. The public library became my best friend."

"I take it that David was not very sympathetic?" Linda said it as a question.

"You have to be present to give sympathy," Mary said quietly, "and David was hardly ever present. Of course, he sold me a bill of goods about how vital it was for the whole family that he should build his career, first at Carnegie-Mellon when he was in graduate school and then at Pitt when he was an assistant professor. If I grumbled about his long hours, his evening committee meetings, and his weekends in the research lab, he would put on his other-men-have-supportive-wives face and make *me* feel like the offending party. He had to publish, he said, or there was no hope of tenure. The few hours he *was* home, it was my job to keep the girls out of his hair so he could grade papers and prepare for the next day's classes."

"Didn't we all grow up thinking that's the way it's supposed to be?" Linda asked.

"God, yes! And at the beginning, I was all in favor of it. You know what my childhood was like after my mother died, the way I was passed around among the relatives. The family that I had with David seemed like a dream come true at first. I suppose that's why I tolerated the rest of it for as long as I did. Even when David was pitching a fit over my being pregnant with Carol—as if I did that all on my own—I made excuses for him to myself. I thought it was my job to tolerate his moods, to soothe his anxieties. All that shit we grew up with."

"Oh, you're talking about juicy stuff," Sharon called from the dining room. "Wait till we get over there before you say anything else." She pulled her long frame upright, groaning in a stagy way as she massaged the small of her back. Peg gathered the cards into a neat stack before getting up to follow her. When they were settled, Sharon sighed noisily and said, "Okay, dish."

"Oh, I was just rehearsing the stages of my first marriage," Mary said, shifting a little in her chair. "Most of this is old news to you guys. I was saying how much I was willing to tolerate by way of neglect, how willing I was to give ninety percent to keep everything afloat and was actually grateful for the ten percent I was getting back. But I *did* resent David's indifference to the girls, suffered over how little time he spent with them. Carol was actually scared of him, the way she was of complete strangers like the postman. I remember the night I found out about the truce in Vietnam. I was alone watching

the news about it on television when bells began to ring all
over the city, some of them close, some far away. I got the
girls out of bed and took them out into the backyard, just me
and those two babies in the dark. 'Listen,' I said to them.
'Listen to the bells. It means peace. It means the war is over.
Always remember that you heard the bells when the war was
over.'"

Linda saw that Mary's dark eyes had filled with tears. No
one spoke for a few seconds.

"Of course, I knew they were too young to remember,"
Mary said finally. "But I knew I would remember, and I figured I could always tell them about it, make it into a family
story. I didn't find out until much later that David was not
hearing the bells in his library carrel as he later told me,
but was merrily screwing a graduate student who probably
thought she was having one of those mystic experiences
that induce musical hallucinations."

Sharon gave a snort of laughter, but Peg only looked sad.

"That was when you dumped him, I suppose," Linda said.
She knew the other two women had a clearer idea than she
did of how the Schneider marriage had unraveled. When
Mary had moved back to Wisconsin, Peg and Sharon had rallied around her. Linda had seen her less frequently, had used
the excuse of juggling two jobs to avoid the necessity for
offering comfort to a suffering soul.

"Oh, no," Mary replied, her voice harsh. "I didn't dump
him over that affair or any of the others that followed it. I was
always willing to believe him when he said they were meaningless, that I was the only one he truly loved. In fact, I never
dumped him at all. He finally found one he actually wanted
to marry, and *he* dumped me. I thought you knew that,
Linda."

"No," she murmured. "No, I didn't."

"I was even willing to be a good sport about it when he asked for the divorce, if you can believe anything so pathetic." Mary had sat up straight, curled her legs under herself in the big chair. "He worked on me to be 'civilized,' as he put it, so that the girls wouldn't suffer from any bitterness. And I agreed. But anything I asked for as part of the settlement was too much for him. Not the house, no, that would have to be sold and split. Never mind that it was the only home the girls could remember. Alimony for me until I could get some marketable skills was too much to ask—it would have to be a lump-sum settlement. When he said what sum he had in mind, my lawyer just laughed. Finally I got angry enough to point out to him that I had invested more than ten years of my life in the marriage while he was getting graduate degrees and building a career, that I had given parties for his friends and colleagues, entertained them even when they were openly laughing at me."

"Laughing at you?" Peg exclaimed. "Whatever for?"

"Oh, lots of stuff," Mary sighed. "I kept my Wisconsin vocabulary, for instance, while David was acquiring a more eastern style of speech. I remember once I called a water fountain a 'bubbler,' the way we do at home, and one of the wives said, 'Bubbler? Bubbler? How deliciously quaint.' And they laughed a nasty little laugh. And, of course, all of them knew David was cheating on me."

"Well, what was David's reaction to your little speech?" Linda asked. She was really beginning to find the story fascinating.

"He threw a tantrum," Mary said, tossing her ponytail. "He lectured me for ten minutes about how 'arrogant' I was to imagine that I had ever been any real help to him in his career. I wasn't worth even as much as the 'generous' settlement he had offered. 'You couldn't even give me a son!' he said. That was his coup de grâce. Can you imagine? Right out of the Middle Ages. And he's a biologist! He knows perfectly well how the sex of a child is determined. But there it was anyway—the ultimate patriarchal dismissal of a worthless wife. Bring on the axman. Anne Boleyn has not produced a male heir! And besides, old Henry is already tupping a new ewe."

Everyone was laughing now, and Linda could see that Mary was enjoying her own histrionics, that she no longer felt the full pain of what she was retelling, had made of it a fine story with flourishes to entertain this particular audience. Only at this stage of rehabilitation could Linda enjoy being around the former invalid.

"Do you remember," Mary was saying, "when we used to talk about the 'Click'—the moment when our feminist consciousness was finally triggered? Well, that was my Click. I told him he was a stupid son-of-a-bitch, and I walked out. As soon as I began to fight him, of course, he asked for custody of the girls. My lawyer warned me it was a ploy to keep the settlement amount low, but I already knew David didn't care squat about his own daughters. It was a long battle, almost two years. And in the end, I took a smaller settlement, just so I could take the kids out of Pennsylvania. What you don't know—any of you—because she made me promise not to tell, is that Micky sent me the money to move home. She shrugged it off, the way she does: 'Peter's richer than God now,' she said, but it was a fortune to me."

They were quiet for a moment, the mention of Micky bringing them, temporarily at least, back to the present. But finally Sharon spoke, her voice uncharacteristically soft and thoughtful. "What happened to David?" she said. "He wasn't like that when we were in college."

"What do you think he was like in college?" Mary asked, tilting her head at Sharon.

"Well, you know," Sharon said, spreading her long hands. "He was always at the top of the dean's list. He was president of the only service fraternity on campus, while the rest of those bozos were into the Animal House scene."

"Yeah, I know," Mary said, nodding vigorously. "And we thought he was the leader of the antiwar movement on campus, even though Auggies was mainly a hotbed of student rest where Vietnam was concerned."

"What do you mean *'thought* he was'?" Peg interjected. "I remember that night when a bunch of us were sleeping on the floor in Jan and Micky's dorm room and David came pounding on the door so we could help drag that damned cannon from in front of Main Hall and put it under the statue of Mary on Boyce Hall. Then we stretched that banner over it—"

"Our Lady, Queen of Peace, pray for us," they all chanted in unison.

"That was a prank," Mary said. "To impress us, mainly. And his antiwar sentiment was largely intended to please his profs who were against the war in that detached, wishy-washy way that so many intellectuals were. We were suckered in by David, all of us. We thought he was so amusing, so daring. He would put on that depraved-choirboy face and say things like, 'Whenever I say that prayer about blessed is he who comes in the name of the Lord, I think about the other meaning of come, don't you?' and we would all shiver with delight that he would say that stuff out loud, would be irreverent enough to link religion and sex. But it was just sophomoric drivel. A bad pun, if you think about it. Only sheltered Catholic girls would imagine it was sophisticated."

"Were we really so wrong about him?" Sharon said wistfully.

"We made him up, girls," Mary said emphatically. "We just created him out of scraps and patches. Because his family had some money and he had some brains, we assumed he must be a nice guy, that he must be 'deep,' as we used to say in those days. We set up a suit of clothes, and I fell in love with it. And don't think I didn't feel honored and even blessed when he picked me, because I sure did. I think I kept right on seeing him through our collective eyes as long as we were together at Auggies. And for a long time after that too."

"When exactly did you start to see him differently?" Peg asked, her round face troubled, sympathetic.

"I'm not sure," Mary answered musingly. "I suppose I saw things about the real David long before I could absorb what they meant. It's hard to give up a fantasy, especially when you've made the mistake of marrying it. I believed he was brilliant and ambitious, but he was really just an academic drone, ready to kiss any butt that had *professor* stenciled across it. Do you know why Angela is named Angela, for instance? Because David's thesis advisor at Carnegie-Mellon admired Angela Davis, so David had to claim a deep fascination with the civil rights movement. At Auggies, he was religious because that was expected there. In Pennsylvania, he saw that his associates were completely secular, so the religion had to go. Everything was for show. There was just nothing on the *inside* of him."

"And with Christopher, there is somebody there, inside the suit, I suppose," Linda said, watching Mary's face soften at the mention of her second husband's name. It was this second marriage in 1988 that had turned Mimi Cavallo into plain Mary Morgan.

"Oh, yes," Mary breathed. "Chris is *there*, all right. And you know what else? I finally realized with Chris what an innocent

I used to be about sex too. Here David was screwing half the women on campus, but sex with him wasn't all that great, at least not for me. And until Chris came along, I always thought that was *my* problem, that there must be something wrong with *me* that I couldn't understand what all the fuss over sex was about in books and movies. It never occurred to me that it might have something to do with my husband's ineptitude or selfishness."

"Ahhh," Sharon said knowingly. "An early finisher, huh?"

"Sharon," Peg murmured. "Specifics aren't necessary, are they?"

"Maybe not," Sharon laughed. "But I always think, don't you, that the emphasis men put on the size of their equipment is pure nonsense. I figure it's just like a good punt in football—it's not so much the length that matters as the hang time."

"Oh, Sharon!" Peg shrieked, before dissolving into giggles.

"Why, Margaret Ann," Sharon said, leaning toward her. "I do believe you're blushing."

Linda joined in the good-natured laughter. She had noticed even in their college days that people talked more outrageously when Peg was around because her blushes and giggles were always part of the fun. Peg would often say, "If you talk that way in front of me, what must it be like when I'm not around?" But in truth they were more restrained when she was out of earshot. And when Peg herself said anything even mildly suggestive, punctuating it with a dimpled grin and a sidelong glance, it was always hilarious because it came from such a source.

When the giggling had subsided, Mary stretched and stood up. "It's been a long day," she said, "and all this soul-baring has worn me out. I'm heading upstairs."

The others murmured a chorus of "Me too," and joined

her in the exodus, Peg pausing long enough to turn out the lights in the dining room. Linda was sharing with Mary the one room that contained two single beds, while Peg and Sharon each had a room to themselves. "I'm only thinking of you guys," Sharon had said by way of explaining why she should be in a room alone. "I snore like a buzz saw."

Linda lay awake for a while after the lights were out, listening to the night sounds of the forest and snuggling gratefully under the blankets that were necessary up here even in midsummer. Whenever she heard a woman tell a story like the one Mary had told tonight, she congratulated herself again on her decision to remain single. Not that these friends of hers were cursed in their marriages. Despite Mary's experience, her group of college friends had far surpassed the national average for intact marriages—four out of six were still married to the men they'd found when they were young. Maybe that was the residue of a strict Catholic upbringing, even though most of them had long since bolted from the Church. Of course, cradle Catholics would always think of Catholicism as *the Church* with a capital *C*. But only Peg was still what Linda's mother solemnly called a "practicing Catholic." Or maybe the relative success of their marriages was a testament to the wise choices most of them had made back in those days.

But Linda knew, lying here in the fragrant dark, that her own choice had been a wise one too. She had intuited at an early age that marriage and children would stand between her and the kind of life she wanted to have. As early as high school, she had decided that her art form would be photography, and she realized that she would have to remain mobile, unencumbered, to do the kind of photography she had in mind.

In college she watched her friends and acquaintances

pairing up, but she was careful not to date anybody more than two or three times. In those days and in that setting, boys didn't expect instant sex, so she had little trouble fending them off. She knew there were rumors about her, the whispered suggestion that she was a lesbian, but she didn't mind much—it kept the most callow of the boys from approaching her at all, so it served her purposes. She had gone to college as a virgin and had no intention of leaving it in the same condition. But the boys of St. Augustine were just that—boys—and they could not arouse her sexual curiosity. So she fixed her sights on a man.

One of her art professors, a flamboyant fellow with black curls and muscular hands, fascinated her from the first day in drawing class. Lawrence DeVitis, who insisted that everyone—including his students—should call him Lorenzo, was a married man with six children. Three of them were a six-year-old set of triplets. "You don't think I could have so many at my age unless I went into mass production, do you?" he would say to anyone who commented on the number. Linda began her affair with him during the fall of her junior year, and it continued on and off until she graduated and left Green Bay.

She had never told anyone about the affair. She suspected that these friends of hers here in Grand Marais would still be horribly shocked by the information if she told them now. And she knew that most people today would regard the affair as a classic instance of sexual harassment on the part of the teacher—unprofessional and unethical behavior at a minimum. If she heard about it from someone else, she would think so too. But Linda knew perfectly well that, in her own case, this was untrue. She had quite deliberately "gone after" Lorenzo DeVitis, and it had taken her the better part of a year to get him. He suffered rather touching bouts of guilt for the whole two years they were involved, but Linda never once regretted the affair. She had some low-level fear of pregnancy but felt no qualms about Lorenzo's marital status. She knew absolutely that neither one of them had any intention of seeing his marriage ended. He was a wonderful lover, patiently introducing her to the thrilling variety of pleasurable experiences that sex could give a woman. When she moved to Chicago, Linda missed him for a long time, but it was the sex she was missing rather more than Lorenzo himself. She knew that. And she supposed that the pain she was feeling in her present life, unconnected to Lorenzo DeVitis in any way, was a sort of justice for the callousness of her youth.

The only job she could get in Chicago at first was dressing windows in department stores, something her art major qualified her to do, but a job she hated for its commercialism and its vulgarity—or so she had regarded it then with all of her twenty-two-year-old's "artistic integrity." She smiled sometimes to remember the girl she had been. After a year and a half, she went to work for a studio where the chief source of business was portrait photography and weddings. Eventually she had a studio of her own and made what her father would have called "a good living." But it wasn't what she wanted to do. She didn't like working with studio lighting, and she quickly tired of the vanity her human subjects wanted her to indulge—"What can you do to make me look thinner?" was a frequent question. There were times when she felt one more candlelit shot of the bridal couple's crossed hands would make her gag. This morning when they'd been trying on the "Camp Men-O-Pause" shirts after breakfast, Peg had made that crack, "Linda doesn't take pictures of people," and she had had to bite her tongue to keep from saying, "You don't know what the hell you're talking about."

But the growing success of the studio had finally bought her the time to do the kind of photography she wanted to do—outside, working with available light. Landscape, architecture, and—especially—flora and fauna. No flower asked if she could make it look thinner. No fish wanted to be lit so it could appear ten years younger. Her present reputation as an art photographer made it possible to leave the studio entirely to her employees, so the "day job" of her earlier career had finally sprung her into the work she had always dreamed of doing. And the praise and prizes were gratifying too.

And, of course, the studio had also brought her Tom. He had come in one June morning in 1975 with his two children, then seven and five years old, to have some "nice pictures" made of them for the grandparents. His wife, he said, had the steady job in the family, so he usually did such things with the kids. He was a freelance writer, a compact man of medium height with a slightly receding hairline. Not handsome, no arresting features except for midnight blue eyes, which were so dark that, from a distance, most people assumed they must be brown. Yet it had taken only two more visits to the studio, the second of which he had invented an excuse to make, for them to become lovers. And they had stayed lovers for fifteen years. That he also stayed married had been largely at her insistence, and she had carefully arranged things so that she would never meet Nancy, although over the years she had learned quite a lot about her.

Linda's friends, sleeping in the rooms around her, knew about Tom, of course, and both Jan and Micky had met him. They had always affected a tolerance for the relationship, but Linda could tell that most of them were uneasy about it. They were, after all, wives themselves and must feel torn about offering support to "the other woman," even if she was their lifelong friend. Mostly they avoided talking about it, not a difficult tack for them to take since they were accustomed to Linda's reticence about personal matters.

Linda had once asked Micky directly for a reaction when she and Peter had come to Chicago for a long weekend in 1983—some of Peter's med-school buddies were still in the area, and while he hung out with them, Linda and Micky had some time together. Tom had stopped in for a drink at the apartment, and when he left, Linda had turned to Micky and said simply, "What are your thoughts about Tom and me? Your real thoughts, I mean."

Micky had taken another sip of her wine, her long fingers wrapped around the stem of the glass with the careless elegance that seemed to come so naturally to her.

"Listen, Lindy," she said finally. "I know you. I know you don't do stuff to hurt people. So whatever this relationship is about, I don't think you're planning to wreck any lives. I think you're probably trying hard not to."

"I am," Linda answered. "We both are."

"'Nuff said then." After a short pause, Micky went on. "If you told me you'd murdered somebody, Lindy, I'd think you probably had a damned good reason for doing it."

The end of her relationship with Tom was something Linda had never discussed with anyone, and any impulse she might have to talk to Micky about it could never be acted on. Not because Micky had lost any capacity for empathy, for loyalty— Linda didn't believe that for a minute—but because the issue paled by comparison to what Micky had to deal with on a day-to-day basis. But she mustn't think about any of that—not Tom, not Micky's Alzheimer's—or she would never get to sleep at all. Better just to breathe in the cool scent of pine and—subtly, behind it—the faint aroma of the great lake itself. Better just to drift, unthinking, over the surface of the lovely world until the oblivion of sleep took her somewhere else.

8 / Micky

In the dream she was looking down at herself from a great height, but she knew at once that the woman on the bicycle was herself. She even recognized the skirt, a granny skirt she had made for herself when she was going through a particularly domestic period in the late seventies; it was long with a great ruffle at the bottom and the fabric was a paisley print in earth tones. And she was wearing the bronze-colored silk blouse with poet sleeves she had bought to go with the skirt. It was an outfit Peter had admired, one he took great pleasure in removing one night after a party where they'd both had rather too much to drink.

Only the hair was wrong—the right color, but much longer than she had ever worn her hair, loose and flowing down the back of the shimmering silk. She felt a vague regret in looking at the hair, a sense that she had lost something, misplaced a valuable possession, which she would need again, even if she couldn't quite remember what it was. The path the bicycle was following was white, dazzling, as if lit from underneath, and very straight. Everything around it was black, featureless.

Suddenly, in one of those twinkling transformations so typical of dreams, she was no longer looking down, but had melded with herself on the bicycle, was now looking forward at the bone-white path, at her hands gripping the handlebars, at the billowing sleeves whose movement tickled her arms. From this perspective, the speed of the bicycle seemed much faster than it had looked from above. Yet she had no sensation of effort, was not conscious of trying to pedal at all. She looked down past the paisley skirt, which was hiked almost to her lap, its generous folds blowing backward over her hips, over the bicycle seat. Now she could see her feet, as if in a sharp close-up, and she noticed that they were being held to the pedals with the sort of clips used by bicycle racers.

In a slow dawning, she realized that she wasn't pedaling at all, that she was a passenger on the bicycle as some force turned its wheels and complicated gears. There was no motor; she could see it was an ordinary bicycle. There were the brake levers next to her hands. She felt no panic yet, no sense of danger. With the calm logic of dream, she thought, "I can just reach out to the brakes and make it stop whenever I want. No biggy." But there was something exhilarating about the speed, the rush of wind in her face. She could feel her hair beginning to lift behind her, its weight tugging rather pleasantly at the back of her head. It was like water-skiing, that same adrenaline rush as the surface of the water seemed to sink below the skis until there was no longer any feeling of resistance, only the sensation of being airborne.

She and Peter had taught the kids to water-ski one summer at their lake cabin in northern Wisconsin. Sam had taken to it immediately, able to get up out of the water on her third try. She had been a gangly thirteen then, still flat-chested but strong, supple. She had her father's skin and tanned to a lovely coppery brown after only a few weeks of summer. Matt was a different story—fair and freckled like his mother, susceptible to painful sunburn. And the waterskiing was hard for him. He would get halfway up from his crouch, lose confidence, and topple into the water, throwing the towrope away from himself as he fell. But so determined, dogged in his insistence that they try again. She would hold him from behind, treading water as the boat gained speed, and Matt gripped the tow bar with fierce intensity. "Relax," she'd murmur against his hair. "Just let the boat pull you up until you're standing." But she could feel the trembling in his body, hear his teeth chattering.

Peter tried to hide his disappointment that the boy wasn't as naturally athletic as he was himself, even suggested that they should give it up temporarily—"Next summer, you'll be twelve," he said soothingly. "You'll be stronger." But the child set his jaw and, without looking at his father, growled, "I'll get it this time." But he didn't—not that day or the next or the day after that. "My God," Peter said to her as they cuddled together in the big bed one night. "He's just as bull-headed as his mother." "No, no," she'd answered, jabbing him playfully in the ribs with her thumb. "As determined, as single-minded as his mother. And, unfortunately, just as uncoordinated."

But by the end of the vacation, Matt was water-skiing—all business about it, grim-faced and still a little stiff, but up on the skis, skimming over the water, even attempting a few widely swinging slaloms. Peter sat in the boat, easing it into lazy turns, his brow puckered into a little frown that was some mixture of concern and subdued pride. On the last day, she watched them from the deck, the kids taking turns on the skis, Peter hauling them by turns into the boat by the straps of their life vests. The sun glared up off the wake of the boat, and she couldn't tell if the heat she felt in her chest and neck and face was incipient sunburn or a joy so warm that it threatened to boil over. And she didn't even bother to try to distinguish the feelings that washed over her as she watched the supreme confidence of her sun-worshipping daughter, the brave effort of her still babyish son, the easy willingness of her husband to make his children's fun the wellspring of his own contentment. It was all one bright glow—almost too bright, almost painful in its intensity.

But now her face didn't feel warm. In fact, the air rushing at her was cool, almost cold, and it was sending little shivers up her arms, making the billowing silk along her shoulders chilly and damp feeling as it fluttered against her skin. The bicycle was going much faster now, and the speed was beginning to frighten her a little. She reached the fingers of both hands out for the brake levers, closed on them, and found to her dismay that they folded against the handlebars with no resistance at all. There was no connection between these handles and the whirring wheels. She looked down at her legs, saw them pumping up and down, pushed and pulled by the pedals, helplessly locked into the rushing motion of the bicycle. The skirt was bunched at her waist now, most of it flying out behind her, and she could feel the whipping motion of her hair at the back of her head. Her legs were pale, almost as white as the path that was flying away beneath her. And beside her legs, she could see the gears—immense, outsized gears— and they were far more intricately enmeshed than on any real bicycle she had ever seen; their teeth made metallic gnashing sounds as they engaged and disengaged, faster and faster.

She lifted her head now and looked forward. The path went straight ahead into the blackness, tapering to the vanishing point, but glowing, almost pulsating in its whiteness. Whatever was powering the bicycle seemed to draw its strength from this glow. She could feel the sick, falling sensation of panic now. Was it too late to just jump from the bicycle? At this speed, would she be killed from the impact with the road? Would the pedal clips over her shoes release, or just hold her as the bike wiped out in a terrible crash?

Suddenly she knew, without bothering to question how the knowledge had come to her, that Peter and the children were somewhere behind her, that they were trying to reach her. She opened her mouth wide, almost like a yawn, gulped air, and then tried to shout: "Peter!" But the rushing air pushed the name back into her mouth, shoved it past her teeth and into her throat. There was no sound. Just the whirring of the wheels, the chewing frenzy of the gears. When she looked down at her legs again, she saw that the gears had grown bigger, were almost halfway to her knees on either side, their slicing motion dangerously close to flesh—if she spread her legs, the gears would bite into her calves.

"Please," she whispered, but she didn't have any sense, at first, of a listener. "Please let me go."

And then she knew with incredible clarity that the force propelling the bicycle, surrounding her like an evil fog, could be defeated. All she had to do was speak to Peter and the children, to tell them the one important word, and the headlong rush would stop. But she would have to turn her head, to turn even her upper body, so that the sound could reach them. And if she turned, her hair, perhaps even her clothes, would get tangled in the gears, causing the bicycle to crash, and the crash might kill her. But she also sensed that the turning, the speaking, the crashing would destroy the force that drove her forward at this terrible pace. She had a premonitory vision of that malevolent spirit exploding behind her whipping hair. If she turned.

She let go of the handlebars, lifted her arms at the black sky, and—turning slowly at the waist—felt the shift of her skirt, the lashing of her hair. She wasn't afraid now, only resolute, certain of what she must do. She took a big breath and opened her mouth to speak.

9 / Mary

When Mary awoke the first time, the windows were turning gray—about four-thirty, she guessed. She made the guess even before she realized where she was, before she remembered she was in the "Pine Room" in a narrow bed. The room was cool, almost cold, because she and Linda had agreed to leave the windows open. Mary loved the cool, was grateful for this concession from her old friend who, she knew, preferred warmth. Every fall of their college years, envious classmates would admire the rich shade of pecan brown that Linda could turn her skin by baking it in the sun for three months. "Just baby oil," she would say when they asked her what she used. Mary wondered now if Linda would someday have to pay for that indulgence, whether she had already begun to examine her skin for telltale lesions. Among the plastic bottles on Linda's side of the vanity, Mary had noticed a sunscreen numbered twenty-five.

She turned her head and glanced across the narrow space between the beds, saw the soft outline of Linda's body under the quilt. How many mysteries were wrapped up in that body! Over the years, Mary had found Lindy Tourneau the most puzzling person in all her acquaintance, had admired her cool independence without any wish to imitate it, had resented her detachment whenever she felt most needy. And she knew now, because he had casually told her, that David had lusted after Linda when they were students at St. Augustine. She believed David when he said nothing had ever happened between them—believed him because at that stage he was almost boastful about his various conquests. But still it made her look at Linda differently. She couldn't help it. And Linda had a married lover for over fifteen years. She never talked about what had happened there, about why the affair had ended. Mary had never met the man, had felt only a vague pity for his wife when Jan had told her about him. And now he was history. Linda was alone again, as self-possessed as ever, not giving anything away. But alone. And that was enough to stir Mary's sympathy.

Suddenly the predawn silence was broken by a sound, distant but distinct, seeming to float across the birches from the direction of the lake. It was a sustained musical note, high and sweet, followed by a much shorter falling note. At first, she thought it might be a flute—it had that pure clarity—but several repetitions of the identical pattern, one closer to the house than the other, convinced her that it must be a bird. She knew many varieties of birdsong, but she had never heard this one before. There was something in the note, in the call and response, that made her heart swell with a rush of joy, a feeling that someone had spoken to her, whispered a sweet secret of peace and healing. For some odd reason, the song made her think of Micky.

When she awoke the second time, she discovered that the other bed was empty and sunshine was pouring through the screens. She bounded up and fumbled for her watch. Seven-fifty. And breakfast was at eight-thirty! She would have to race through her shower. What could have made her sleep so soundly that she hadn't even heard Linda get up?

At the table, she remembered the birdsong, asked Steve Olson about it as he was setting down the second pot of coffee.

"I know what you mean," he said. "I don't know what bird it is, but I've heard it often, very early in the morning. A sad sound."

"Oh, no!" she said, surprised, looking up into his long face. "I didn't think it was sad at all. Serious, maybe, but it was sweet, lovely."

He looked down at her briefly from his gray green eyes, the eyes of a fox, and then he shrugged, a slow movement of the muscular shoulders, as if he were afraid that any quick movement on his side might set off a flurry of alarm among these plump hens. "I guess it's a matter of human interpretation," he said, "either way."

Earlier, at the start of breakfast, he had told them that he'd arranged a dinner for that evening at Trail's End Lodge so they could finally meet Ada Thurley. Last summer, they had discussed how they might make contact with the woman whose book they had read and whose life they admired. "We'd better hurry up and meet her," Sharon had commented at the time, "before she dies on us. She must be older than God already." But nothing had come of it then. Now it seemed Steve and Kim knew somebody who was good friends with Ada's son, and they had conspired to bring together the old woman and this group of fans. As an added bonus, the meeting was to be at the lodge Ada had helped her husband build when the Gunflint Trail was truly a "trail," a narrow path through the wilderness. Ada's memoir about her pioneering life as a trail guide and a leader of hunting parties had created a small sensation in the Midwest some years before; one of her "clients," as she invariably called them in the book, had been Ernest Hemingway. She was eighty-six years old and living in retirement at Trail's End, which was now operated by her son.

"As long as it's such a beautiful day," Steve was saying now, "you might as well go up early and get in some canoeing. I could pack some shore lunch for you, if you'd like."

"Where could we canoe?" Jan asked, interested immediately.

"You could try Big Sag," he answered, "if it's calm. Or Sea Gull."

"No way," Sharon cried, looking up from the last bits of the breakfast burrito that had generated noisy enthusiasm when it was served. "Not Big Sag. I heard you last year talking about the wind and the choppiness up there. I'm not eager to be drowned."

Big Sag was the local nickname for the larger part of Lake Saganaga, a huge body of water at the mouth of the series of interconnected lakes that formed the boundary waters between the United States and Canada.

"Well, Sea Gull Lake then," Steve said with a little smile at Sharon. Mary suspected that, like the rest of them, Steve Olson found Sharon's loud bossiness amusing rather than annoying; he seemed to understand that it was a mask for a tender heart. "It's closer to Trail's End and much quieter. If you stay among the islands along the shoreline, you'll hardly need any muscle at all."

"Isn't it short notice to get outfitted, though?" Jan asked.

"Nah," he said. "Not on a Wednesday. I can make a few calls, and they'll be ready for you. Some of my buds run Voyageur Outfitters up there, and they've got good, reliable equipment."

One of the things Mary liked about the Arrowhead region was this folksy interconnectedness of the people who lived here the year around—they knew each other, cooperated rather than competed. No doubt they had learned that stay-ing solitary in a place so big, so capable of swallowing up puny human beings, was not a preference they could afford to indulge.

"Well, what do you guys think?" Jan asked. "Are you up for this? We'd have to take along a change of clothes, I suppose, but it would be a bona fide adventure."

"I'm for it," Mary said quickly, hoping to forestall Sharon's typical grumbling. Sharon was actually a skilled canoeist, as everyone knew, perhaps the most seasoned camper among them, but for some reason she always felt obliged to pretend that strenuous activity of any kind might put her into traction.

"I won't have to paddle, will I?" Peg asked, blushing slightly at having to admit her ineptitude. "You know me. I'd tip us over for sure."

"You could be a duffer," Jan said soothingly. "We'll only take two canoes, I think."

There was a silence now. Mary, impatient as always at the reticence she associated with Americans of northern European extraction, smacked her spoon against her saucer and exclaimed, "Well, come on, you guys. What do you say?"

"I'd like to go," Micky said, her voice clear and firm. "It sounds like fun." And that was the deciding vote.

They were lacing and zipping themselves into their life vests, having found the launch site after only two wrong turns. The outfitters had been waiting for them with two huge Grumman canoes already hoisted off the truck and beached with their battered noses in the lapping water of Sea Gull Lake. Mary was having trouble loosening a knot that was preventing her from restringing the side vents of her vest. She picked at the knot with her weak fingernails, trying to suppress the rush of irritation that threatened her good mood. What she had once attributed to her Italian volatility, she now ascribed to her menopausal hormone imbalance—she found it strangely comforting to have such a nail onto which she could hang her unlovely feelings. But the knot, locked in by repeated wetting and drying, was being especially resistant. When "Damn!" had turned into "Oh, fuck!" she heard a melodious voice say, "Here, let me see." And she looked up to see Micky striding toward her, a life preserver neatly zipped around her lean torso.

Mary began to back up, almost ready to fend off her old friend; if she tried the knot and couldn't budge it, what then? Would the frustration trigger an incident? But Micky looked so calm, so competent, that Mary stopped herself and pushed the offending string into Micky's outstretched hand. She watched as the pale fingers went to work on the stubborn tangle, turning the knot carefully, feeling for any give. Micky's cropped head bent over the string, just inches below Mary's face; a fragrance of coconut drifted up from the clean hair.

"Oh, yarbles," Micky whispered. "This really *is* a bitch, isn't it?"

The first epithet surprised a sudden laugh from Mary, followed by a choking gulp as the memories flooded her. At St. Augustine, most of the undergraduates of the sixties claimed *Catcher in the Rye* as their cult book, generally oblivious to the fact that it had already been "discovered" by millions of other would-be rebels. But the honors-program group favored *A Clockwork Orange,* that stranger, darker vision of youthful assertion. Micky had adopted much of the eccentric vocabulary Burgess had invented for his futuristic street toughs. And years after she had abandoned, perhaps even forgotten, most of it, she retained *yarbles* as an expression of general disgust or dismissal. Sometimes when she was feeling especially exercised, she would say, "Great leaping yarblockos!" People in her acquaintance who had never even heard of *A Clockwork*

Orange understood from usage exactly what the expression was intended to convey.

Mary had noticed at breakfast that Micky seemed more alert today, more "with it" than she'd been yesterday. She'd asked Steve about the ingredients of the burritos, had talked easily with Peg about flowers—Peg had a gorgeous garden at home and had picked some wildflowers on an early walk that morning. On the trip up the Gunflint Trail, Micky watched the landscape slide by, commented on the colors of the rock face through which parts of the trail had been carved, listened attentively as Peg pointed out the two-hundred-year-old white pine forest they passed through. And she asked Mary, "Did you bring along that tape you were telling me about? Maybe we could listen to some of it." They had talked about the tape Sunday evening at Jan's house, so this was an impressive feat of memory for a woman with Alzheimer's.

"Got it!" Micky said triumphantly. She lifted her head and flashed one of her wonderful smiles at Mary. Sure enough, the two ends of the string were separate now, one in each of her slim hands.

"Bless you," Mary said, giving Micky a quick hug. "You know what a putz I am. I'd still be here struggling with this damn vest while the rest of you had paddled to Canada."

"Oh, we would take you along anyway," Micky said against her ear. "If you fell in, we'd rescue you."

"I'm sure you would," Mary whispered, fighting tears.

When they stepped apart, she occupied herself with restringing the vent so that Micky wouldn't see her face.

They had listened to some of the tape in the car. It was "Mozart Portraits" sung by Cecilia Bartoli. Christopher had bought it for Mary more than a year ago, because he knew how much she loved the young coloratura's voice. It was opera that had brought Mary and Chris together in the first place. Not an opera on stage—that was something Kenosha didn't provide. But one day in the summer of 1986, Mary had come out of her bank and had been brought to a stand by the sounds coming out of a car that was parked next to her own—it was a convertible, top down and motor running, and no one at the wheel. The sounds were coming from the speakers—an elaborate, customized set built into the corners of the backseat. The music was from *Rigoletto*. The incongruity of such music coming out of such a vehicle brought a vague smile to Mary's face as she stood listening, her hand on the door handle of her own car.

"Do you like it?" a voice said behind her.

She jumped and whirled to find a trim, bespectacled man at her elbow.

"What?" she blurted. "The car or the music?"

"Either," he said, grinning. "Both."

"I like the music," she mumbled, opening the door of her car.

"Oh, good," he said, "because the car isn't mine. It's my partner's. But the sound system is so good, I keep borrowing it when I need to run errands for the firm."

She sneaked a look at him now: narrow, intelligent face; dark hair laced with gray; a thick mustache, almost white; beautiful eyes, caramel colored and fringed by long lashes. *Way* too good to be true, she thought, her suspicions aroused. Married for sure and trying to pick up a woman in the bank parking lot.

"Yes," she said tightly. "It's a wonderful sound." And she climbed into her car and slammed the door.

The next day he appeared in her shop. He had simply gone back into the bank, he explained, and asked who the woman in the white Pontiac was—she'd dropped something he wanted to return, he fibbed. That day in her store he'd told her about himself, almost as if he were presenting a resumé for a job interview. He was a lawyer specializing in workmen's compensation. He was fifty years old. His wife of twenty-five years had died of breast cancer two years earlier. They'd never had children. And then he asked Mary to go with him to an opera in Chicago.

She had dated him for two years, delighted with his company, pleased to have a sex life again—a *satisfying* sex life for the first time. But she remained skittish, fending off his marriage proposals—"What's the hurry?"—afraid to trust after what David had put her through. Besides, she was beginning to really enjoy her independence, at last confident that she was a person of substance in her own right—not just an adjunct or auxiliary of someone else. And then she got sick, a bad case of salmonella poisoning that put her in the hospital for four days. Christopher came every day, held the basin when she vomited, mopped her face with a damp cloth when she was through. She knew how she must look, how she must smell, but she was too sick to care. But Chris treated her as if she were a beautiful princess, kept murmuring, "Poor darling. I'm here. It'll be all right." When he drove her home from the hospital, she told him, "If you still want to get married, let's do it."

In the years since the wedding, she had relaxed into a good marriage, had come to see that Chris didn't expect her to be an adjunct; he was proud of her success, boasted about her to his associates in the legal profession. And he remained full of surprises. While David had considered any outdoor activity besides golf "unsophisticated," Chris loved hiking, camping, canoeing, birding. So in her early forties, Mary Cavallo, city girl, opera buff, and business woman, had become "outdoorsy," as her brothers put it. And she had come to love it, quite independent of Chris's influence and company. Many of the surprises from her husband took the form of little gifts, thoughtful reminders that he listened to her, remembered her interests and enthusiasms. The Bartoli tape had been one of those surprises. "So you can listen to her in your car too," he had said, since they had CDs for home use.

She remembered vividly the day she had first listened to the tape. She'd been on a buying trip for the shop, listening to the car radio, when a newsbreak had identified Timothy McVeigh as the person arrested for the bombing in Oklahoma City: a domestic terrorist, militia wanna-be, twenty-five-year-old filled with the hatred born of ignorance and envy and the refusal to admit his own inadequacies. She had listened, horrified, as the analysis continued, mile after mile, until she could stand not one more word. She pushed the tape into the player and let the wonderful voice flood the car— *"Exsultate! Jubilate!"*— moved as always to awe not just at the tone quality, the range, but at the discipline, the control, the sheer labor that surely went into the making of such beauty. And Bartoli was twenty-six years old when she made the recording. Finally, Mary pulled off the highway to a phone booth and called Chris at his office.

"I had an insight today," she told him. "Timothy McVeigh and Cecilia Bartoli are both *facts* about the species I belong to. They might pretty much define the limits, both ways, but they are both distinctively human. They are *us.*"

And she had wanted to call Peg and Jan and Micky and Sharon and Linda, too, but that would be unreasonable, and Mary Morgan had become a reasonable woman in the middle of her life. They had begun the habit of calling each other in times of national crisis soon after they graduated from St. Augustine. But the crises had begun while they were still in school together, especially during their senior year, that remarkable time in 1968 when the nation seemed about to tear itself asunder.

Even as freshmen they had identified themselves with the civil rights movement; their idealism was abstract because the worst instances of racism were remote from their own experience. The only black people in Green Bay in those years played for the Packers and lived somewhere else during the off season, and St. Augustine had exactly two black students: Tim Hilton, a biology major, and John Evans, a seminarian from Philadelphia. But they felt passionate enough in their devotion to justice. When they were freshmen and didn't even know each other very well yet, George Wallace came to campus to speak against the Civil Rights Act of 1964. He had brought with him a group of Alabamians, who sat behind him on the stage, and he introduced them as representing the major constituencies of his state, all of whom supported him on the principle of states' rights. The one glaring omission was too obvious to pass unmarked, even though the packed auditorium had agreed ahead of time to react with total silence to Wallace's presentation, a tactic that so unnerved the little man that he cut short his remarks and made the error of asking for questions.

Michelle Marie Jaeger, as the newspaper accounts later named her, popped to her feet and said in a ringing voice, "You say you've brought with you representatives of all Alabama's constituencies. Where is the black person in the group?" A sustained cheer went up from the crowd, and Wallace reddened. When near silence had been established again, he leaned forward over the podium and drawled, "Well, little honey . . ." and leered at her. Instantly, before he could go on, Micky snapped, "You may call me Miss Jaeger, Governor Wallace." An even louder roar went up, and Mary sat there thinking, "That's somebody I have to get to know."

They were devoted to Dr. Martin Luther King and his principles of nonviolent protest. Jan had actually attended the March on Washington the summer before her senior year in high school, had heard the "I Have a Dream" speech, though, she said, she was so far from the speaker's platform, that she couldn't see King at all. On the morning of April 5, 1968, they all huddled together in the Honor's Lounge, alternately weeping and raging, as the small black-and-white television set reported the details of King's assassination the previous evening. There they learned that King had been shot through the throat, that he was conscious enough to move his lips, but that he couldn't speak.

"They knew what they were shooting at," Linda said softly. "They killed that voice, that wonderful voice."

By that time, of course, they were expanding their attention to include the Vietnam War. In Mary's mind, there was still no difference between the civil rights movement and the antiwar movement: racism, violence, and injustice were targets in both causes. During their senior year, they got "Clean for Gene," working as volunteers in the campaign of Senator Eugene McCarthy, gloating over his good showing in the New Hampshire primary, increasingly convinced that he could take Wisconsin at the beginning of June. They spent much of their days distributing leaflets, drumming up the crowd support for celebrity speakers, who included such dazzling figures as Edward Albee and Paul Newman; they spent their evenings before the TV set, watching the nightly parade of horrors from the other side of the world: the body count of the Tet Offensive, the surreal film—played over and over—of Colonel Nguyen Ngoc Loan raising a revolver and shooting a handcuffed prisoner through the head.

They were so dedicated that they imagined McCarthy couldn't lose; every rally they attended was crowded with supporters, the headquarters was staffed by people of almost fanatical faith, and almost everyone they knew well was against the war, even some of their parents. When Robert Kennedy entered the race, they vilified him as an opportunist, but Sharon remarked shrewdly that perhaps Kennedy had a better chance of winning the nomination and then, in the long run, the election. They graduated in the middle of May on a sunny, hot day, their spirits high, their idealism intact.

And then all hell broke loose. President Johnson bowed out on the eve of the Wisconsin primary, so McCarthy's victory was rendered meaningless. And on the morning of June 6, Mary, still living with her father, awoke to the ringing of the phone. It was Peg calling from across town to tell her that Bobby Kennedy had been shot the night before. When his death was confirmed, Mary called Micky long distance to Augsdale. The first words Micky spoke were, "Oh, Mimi, I'm so tired of having tears for breakfast." The long summer passed in the slow motion of nightmare, the Chicago convention that nominated Hubert Humphrey coming as the penultimate horror. In early November, Richard Nixon was elected president, and at Thanksgiving, Mimi Cavallo married David Schneider and moved with him to Pennsylvania.

For Mary, 1968 became one of the great dividing moments of her life, slicing like a knife between her childhood and her adulthood. She had been living in her father's house on her wedding day, and one year later she was a mother. She had been a political and social idealist, but after 1968, she was never active in a political campaign. In the summer of 1969, she sat alone in front of the TV, watching Neil Armstrong walk on the moon while her husband was sleeping and her unborn daughter was quiet in her womb. Fifteen minutes later, she picked up the phone and dialed

Peg's number in Lafayette, Indiana, where Peg and Jerry—
married that spring—were then living. She had missed Peg's
wedding—no money to travel, David said—and so felt perversely justified in the impulsive phone call. They talked for
half an hour—"It doesn't seem *real*, does it?" Peg exclaimed—
and later David complained bitterly about the phone bill.

And so it went as the years flew away—the Kent State massacre in 1970 brought a call from Micky at Columbia where
she was finishing her master's degree, still fiercely active in
the antiwar movement. The massacre had resulted in a brief
estrangement from her policeman father who, she told Mary,
had said, "The little punks should have expected it." Nixon's
resignation brought a flurry of phone calls, most of them
self-congratulatory—"Didn't we just *know!?*"—and the hostage
crisis in Iran prompted Linda to call from Chicago. Even
years later when Mary had moved back to Wisconsin, the
explosion of the Challenger sent most of them to the phones
to discuss it across the miles. Letters seemed to serve just fine
for personal news and even personal crisis, but the national
and international upheavals seemed to require the sound of
each other's voices, tsking and soothing, complaining and
analyzing, their old bonds reinforced by making sure—listening to tones of voice, nuances of expression—that they were
still as one over the big stuff.

Now, secured in her expanded life preserver, Mary
watched as her friends headed for the beached canoes,
chattering and laughing, lifting their heads to watch a loon
soar overhead and then settle with a great plop onto the
water they were about to invade.

"Have you got your sunglasses, Mick?" Mary asked as she
caught up with the group. "It looks like we're going to need
them."

"Right here," Micky said, grinning at her and pulling the

sunglasses out of her shirt pocket. "And I've got my hat too." She tugged a battered fishing hat from the back pocket of her jeans. "I just fry in the sun, you know."

"Yes, I remember," Mary laughed.

At the beach, there was some discussion as to who would go in which canoe and who would paddle stern.

"I'm duffing," Peg reminded them, standing at the side of one canoe. "You promised I wouldn't have to paddle."

"Me too," Micky said, stepping forward to the other canoe and pulling the khaki-colored cap firmly over her hair.

The others looked at each other in silence; Micky had always been the first to volunteer for stern, a skilled and confident paddler even over white-water rapids. She turned back to them now, her own eyes hidden behind the dark lenses of her sunglasses.

"I'd be a liability now," she said softly, as if answering an unspoken question.

It was the first time on this trip that they had heard her allude to her condition, and it occurred to Mary that hearing it together like this, in a group, had suddenly made it real.

10 / Sharon

They were stowing the trash from lunch in a plastic bag, and Sharon was hunting for an apple core she had seen Micky drop. There were strict rules up here about trash—even biodegradable stuff must be policed up and carried out. Mary was standing apart from the group puffing on a cigarette, and Linda, who had brought one of her smaller cameras along, was taking pictures of the rock formations against the background of the lake's brilliant blue. At one-thirty, they had decided to put in at the first island that presented a place to beach the canoes, and Sharon was grateful for the break, her shoulders and biceps beginning to ache from paddling. Managing an office was not a good way to stay in shape, she thought. They had left the canoes and bushwhacked up to a flat rock outcropping on the island's windward side, a formation typical of the Boundary Water's islands. A nice breeze kept the site relatively bug free, and nearby trees provided shade. Steve had packed big sandwiches on crusty whole-wheat bread, trail mix, and fresh fruit. A thermos jug of lemonade and gooey brownies for dessert finished off the meal.

"Hurry up," Jan was saying to everybody. "We've got an hour and a half at least before we get back to the cars and then we have to shower and change before we go to Trail's End. What are you looking for, Sharon?"

"For your whip, Ms. Legree," Sharon said sweetly. "The better for you to drive us galley slaves with."

"Oh, for heaven's sake," Jan said, and she sounded genuinely peeved. "Must you make such a production out of everything? You make it sound like you're an invalid or something." But by now she was beginning to grin. "It's very elderly of you, Sharon."

"Oh, I suppose I can suffer through it," Sharon said, putting the back of a brownie-stained hand against her forehead and gazing up at the sky. "But I'm not paddling stern on the way back."

When she looked down again, she spotted the apple core and bent quickly to pick it up. She sometimes wondered herself why she groused so flamboyantly about things she really didn't mind doing. It was as if she had created a persona while they were in college together, a comic complainer who was always dragged kicking and screaming into the plans and activities of the others. And now she seemed stuck with the role. Maybe, she thought as she wiped her hands on a paper towel, it was because she *felt* herself so different from the others that she had to exaggerate the differences in order to prevent anyone else pointing them out. The truth was that she'd always felt a little awkward, bumpkinish, among these women she loved and admired so much.

And college hadn't seem to "take" with her the way it had with the others. They were professional women with higher degrees, Peg a school social worker, Jan a fancy Ph.D. psychologist you had to be afraid to tell a dream to, and Micky a college professor. Linda, of course, was a Chicagoan with a national reputation as an artsy photographer, and Mimi— for whom she'd been able to feel comfortably sorry for quite a few years—had founded and fostered a now successful business of a particularly feminine variety; she was practically Martha Stewart, for God's sake.

Once, near the end of their junior year at St. Augustine, Micky had encouraged Sharon to apply for a Woodrow Wilson Fellowship for graduate school. Micky was planning to apply. And, to no one's surprise, the next year Micky won, making Columbia possible for her.

"Are you nuts?" Sharon had cackled. "Me? Not unless they've got one for advanced cowshit hauling. I'm good at that."

Micky hadn't laughed, not even a smile. She just cocked her head at Sharon, eyeing her speculatively for a moment. "Is it possible," she said finally, "that you really don't know how smart you are? Do you think you were invited into Honors by mistake or something? You have a steel-trap mind and great insight, so stop putting yourself down."

Sharon had been so pleased, so close to tears of gratitude, that she had immediately cracked a joke playing off "steel-trap" to hide her feelings. And she *had* loved her college coursework, especially in her major. The sweep and grandeur of history was so impressive, so *big* compared to what she had known of the world. And the efforts of historians to discover cause and effect, to separate the accidental from the essential across eons of time, seemed noble to her. But when she went to Oconto to teach history to high schoolers, that was swallowed up in daily aggravations: trying to manage the behavior of physically twitchy, intellectually dull adolescents; composing and grading quizzes, which emphasized only the trivial details of time and event; struggling to please administrators who considered a clean blackboard a greater sign of pedagogical success than an awakened mind. She had fled into marriage with a great sigh of relief.

Then, four years later, when Kaz finally brought himself to tell her that his business was going under, she pitched in, sorting through the mountains of disorganized documents he had flung willy-nilly into file drawers, setting up meetings with bankers, negotiating with creditors for more time, even laying off some of the salesmen when Kaz proved too soft-hearted to do it. In three years, they were back on their feet, and in five they were doing quite well, thank you very much. Kaz was great with people, beloved throughout the region, able to stand for hours in a field with a local farmer, kicking at clods, and allowing as how a new haybine would be just the ticket to take care of that extra acreage the man had rented to plant a cash crop. And she discovered that she had a knack for the paperwork, the numbers, the management end. Eventually, she bought and learned how to use a computer system for ordering, billing, and accounting. Kaz took to saying to anyone who would listen, "I don't have no clue how much we're hauling in. I leave that all to the little woman." And she took a secret pride in knowing that this was literally true.

But it was still farm machinery, for Christ's sake—you didn't need college for that. So whenever she was with her old friends, she felt defensive, and she knew it too; there was nothing subconscious about it. She also knew that they laughed at Kaz a little, compared him unfavorably to their own husbands. And *that* she resented, felt a hot urge to slap them sometimes when they exchanged glances over his grammar, his politically incorrect attitudes. But, instead, she made jokes to redirect their laughter at her. And she bought things. Expensive camping gear if they were going on a trip with any of the other couples; a dazzling beaded dress for the twenty-fifth reunion at St. Augustine; a top-of-the-line imported car with a sunroof and enough electronic gadgetry to impress even the Ph.D.'s. Dumb. But, what the hell, she could afford it now, and it bought her a little edge.

"Here, Mimi, catch," she called and tossed the tightly bundled trash bag at her old friend just as she was turning.

"Hey!" Mary cried, reacting in time to catch the sack in her free hand. "We don't call me Mimi anymore, remember?"

Sharon was sometimes rankled by Mary's insistence on this point. After getting her consciousness raised, Mary had simply trashed all of her names; Mimi had always been a nickname, anyway, she said, and a "degrading diminutive" at that. Her other names, surname and married name, had been foisted on her by a patriarchal culture. Only "Mary," a name given her by her mother, was acceptable. As usual, when she felt angry, Sharon made an attempt at humor.

"Okay, so sue me," she cackled. "One of my old synapses fired, I suppose, because my new ones are so sluggish." The moment the words were out, she gasped and snapped her head around to see where Micky was. Shit, shit, shit! Here was a new worry. They would all have to edit their words now, avoid any references to the brain, to forgetfulness. Micky was standing behind her to the left, close to the edge of the rock outcropping. She was holding a tiny bunch of wildflowers, and she was looking at Sharon with a wry smile that made her seem like her old self.

"Don't worry, Sharon," she said gently. "It's all right to say *synapse* in front of me."

Sharon dropped her gaze to the flowers, unable to bear the look of sad tolerance in Micky's eyes. "What are those flowers called?" she asked. Lame, stupid. Why could she never say the right thing?

"I have no idea," Micky said simply. "I just liked them."

"Are you going to take them along?" Sharon said, stepping toward Micky.

"No," she said. "I'll just leave them here." And she went into a graceful stoop, tucking the little bouquet into a crack in the rock near the edge of the drop-off to the lake below. The breeze set the little blossoms to ruffling as Micky stood up again. "So we can find this place again next year," she finished.

Sharon looked up quickly at Micky's face, saw at once that she was quite aware of the "joke" she had made, aware too of the underlying irony—*she* wouldn't remember any of this next year. Sharon reached out and put her hand on Micky's shoulder. Sometimes, she thought, even *she* knew when words were both unnecessary and inappropriate.

The canoes were drifting along close to the shore with Jan and Sharon paddling stern. Sharon had simply taken the position, and no one had reminded her of her earlier assertion that she wouldn't do it. They had discovered that the wind would simply float them back to the spot from which they had launched—all that was needed was an occasional directional adjustment. Without any work to do, their natural disposition to talk had emerged, so they had simply formed a catamaran by coming alongside each other and having Peg and Micky, both seated on the floor in the center of the canoes, reach out and grasp the gunwale of the opposite canoe. It was one of those days, Sharon thought, that postcard makers must love: cloudless sky, dazzling sunshine, cooling breeze, and the colors of everything so bright that trees seemed to pop out at them from the shoreline, loons bobbing on the water seemed lit from the inside like glass ornaments. Sharon noticed that Linda, seated on her heels in the bow of the opposite canoe, seldom took her camera away from her face. Right up her alley. Still it seemed almost sad that Linda could appreciate such a day only through a viewfinder. You should put a day like this straight into your eyes, your ears, your nose, your fingers. You should just swallow it whole. Seated behind Peg, Sharon trailed her fingers in the icy water and watched the two duffers lean toward each other as they talked.

"Did I ask you about Jerry already?" Micky said.

"Yes," Peg answered, her ears reddening. Every uncertainty, every embarrassment—even for others—seemed to make her blush. "Sunday night."

"Well, you'd better tell me again." Micky said it with a smile. "I know he had that surgery."

"That was two years ago now," Peg explained patiently. "Heart bypass surgery, and he's recovered from that quite well, the doctors say. But you know how Jerry is. If you looked up 'Type-A Personality' in some psychology textbook, there would be a tiny photo of Gerald Brunner next to the definition. I finally had to accept it that *forcing* him to take it easy would be more stressful for him than working hard. We just have to monitor his blood pressure and keep him on his meds."

Sharon remembered the anxious round of calls that had followed Jerry's emergency surgery. Since Mimi's divorce from David Schneider, Jerry, Peter Shaw, and Mike Werden were the only male college chums they still claimed as "family" and the horrible possibility of losing one so early had sobered all of them, made them look at their own husbands with new eyes.

"Hard on *you*, huh?" Micky said, reaching over briefly to pat Peg's freckled hand.

"Oh, yeah," Peg breathed. "It's a wonder *my* blood pressure isn't spiking every other day. And my parents haven't been well either. They were all set to move to Menominee to be near us, and then they changed their minds at the last minute. Just last month. I know I'm lucky to still have my parents, but honestly, sometimes I could just shake them."

Mary, at rest in the bow of one canoe, turned at the waist to get in on the conversation. "I suppose it's hard, too, for you to have Lizzy so far away," she said to Peg.

"Sure," Peg answered. "But even if she lived close by, she has her own life now. I don't think we should expect our kids to take on *two* generations. Still, I miss her, of course I do."

Sharon felt the beginnings of a familiar sinking sensation. They were going to talk about their kids again. She glanced over at Linda, the other nonmother, but that intent photographer seemed not to have heard.

"When Carol went away to college," Mary said, "I thought I was never going to stop crying and brooding. Chris practically turned himself inside out trying to cheer me up. But, you know, I'm used to it now, and I really kind of enjoy finding the scissors in the exact same place where I left them. And now, when they come to visit, I'm just exhausted when they leave."

"But it must be such a joy to have the baby in the house," Peg said, her voice full of mild reproach.

"Oh, of course it is," Mary said immediately. "But come on, you guys, 'fess up. Don't you ever find yourselves resenting the way your kids do things when they come home—sleeping late and expecting you to wait on them the way you did when they were four? And when they help, they just do stuff wrong."

"Like what?" Peg asked.

"Like when they load the dishwasher wrong," Mary answered. "Like they've never bothered to learn that you want the table knives blade up in the baskets and the other silverware separated in the little compartments so it's easier to put away later when you unload." Her round face was almost comically outraged, and they all gave a shout of laughter.

"Oh, Jesus," Mary breathed, her face reddening. "Listen to me. And we used to swear we'd never be like that. Never rigid and stuffy like—like *parents.*"

"Oh, hell," Jan said, recovering her voice sooner than the others. "We *are* parents. And I know what you mean. Kevin still thinks he can raid the refrigerator, and most of the time I think it's cute, but this spring he came for a weekend and gouged a big chunk out of the torte I was planning to take to Mike's department picnic."

"Matt leaves his underwear on the bedroom floor," Micky said brightly. "Sometimes when he goes back to school, there are still socks under his bed. Not even pairs. Just stray socks."

Sharon set her jaw and adjusted the bill of her cap lower to hide her eyes. She should be used to it, this mock complaining about their children when they were really trying to one-up each other, just busting their buttons with pride. Even Micky. Even now. But they never seemed to give a thought to how it would feel to listen to such talk if you'd tried for twenty years to have a child—just one child—and you couldn't do it.

"But most of the time," Jan was saying now, her voice suddenly serious, "I can hardly believe that they're gone. It feels as if they're away at camp, and pretty soon the house will be full of their noise and bickering again. At Easter, Douglas was sitting next to me at the table, in his old place, and I noticed a scar on his thumb that I'd never seen before, a long line already white. When I asked, he said he'd cut it when he was scraping some paint off the woodwork in his condo—three stitches. 'When?' I said. 'Oh, last year sometime,' he said. 'Why didn't you tell me?' I said, and I was really feeling angry about it, outraged. How could he have a scar from a wound I hadn't patched, hadn't suffered over with him? And already an *old* scar. That was somehow the worst, that he could have been gone from me so long that wounds I didn't even know about were already old scars."

"How did he react when you fussed?" Linda asked, turning from the front of the canoe Jan was steering. So she had been listening, Sharon reflected. How often, when she seemed pre-occupied with her lens settings and shutter speeds, was she actually paying attention to other things as well?

"Oh, you know how he is," Jan shrugged. "He hates any expressions of concern about his health. Always acts as if it's a criticism. *Way* too sensitive, that one."

Sharon knew the subtext of these remarks, as did the rest of the women. Douglas Werden was gay, had come out to his parents when he was in his late teens. Even parents as loving and supportive as Jan and Mike could not shake the specter of AIDS, could not wholly restrain themselves from "advis-ing" their adult son about safety. So not being told about even something as innocent as a cut thumb could seem omi-nous. Maybe they wondered what else he might be keeping from them. The aftershocks of Douglas's revelation in 1987 had resonated through the group for years until it was finally "all right" with everybody.

Sharon herself had very little struggle with acceptance. She was surprised because Doug had seemed a very "mascu-line" little boy, good at sports, gregarious. But she had long since decided that conventional and religious attitudes about sex were mostly a lot of hooey—designed and enforced for the purpose of social control rather than from any sincere respect for individual human beings. Kaz was too tied into the old taboos by which he was raised to ever be comfortable around somebody he knew for sure was "a homo," as he would say. Sharon suspected that Jan felt his discomfort and had added it to the list of things she had against Bob Kazmerinski.

"I always envied you your boys," Peg said suddenly, after a little silence in the boats. "I guess I just envied the *number* of kids you and Mike had. I did so want a big family. When my mother was my age, she still had a fourteen-year-old and a ten-year-old at home."

"Jesus!" Linda cried. "Would you really want that? It makes me tired just to think about it."

"Yes, I would want that," Peg said, her mouth tight, her voice unusually sharp. "And it was taken from me—stolen away. Those damn doctors made us believe that there was nothing else to be done—that surgery was the only cure for the pain."

Sharon knew, as did the others, that Peg had suffered so horribly from endometriosis after Elizabeth's birth that she would pass out, that she had collapsed at work and been rushed to a county hospital when Jerry had just started at a small PR firm. The insurance would not cover a "pre-existing condition."

"But it wasn't true even then," Peg was saying, her voice rising, flying out over the quiet lake. "They just didn't want to undertake the longer, more difficult, treatment without any guarantee of payment. So they just ripped everything out, sterilized me." Her voice rose half an octave on the second-last word. There was a long silence now, broken only by the splashing of a nearby loon.

"Oh, I know what you're thinking," Peg said finally, her voice calm again. "We could have adopted children. You used to say that in your letters, Jan. We waited too long, I guess. It took a few years for me just to get over the loss and then we kept moving around so much. In Lafayette, we had our application all finished, home study and everything. Then we had to move out of state when Jerry's job took him to Ohio. It would have meant starting all over again. And the waiting period was so long by then—five years. It was so disheartening that we finally just gave up. And we had our Lizzy, of course. She was such an angel that it always seemed mean-spirited and greedy to complain about not having more children. But I would have loved a crowd. That's what makes it so hard to forgive those doctors."

There were tears on her face. Sharon could see her profile, could see the glistening trail of moisture making its way toward her chin. Micky, who had been watching Peg intently, lifted her hand from the gunwale and brushed it quickly over Peg's cheek. The canoes drifted slightly apart, and Micky's slim hand fell away from Peg's tears. Peg pulled hard, and the two crafts came alongside again. Micky resumed her grip on the gunwale and turned her own profile toward a small island that was drifting by on the right.

"Doctors always act like they're God," Mary said suddenly. "But they're just guessing a lot of the time. Twenty years ago my brother Tony and his wife lost a baby to SIDS, and every doctor they'd talked to said it was just a mystery, that nobody could prevent a baby from dying that way if that was the way they were going to die. It took my sister-in-law *years* to accept that, to stop blaming herself for not watching that baby every second. And now doctors are saying that SIDS is caused by putting infants on their stomachs to sleep, by putting soft pillows too close to their faces. So poor Joan has that horror stirred up again, the guilt fresh like a raw wound. Because she did put the baby on his stomach to sleep, and she did have soft pillows in the crib. But it was the goddamned experts who told her to do it that way back then. You can't win for losing."

"Of course, there are plenty of good doctors," Jan said, nodding significantly at Micky to remind them that Peter Shaw was, of course, a doctor and that their old friend might take offense at any blanket indictment of the medical profession.

"Well, of course," the women murmured in chorus, but Micky seemed not to have picked up on the anger, only on the sorrow, for she turned back to them now, her face filled with a kind of wonder.

"You know," she said slowly, "whenever I hear people talk about this sort of thing, I always think how lucky we've been, Peter and I. Nothing bad has ever happened to us."

Now the silence was a stunned one, punctuated by small gasps, that betrayal worked by the body when the will is struggling to maintain the appearance of calm.

"Oh, Micky," Peg breathed, and she reached over with her free hand to cover Micky's hand on the canoe.

But Sharon could see that the truth of Micky's words was also dawning on her other friends. Until this awful thing had fallen on Micky, she and Peter had led a charmed life—the American dream, really: happy marriage, beautiful children, wealth, position, a sense of achievement and social purpose—the whole package. The rest of them, Sharon thought, had been tested in dribs and drabs, facing sorrows and setbacks over the years in the usual pattern of life. But Micky was getting her "test" in one huge lump.

"Hey," Jan said suddenly. "Am I the only one who's getting warm? I'm sure it can't be a hot flash. Men are allowed to pull off their shirts in circumstances like this, so why shouldn't we?"

"You mean strip?" Linda asked, her voice amused. "I'll be happy to record that for posterity." And she swung the camera around toward Jan.

"Just to the waist," Jan said. "There's nobody else out here for miles around, except for the loons. Why shouldn't we get a little breeze to dry off our backs? And you can take pictures if you want."

"I'm game," Mary said cheerfully. "But you'd better holster that camera, Lindy. Only you guys and the loons are going to

get this particular view." She pulled off her cap and slipped
her T-shirt straight up over her head—her paddle had long
since been placed inside the canoe as there was no need for
her to use it. She undid her bra and let it slide down her
arms, which were browned below the elbows, paler above.
Then she lifted her fists up at the cloudless dome above
them, raising her ample breasts into the wind.

"Here we go," Jan laughed as she balanced her paddle
across her canoe and began struggling out of her shirt.

Sharon could feel the onset of panic. If they all did it, she
wouldn't be able to get out of it. It would be the agony of
gym class all over again. And, worse, the labor of hiding the
agony, of pretending that she felt no embarrassment.

"If Jan's willing to advertise her deficiencies," Micky
laughed, "I can do it too." When she was naked to the waist,
she sat forward, thrusting her chest out like a masthead figure. Her small breasts were stark white, still firm and high on
her body. "Come on, Peg," she cried. "Free yourself from
bondage."

"No way," Peg said, blushing predictably. "Even the loons
don't need the shock of seeing me naked."

"Me either," Linda said. "So don't even ask. I'll refrain
from snapping the shutter if it would make you nervous, but
I'm not joining in this invitation to be arrested."

"And somebody's got to steer this damned flotilla," Sharon
said, relieved gratitude toward Linda and Peg pouring over
her feelings. "So I'll just keep on paddling while you brazen
hussies flap your boobs at passing boats."

"Oh, there aren't any other boats," Jan said. She had
grabbed up her paddle again and had lifted it over her head.
"There should be a name for this. You know, like sticking
your bare butt out a window is called 'mooning.' Come on,
Sharon. This will be your contribution. What's a good name

for this? It can't be 'flashing' because that's just lifting your blouse fast and then putting it down again."

"Okay, okay," Sharon said, her equilibrium restored. This was a familiar role for her, a comfortable assignment. "I got it. This is called 'boobling.' The verb 'to booble' means to deliberately expose the entire female chest, for more than sixty seconds, in a public place."

"Is it boobling if there's no chance that strangers could see it?" Linda asked. "This doesn't seem very 'public' to me."

"Oh, we don't know when a canoe could come around one of these islands," Mary offered. "And it could be filled with strange men. Or even normal men. You know there are no motorized vehicles allowed up here, so somebody could creep up on us without a sound."

"Okay, then," Linda said, "we can accept the definition."

"We should sing," Micky said. "That should scare off any spies."

"Good idea," Jan chimed in. "Some of the old songs we used to sing at Auggies."

"What were those verses we used to sing to 'She'll Be Comin' Round the Mountain'?" Linda said now. "You had one, didn't you, Jan?"

"Let's see," Jan said, lowering the paddle to her side, forgetting apparently that she was naked. "Oh, I got it." And she began to warble: "She'll be sucking on a beer when she comes." The other voices joined in lustily. "She'll be sucking on a beer when she comes. She'll be sucking on a beer; she'll be loaded when she's here. She'll be sucking on a beer when she comes."

"And Mike made up an even better one," Micky laughed, her face alight with the pleasure of remembering, of joining in. And once she had intoned the first line, they all joined in, shouting the notes in the old competitive spirit. "She'll be smokin' good green grass when she comes. She'll be smokin' good green grass when she comes. She'll be smokin' good green grass; she'll be stoned right on her ass. She'll be smokin' good green grass when she comes."

"And we used to think that was so damned daring," Jan cackled. "A bunch of good Catholic girls and an ex-Jesuit seminarian who had maybe smoked grass three times in our lives."

And some of them, Sharon reflected, had never smoked grass at all. Sharon Lee Gill, for instance, who sang the verse more loudly than the others, and with more knowing winks. No, alcohol was her drug of choice. Conventional. Acceptable. Safe.

"Puff, the Magic Dragon," she began now in her firm alto—of the group members, only she had some formal voice training. One by one the others picked it up: "Lived by the sea. And frolicked in the autumn mists in a land called Honalee."

Now all irony had gone out of their voices. The sweetness of the music subdued them, the tenderness of the lyrics softened them. "Little Jackie Paper loved that rascal Puff." Three of them naked and three clothed, they sang of lost innocence and the end of dreams. "One gray night it happened, Jackie Paper came no more." Over the still waters of Sea Gull Lake, their voices lifted and fell. "A dragon lives forever, but not so little boys." And, this time, the harmony was true.

11 / Peg

"When they first started talking about paving the trail, all of us old-timers was dead set against it." At a long table in a corner of the dining room, Ada Thurley was holding forth. "We thought it would ruin the woods. They'd have to blast through the hills to straighten it out. And we figured it would just make it easier for the riffraff to get up here." She laughed, a wonderful, high-pitched cackle. "But when it was done, all we could talk about was how easy it was to get back and forth to town. We just loved it."

Peg was sitting opposite the old woman, listening with respectful fascination, as were her other friends. They had seen photographs of Ada before, but pictures could not prepare them for the living fact of Ada Thurley. The face was as ruggedly lined as it looked in the book picture—deep valleys scoring the leathery skin, a series of foothills leading to the imposing mountain range of her beaked nose and her craggy brow. The hair was the same steely gray, cut short and spiky on the bony head, looking for all the world like the wolf fur of her famous parkas. But the animation, the sparkle, couldn't be caught by any camera. Her knobbed fingers slashed the air to punctuate her speech, the smile split her lower face with almost ferocious mirth. And her eyes were quite remarkable—not the eyes of an old woman at all. They were light brown, almost yellow eyes, glittering and sharp like some bird of prey, darting from face to face with keen attention. Whenever she thought something was funny—and frequently this was her own speech—she would throw back her head, lift her hands in a forward-sweeping, dismissive gesture, and let loose that distinctive cackle.

When Jan, as self-appointed spokesperson, had thanked her for having dinner with them, Ada had fired back, "Well, I gotta eat anyway, don't I? And I'd rather spend my time with young people like you than with folks my own age. I'm telling you, all they ever do is talk about their aches and pains. It's just one organ recital after another." Peg could tell it was a frequently uttered remark, a sort of conscious role-playing as the wise woman raconteur, but that didn't stop them from laughing appreciatively. And it didn't stop Ada from laughing along.

The dining room of Trail's End Lodge was a huge room with vaulted ceiling, rustic in a stagy sort of way with rough-hewn beams and curtainless windows. Above the main doorway, mounted on a big slab of oak, were the intertwined antlers of what must have been two impressively big stags, whose long-ago battle over some harem had inadvertently led to their mutual demise, locked forever in the embrace that kills. Peg and the others had showered and changed at the shiny new facilities at Voyageur Outfitters and had arrived at Trail's End only a few minutes after six, the hour they had agreed to meet Ada. Linda had asked the old woman if she would mind being photographed, and Ada had boomed, "Hell, no. Knock yourself out. I ain't no model that gets paid by the picture." Peg had read Ada Thurley's book—there had been no ghostwriter—and had admired the simple eloquence of its style, so she knew that the bad grammar must be an affectation. The whole dinner was a species of performance art, but a very entertaining one. And it was clear that the performer was having a hell of a good time too.

"What kinda car you drive?" Ada asked Jan, who was sitting to her left. It was the sort of abrupt and personal question they had already got used to by the time the first course was served.

"A Toyota," Jan answered. "A Camry."

"You like them foreign cars, do ya?" Ada said, her hawk's eyes fixing Jan with an accusatory glare.

"It's very reliable," Jan said with a slow smile. "Good mileage too."

"I got me a new Chevy Blazer in June," Ada said smugly. "I love that four-wheel drive. Bill—he's my son who runs the place now—don't like for me to be driving any more, but I told him, 'Hell, I gotta get into town now and then, don't I?'" Town was forty-five miles down the Gunflint Trail.

Linda was prowling up and down with her camera in front of her face—didn't the woman ever eat? Peg kept wondering—but it was hard to tell when she was actually taking pictures because there was no flash, and there was too much noise in the room to hear the click of the shutter. Probably, the secret to getting pictures in this light was in the kind of film and the shutter speed. Peg thought it was odd that when she got her pictures back, Linda would be the only one not in them. Maybe she should offer to take a few with Linda at the table too. But, no, Linda was a professional photographer, and Peg's shots would be amateurish—probably she wouldn't even be able to work such a fancy camera.

She glanced over at Sharon, who had a bit of sunburn on her nose. She was holding her third drink, a Tom Collins. Peg had often thought that it would be better if Sharon didn't drink so much. In the past fifteen years, Peg and Jerry

had spent more time with Sharon and Kaz than any of
their other college friends, ever since they had settled in
Menominee, because that was only about twenty miles
from Oconto where the Kazmerinskis lived. So Peg had
many occasions to notice how Sharon would get progres-
sively louder and more bawdy with each drink, how heads
would turn toward their table in restaurants when they ate
out. Jerry would sometimes come home grumbling that he
never wanted to go out in public with the other couple again.
But tonight, here at Trail's End, Sharon was being uncharacteristically quiet, not even seeming to pay much attention to
the stories Ada was regaling them with, and Peg would have
guessed that these tales of hunting and camping would be
right up Sharon's alley.

But Sharon was staring at her own hands, which were covered in the jewelry she must have brought along with her
change of clothing. She had worn no rings on the canoe
trip. One of the rings was new—Sharon had bought it in
town yesterday while they were strolling from shop to shop.
It was a pinky ring with four rubies, channel set into a high
gold crown. "How much?" Sharon had said casually while
her friends gathered around her. When the shopkeeper
answered, "Nine hundred," Sharon had announced, "I'll
take it." And then she plunked down her gold card while the
other women exchanged stunned glances. "Don't bother
with a box," Sharon brayed. "I'll just wear it." Why did she
have to flaunt the success of her husband's business like that?

Peg shook her head now, feeling herself blush. It was
unkind to have such feelings about one of her oldest friends.
So what if Sharon spent her money the way she wanted to?
And Peg knew that her irritation had more to do with her
own current worries about money than with any real grudge
against Sharon. Since Jerry's operation, his advertising firm

hadn't been bringing in as much as expected, and things were more than a little tight for them. Insurance didn't cover all of the medical bills, which were staggering; the intensive care room—just the room!—was fifteen hundred dollars a day. And now Peg's parents were becoming more and more dependent—

No, she had to stop this! She was obsessing, and she had sworn she wasn't going to do that while she was up here. She shouldn't have got so serious on the canoe trip, crying like that, talking about her hysterectomy. The trouble with confiding a feeling like her disappointment over having only one child was that now her friends would think it was "the real truth" about her life, that she'd been hiding this core truth, this pain, behind a false front—putting on a brave face for years, only pretending to have a happy and fulfilled life. But, of course, her life *was* happy and fulfilled—for the most part. The stuff about her hysterectomy was only a truth, among all the other truths. How could you live to fifty and *not* have one such truth in your repertoire?

What she could never tell them—too embarrassing, too personal—was that the operation, back when she was twenty-four, had provided a wonderful bonus in her marriage. It had permanently improved her and Jerry's sex life. As long as sex held the possibility of unplanned pregnancy—and they had hoped to space their children pretty widely until Jerry was more financially secure—she could never be completely relaxed about it, never have sex when she felt most eager for it, because abstinence was the only contraceptive the Church allowed. After her physical recovery from the surgery, she and Jerry had found a great comfort and, finally, a great joy in their sexual union. Over the years, she had met so many Catholics who had parted ways with the Church over the issue of birth control, and she did sometimes wonder if her own continued faith owed something to the fact that, for her and Jerry, that was never an issue at all.

Jerry had always found her desirable. He was one of those thin, wiry men of high energy who found pillowy breasts and a languid ampleness in a woman a real "turn on," as Lizzy would say. She had read about this in magazines and had good reason in her own experience to believe it. Her husband craved her body, just as he had when they were kids together, and being able to answer that craving with a physical delight of her own had given her a deep and unshakable confidence in herself as a woman. She was always puzzled when women expressed sexual curiosity about men other than their husbands. She never had such thoughts, never felt the itch of unsatisfied longing. And now that Jerry's heart condition had reintroduced an element of fear into their bed—never mind that the specialist had said there was no reason to worry on that score—she realized for the first time how much they had taken their easy and confident sexuality for granted.

Of course, her marriage was so much more than sex. She and Jerry had spent their first date, in 1965, talking for four hours in a parked car, both of them forgetting the time so that her 2 A.M. return to her parents' house could not help but look suspicious. But the truth was that they had kissed only once, a short peck when he took her to the door. Their mutual lust for conversation had never changed; in more than thirty years, they hadn't run out of things to say to each other. Two years ago, when she'd been sitting in the hospital waiting room with Jerry in the operating room, she had suddenly realized that, if he should die on the table—a possibility the doctor had gravely mentioned—three quarters of what she would ever have to say again for the rest of her life would have to remain unspoken because all of it—every word—would be stuff she would have said to Gerald Brunner.

"That big, stupid man would not put them snowshoes on his feet," Ada was saying, "and I told him he was gonna bury himself every time he tried to take a step. But there's no telling nothing to some of those city folk. And he thought he was going to shoot a moose!" She made a derisive noise, blowing air through her impressive nose. "Why, the moose would more likely die laughing at the sight of that whale floundering around in the snow."

Peg glanced now at Micky who was seated at the far end of the table. She was wearing the blank expression again, staring into the middle distance and apparently making no effort to follow the conversation at all. In the car on the trip up to Grand Marais on Monday, Jan had told them about "sundowning," a condition of Alzheimer's patients that made them more distracted and out of it in the late afternoon and early evening. Peg wondered if that could already be happening to Micky who had seemed so alert, so like her old self on the canoe trip that it had been possible for a few hours to almost forget that there was anything wrong with her. Seeing her now, with her wonderful eyes glazed, her face slack, Peg felt a wave of outrage at life's ironies. Here was this woman, still young and beautiful, her body upright and healthy, but her brain dying by inches. And seated at the same table was an eighty-six-year-old woman whose flesh was folded in on itself, whose once-strong back was bent by osteoporosis, but whose mind was gloriously intact, sparking out of her young woman's eyes, ringing in her boisterous laugh.

Not all the old were so lucky. Some of them, like Peg's parents, were losing the fitness of both mind and body, rolling backward into the dependencies of childhood without recovering any of the charm of children. They still lived in the old house in Green Bay, clinging stubbornly to the world that was now too much for them—too many rooms to keep clean, too many steps to climb, too much sidewalk to keep shoveled in the winter, and too much lawn to keep mowed in the summer. Her father had suffered several bouts with phlebitis, had had his right foot amputated. Her mother had painful angina and arthritic hips. And they were three years younger than Ada Thurley.

But worse than the physical deterioration was the psychological change that Peg had seen developing over the past few years. Once decisive, bright, and cheerful people, her parents had both become emotionally frail. Her father wept easily now over seeming trifles. Her mother forgot to pay bills, sent delivery people away without opening the door because some house down the block had had a break-in. And every crisis brought distraught phone calls to Peg's house in Menominee: "You'll have to talk to that kid who's supposed to shovel the walk," her father would say, his voice quavering. "He does a piss-poor job, and he doesn't come until everybody's packed the snow down by walking over it all day." Peg's older brothers lived now in distant cities—Los Angeles, Phoenix, Toledo—but even if they were closer, they would assume what all the families of Peg's childhood neighborhood assumed: daughters take care of aging parents. Peg's only sister, the baby of the family, lived in Milwaukee and used the two-hour drive as an excuse to leave the "parent problem" to her big sister.

And Peg tried hard to cope. Within a few months of Jerry's surgery, she had begun to look for a place in Menominee where her parents might move and, at the same time, began "working on" them to convince them that such a move was the best solution. They waxed and waned, sometimes ignoring her blandishments about the various wonders of Menominee, Michigan, sometimes sounding enthusiastic about how nice it would be to have her closer. Sometimes, she felt it was just like trying to persuade Elizabeth, at four years old, that broccoli with cheese on it was really yummy—not just good for her, but tasty too. Finally, this past Christmas, an opening was announced at a townhouse development just two miles from Peg's house—two bedrooms, all on one floor, attached garage. A nice, tidy place, and—*mirabile dictu!*—affordable. She snapped photos, inside and out, and took them to Green Bay. When her parents showed some tepid interest, she persuaded Jerry that they should put down a deposit on the place. She contacted realtors in Green Bay to set up a listing for the old house. She made several visits to help her parents decide what furniture should be sold and what should be moved. When they got a good offer on the house, she contacted a lawyer to help the sale go smoothly.

Then in June, her parents announced, in a brief phone call, that everything was off—they were staying where they were. She had driven straight to Green Bay—too fast, gripping the steering wheel until her knuckles were white. "Our life is here," her father had said, after she had exhausted herself with pleading and cajoling. "We always expected to stay. We've never had any other house." There were tears in his eyes. "We raised our children here," her mother said, "and we expect to die here too. Benny is buried at St. Paul's." Benny was Peg's brother who had died of leukemia when he was seven.

She knew it was no use. Her parents had grown up with the expectations of another America, the one where your children got married in the parish, went to work for the paper mills, and settled in houses down the block, so that grandsons could come over to mow the grass when your foot had to be taken off, and granddaughters would be sent, sulking a little, to houseclean every spring when raising a dust mop to sweep spiderwebs out of the corners of the ceiling made your heart hurt. It wasn't their fault that America had changed on them, not part of their plan that children ran away to Phoenix or Milwaukee, not their style to have traveled and broadened their horizons so that Green Bay would not be the only world in which they could feel at home. She understood. She loved them, honored them. They had been good parents, had sacrificed to send her to college when all their friends were telling them that education would be wasted on a girl. She couldn't force them, could she?

But none of that stopped her from seething with rage on the way back to her own home, from weeping with frustration that the deposit she put on the townhouse was lost—she couldn't ask her parents to reimburse her. And when the first call came after that, as she knew it would—"That fool doctor won't change my medication, and I told him and told him it makes me light-headed. I'm not going to take it any more"— it had crossed her mind that perhaps an overdose of medication would solve their problems—and hers. Of course, she had recoiled in horror from the thought almost as soon as it was formed.

Two years before, when Jan's parents had died within days of each other just a few weeks after Jerry's surgery, she had wept for Jan, of course, but the tears she'd shed at the funerals weren't just for her old friend. Sitting there, smelling the incense and listening to the swelling music—"Be not afraid, for I am with you always"—she had for the first time fully imagined the funerals of her own parents. And Jerry was still too ill to be with her, wasn't there to put his arms around her when she couldn't stop sobbing in the cemetery. So when she found herself thinking almost wistfully about her parents overdosing on medication, she imagined herself the worst daughter ever born. And she had raced out into the blistering afternoon sun to bury her guilt in her flower garden. She could drive away all mean-spirited thoughts by digging her hands down into the rich dirt, holding and pinching back her petunias, wrenching weeds up out of the bed of moss roses.

She always felt soothed by working in the garden, felt tension and stress flowing off her hands and away from her when she was wielding a spade or a pruning shears. And she loved the flowers themselves, the textures, colors, shapes, the variety of smells. Every summer, she marveled at the pregnant buds of her perennial hibiscus. She would check on them every day, counting them, wondering at how the slim stalks could support such swelling weight. When they finally opened to thrust forth the dazzling blooms, she always felt a rush of joy, as if she herself had given birth to this beauty.

And the work of cleaning out whatever was unlovely, the faded petunia blossoms, the stubborn thistles, was satisfying in another way: she could make of this little world a constant order and symmetry, a disciplined universe. Sort of like God. No, better. Because she didn't have to respect the thistle's free will, didn't have to helplessly allow the deadly nightshade to strangle the dwarf hollyhocks or crowd out the delicate primroses. How sad God must be sometimes.

"Excuse me, Peggy," Linda murmured close to her right ear. Peg jumped a little as the camera moved past her face. Doubtless a close-up of Ada's face was the object at the moment. She felt embarrassed at having been so far away in a reverie, could feel the heat of a blush rising in her cheeks. Why, she must have looked just like Micky, blank and distracted. Maybe that's what it was for Micky too. Maybe she was just thinking about something personal while Ada Thurley was recounting the trips she had made into the Boundary Waters with various celebrities.

The women were beginning to stir now, to get up from the

table—last sips of coffee, folding of napkins. Jan offered her arm to Ada, who took it immediately, bracing her other hand against the tabletop as she hoisted herself out of the chair. They created a mild stir among the other diners as they crossed the room—Ada was a certified celebrity up here, and according to Steve, she didn't make many public appearances anymore. Even from her bent position, the old woman noticed the stir, bowed and saluted people at each table she passed. What a delightful old ham she was, God bless her. Peg waited for Micky to rise and then walked next to her as they passed into the lounge area at the front of the building.

This lounge was actually the original building—the larger dining area had been added later—a lower, simpler room now containing sofas and upholstered chairs. Its focal point was an immense fireplace, almost filling one wall and rising up to the roof in a graceful taper. It was made of the various stones of the Arrowhead region—granite, volcanic basalt, lintonite—some of them boulder size. The fire pit was almost as tall as the people who passed in front of it. Here, the group paused.

"Would you pose for a picture with us in front of the fireplace?" Jan asked the old woman, stooping respectfully so she could look into the leathery face. "Maybe we could ask one of the waitresses to take the picture for us."

"Sure," Ada said cheerfully. "I'll ask Elaine. She's my daughter-in-law. Over there at reception. She won't mind. You know, the mister and I dragged most of them stones in here by dogsled. Didn't have the sense to wait for summer. That's being young, I guess. Impatient."

They began arranging themselves, placing Ada at the center, taller people at the back, shorter ones in front.

"You got some sunburn there," Ada said, pointing at Sharon's throat, which was just at her eye level.

"It was a sunny day," Sharon said.

"I don't burn," Ada said. "Never did. I got some Indian blood in me. But these brownies on my face come from the white folks in the family." And she gestured at the dark moles, which dotted her jaw line.

Micky, who had been allowing Peg to pilot her into a position on the left, turned sharply toward the old woman. "Brownies?" she echoed, incredulous. "You put brownies on your face?"

Sharon and Mary began to laugh. They must have assumed that Micky was making a deliberate joke, but Peg could see her face, knew she had really believed the old woman meant chocolate brownies. Jan who was standing to Micky's right, lifted her palms to waist level and waggled them at Sharon and Mary, forming a *no* with her lips. The motion, just at the edge of her peripheral vision, caught Micky's attention, and she looked quickly at Jan, caught the *no* and the agonized expression. Peg saw sharpness come back into Micky's blue eyes, saw them flash the way they had in the old days when something displeased her.

"Stop that," she snapped at Jan. "Stop making hand gestures behind my back. I'm not a total idiot yet."

A horrified silence fell. Jan looked as if she might begin to cry. Ada Thurley, who had not been told that Micky was in any way different from her other dinner companions, seemed to grasp the situation at once. She took Micky's rigid arm by the elbow, patted her forearm.

"It's a silly habit of mine," she said casually, "calling things by the words my kids used when they were little. Louann always called my moles 'brownies.' Bill used to say 'Rice Krip-sies' instead of Krispies, so we still call it that when we have it for breakfast." And she cackled noisily. Micky relaxed, moved back into the grouping for the picture. But she didn't look at Jan again.

And when they divided up outside to get back into the cars, Micky walked with Sharon and Linda to Sharon's car. In the glow of the parking-lot lights, Peg caught the pained expression on Jan's face.

"Will you drive my car?" Peg asked her. "I don't do so well with night driving these days." And she held out the keys.

"Okay," Jan said absently. "Sure."

They waited for Sharon's car to pull out onto the Gunflint Trail, and then Jan maneuvered the Lumina into position to follow. It was very quiet in the car. Peg hadn't made it up about having trouble with night driving. She hated it now, almost never did it anymore. She thought in awe of the year when she was working on her advanced degree in counseling and would deliberately set out late at night to drive the 120 miles from Marquette, Michigan, back to Menominee where Jerry and Elizabeth were waiting for her. She had done it easily then, glad that there was so little traffic, energetic enough to add that night trip to a four-day class schedule so she could have the full three-day weekend with her family. But no more. Something must have happened to her night vision about four years ago. She'd noticed it first on a short trip home from a bridal shower for a friend's daughter, and it seemed to get worse after that.

Even familiar roads and streets looked strange and distorted in the dark, like those grainy landscapes on the moon she remembered from the first televised space shots. She had the eerie sensation that the car was hovering slightly above the surface of the road and might suddenly rocket off into a field or plunge straight into the side of a building. Trees along the streets seemed to crowd in, threatening to topple onto the car; a few times she could have sworn she saw them beginning to fall. She found herself driving very slowly just like those little old lady drivers who had once filled her with such righteous anger. Other cars would come up close behind her, their headlights shining all around her own car and casting spooky shadows into the ditches, as if living creatures were hovering there, making ready to leap onto the road. These days Jerry did the night driving in the family.

Maybe that was what Alzheimer's felt like for Micky—her own neighborhood turned into a moonscape, a giddy feeling of racing out of control, of hurtling headlong on a road where terrifying shadows had taken the place of all the familiar trees and hedges and ambling dogs.

12 / Jan

Jan tried to keep her eyes closed, tried to ignore the throbbing in her shoulder muscles, the prick of mild sunburn
on her chest. So much for "boobling"! If she could will
her lids to imitate sleep, maybe sleep would come. She was
stretched rigidly at one edge of the big bed, as far from
Micky's still body as she could get. They had prepared for
bed with only the most superficial exchanges, both pretending that the incident at Trail's End hadn't happened, but
Jan could tell from the wounded look in Micky's eyes that
she hadn't forgotten. So what was so terrible about trying to
spare a friend's feelings? Why was she the bad guy when all
she meant to do was make this trip easy and fun for Micky? It
seemed like a month since they'd left St. Paul, and it was only
Wednesday, for God's sake!

She knew she had to relax, to leave some of the Micky-
watching to her other friends. It was a lifelong habit, though,
this urge to manage every situation. The eldest of six children, Jan had been given the burden of taking care of others
at an early age. Her major professor at the university had
rightly guessed that part of her motivation for pursuing a
Ph.D. in psychology had been her need to "direct" other
people, to point them in the way that they should go when
they were always, perversely, going in ways she knew were
wrongheaded. Control freak. That was what Adam would call

her when he was most angry, most rebellious. "Get off my fucking back!" he would shout, when all she'd said was "You've got to *plan*, darling. You can't just let your life happen to you." That was when he should have been narrowing his choices for college, should have been arranging campus visits. And now he was a college graduate already, a computer consultant helping small businesses coordinate their software—whatever the hell that could mean.

So she hadn't been such a bad mother, had she? Peg was right to envy her those four boys. They were all nice kids, all smart, all good-looking. That last was due to Mike's genetics, really, because the boys looked more like their father—dark hair and eyes—although Ryan had a reddish cast to his beard and some of the Farrell Irishness in his upper face. Funny to think of Ryan having a beard; he seemed still so young to her, her baby. But he was twenty now, had chosen to stay in South Bend for the summer, working full time to get money for his junior year at Notre Dame; his scholarship would be a little less than last year. Odd, really, that they didn't have to worry so much about money for that sort of thing anymore; her private practice was finally beginning to bring in a nice income. That one year when they'd had the first three boys all in college at the same time, the family income was only half what it was now, but they had managed it somehow. And Douglas had already paid back all of his student loans in the four years since he'd graduated. Who would have guessed that hospital administration paid so well?

Whenever she thought about Doug, Jan felt a squeezing sensation around her heart. It was a feeling made up of equal parts love, pride, and fierce protectiveness. He was her firstborn, and he was gay, and he was brave and wonderful. Whenever she heard someone telling a "queer joke," whenever she saw any celebrity on television do a mincing and mocking imitation of homosexual men, she was moved to an almost murderous rage. Mike sometimes had to take her away from parties after she'd delivered lip-quivering speeches about tolerance and fairness. Kevin, just a year younger than Doug, had said to her recently that he had come to think of the family history as divided into two halves, one before they knew Douglas was gay and one after they knew Douglas was gay, and she felt this was a true insight. Almost everything was changed by that knowledge.

That spring night in 1987 had seemed like so many others. They'd had almost a full house at dinner—only Adam was missing, a chess club meeting—and Mike had been teasing Doug about finding a date for the prom. This had been a theme with Mike for several days already: "Are there so many girls chasing after you that you can't make up your mind?" Later that evening, after the boys had gone up to bed, Doug came back downstairs and padded barefoot into the living room where Jan and Mike were reading; he was wearing only pajama bottoms, and Jan's first thought on seeing him was that he was thinner than he looked with clothes on.

"I have something I have to tell you," he said, coming to a stop halfway between his parents. He was ghastly pale, and Jan's mind began racing: he was flunking trig; he had been caught shoplifting; he was hooked on drugs. "You've got to lay off about the prom, Dad," he said without looking at them. "Because I'm gay. I've known about it for a long time."

Jan's instant reaction, inside her mind, was "So *that's* what it is. That's what I couldn't pinpoint, couldn't label." But, of course, she began at once to argue with him. *How* did he know? He couldn't be sure. It was just a phase. He was only confused. That wasn't so unusual at his age. But at the base of her mind she *knew* he was saying what was true, what had always been true. Mike sat rigid, silent, while she and Doug went back and forth, both pacing now, Doug recoiling from his mother's attempts to put her arm around his shoulders. Finally, after five or six minutes, Mike sprang up, so suddenly and so violently that Jan was afraid for a second that he would fly at Douglas, attack him. But he only walked straight across the living room, stopped at the front window, and stared out into the night. And then he began to sob—a painful, barking noise coming up from his diaphragm and tearing out of his throat. Jan had never heard him make such a sound before, and it terrified her, froze her blood. She saw Doug's face crumple, watched as he sank to his knees, his naked torso folding over as he began to rock back and forth. Then he, too, began to wail, the same piteous cry he had made when he was a little boy and they had to tell him that Grandpa Werden was dead.

That wasn't the only night for weeping either; there had been plenty of tears in the following weeks. Tears and avoidance and recriminations. But, gradually, by the end of that summer, they had begun to come to terms with it. Jan had never experienced any feelings of rejection toward Doug, only desperate worry, horror over what it would mean for her son to deal with society's revulsion from what he was. Mike had more trouble with disappointment—that was the word he used to her; the expectations he'd had for his sons, the emotional investment in their identity as projections of his own best self—all threatened.

One night, Jan had awakened to find Mike sitting hunched over in the big chair that angled across a corner of their bedroom.

"What is it?" she whispered, alarmed. He mustn't be ill, not now.

"I've been thinking," he said in a normal voice as he sat upright. "About Douglas. I kept on teasing him about girls, all that crap about the prom, because I must have guessed he wasn't interested in girls in that way. I was needling him, really, wasn't I? Why was I doing that?"

"Why do you think?" Jan asked, sliding over to his side of the bed so she could reach out to touch his knee. He covered her fingers with his right hand.

"I suppose I was trying to goad him into talking," he said. "Maybe I hoped he would tell me there was one special girl that he just couldn't have and that would account for his not being interested in other girls. I was looking for reassurance."

"It's not the end of the world," she said quietly, half embarrassed that she could find nothing to comfort him except this lame cliché.

"I don't know," he breathed. "When I look at him now, I can't see the same boy. He doesn't seem like our Douglas anymore."

Jan had snatched her hand from her husband's grasp, had felt along her arm the twitching impulse to strike him. From the second she'd first held Douglas, pink and clean in the hospital blanket, she'd felt the connection of her flesh to his as still unbroken. This mewling scrap of life was hers, was *her*, in a profoundly personal bond. She'd never had the feeling as strongly again when the other boys were born, not even with Ryan whom she'd touched and held while he was still literally connected to her by the umbilicus. When Douglas was an infant, she would sit and watch him, sometimes for as long as an hour, while he fanned the air with his plump fingers, examined his own toes with rapt interest, lowered his finely veined eyelids in slower and longer intervals until he slept. Over the years, she'd seen those fingers and toes elongate, watched the narrow hands flying over the piano keys when he practiced after school. And now when he lowered his eyelids to avoid his father's gaze, they were still so pale that the fine lines carrying the blood across them showed in the identical patterns she'd watched as he slept his infant sleep. Not our Douglas anymore! How could Mike be so blind? She crawled back to her own side of the bed, rigid with unexpressed anger, and she thought, "If you keep on like this, I'll never forgive you."

The whole family was still Catholic then, still churchgoers. Mike had taught chemistry for fifteen years at St. Cecilia's, a small college in St. Paul, and they belonged to the campus church. Mike, who had once studied for the priesthood himself, turned for help to Father O'Brien, the pastor of that church and also the head of St. Cecilia's theology department. O'Brien was sympathetic, kindly, but absolutely wedded to the Church's position that, while a tendency toward homosexuality was not in itself sinful, any homosexual behavior was a sin before God, and a mortal sin at that. They must get Douglas into therapy, which would help him avoid sinful behavior, which might even cure this "vice"; he was still very young, after all.

Somehow the word *vice* was a trigger for Mike. He left O'Brien's office in tight-lipped silence, but once they got to the car, he turned to Jan and cried, "I don't accept that my son is some sort of vicious character. And what the hell does it mean that he should be 'cured,' as if he was sick or something?"

That outburst was the beginning of her husband's movement from resignation to acceptance. Jan had been present some weeks later when Mike said quite calmly to Father O'Brien, "I don't believe in God as some sort of practical joker. I don't accept that he could create about one-tenth of the human race this way and then send them to hell if they act on it."

"Oh, Mike," O'Brien had said, shaking his head sadly.

"The Church is not going to change its position on this. You'll have to conform your beliefs to the eternal verities."

Their Catholicism couldn't hold against such a choice. If the Church rejected their son, they would reject the Church. They had found no substitute religion. So now she and Mike spent their Sunday mornings reading newspapers and, weather permitting, jogging along the river. The other boys were now "cool" about Doug's identity and relieved not to be forced into churchgoing. Ironically, Douglas himself had hung onto his religion the longest. Only two years ago, when he had finally embarked on what he called a "committed relationship" with Tim, a nurse at the hospital where he worked, did he stop yearning after the acceptance he would never find inside the doors of a church.

The extended family was another matter, of course. Jan's brothers were distant and noncommittal, not overtly disapproving, but never accepting. Mike's widowed mother responded by resolutely pretending that she hadn't been told. Her code name in the family was "Grandma Cleo" because, as Kevin said, "She's the Queen of Denial." Jan's parents had caused her the most heartache. Douglas had been their first grandchild, and because they'd lived so near when Mike was in graduate school, they'd spent a lot of time with the baby in the first three years of his life and had always considered him a pet. They'd been devastated by the news that he was gay, expressing the shock and revulsion that sheltered people of their generation had been socialized to feel about "perversions"—her mother's word. Jan's father would regularly tell her over the phone that they were praying every day "for Dougy to be healed." She would say, "Daddy, don't you realize how insulting that is?" and he would say solemnly, "We pray for you, too, Janet, to give you strength."

She knew now, lying here in the dark, that part of the

reason she had gone back to graduate school was to find the key for healing *them*—her parents, specifically—of their intolerance, their smug certainty that they knew the mind of God. And two years ago, her parents had cheated her out of the chance to apply her newfound wisdom. Her mother had suddenly sickened—liver cancer, already metastasized into several other locations in her body, one of them in her brain. In the last weeks, her father had insisted on taking his wife home to die. He had rejected help from a visiting nurse, wore himself out caring for her.

Jan had made weekly visits, shocked at her mother's rapid decline from a robust woman to a feeble invalid. In the bedroom Jan had always remembered as airy and warm, the smell of disinfectant blended with room deodorizer, a sickening floral disguise for decay. Sitting quietly next to the bed watching the morphine-induced sleep, Jan would reach out to touch her, as if she were trying to hold the flesh in place; she couldn't shake the impression that her mother's face was sliding off her skull. But her father rejected all other offers of help from her. He would allow her to be in the room when he gave the dying woman sponge baths, lifting her arms tenderly as if he were handling tubes of paper-thin blown glass, but he permitted his daughter no active role.

What she couldn't see then was that there was nothing personal in the rejection; it was just that he couldn't bear to have any service, however small, administered by any hands besides his own. Like a jealous lover, he could not bear to have other hands touch her. They had wed later in life than most people of their generation—Jan's mother had been twenty-eight—had been devoted their entire married life, still held hands in public when they were in their seventies. When she died, on the eve of Good Friday, he was cradling her in his arms in the bed they had shared for almost fifty years. Easter Sunday morning, the day before her funeral, Jan's brother Patrick found their father dead in the same bed. Heart attack, the doctor said, but his children knew he couldn't keep his heart beating without having his Maggie there to rest her head against his chest.

The agony of that double passing was still acute for Jan. Of course, she knew, rationally, that her parents would have chosen this finale, to go so nearly at the same time, so one of them wouldn't have to linger in a lost and diminished existence. Her brothers were saying that all the time. But she couldn't stop the feeling that she had been orphaned, cut off too soon from the love and support of her parents. Sometimes, when she read something or heard something on the news that would have interested them, she would think, "I should call Mom" or "I wonder what Daddy is making of this." But part of her anguish was knowing that they had died before she could make them "see the light" about Douglas. At Easter this year, Doug had brought Tim along home for the weekend, and remembering that it was the anniversary of his grandparents' deaths, he had said, "I wish Gran and Gramps could have met Tim. I think they would have liked to see me settled." And she had thought, "Oh, my poor boy! If you only knew what your Gran and Gramps would have liked." For she had never told him about their reaction, about those phone calls.

"Are you awake?" Micky's voice startled her. She didn't answer, didn't open her eyes.

"I know you're not sleeping," Micky said calmly, "because you're not snoring."

"I do not snore," Jan said peevishly.

"Well, you breathe loud then," Micky responded, chuckling

softly. "Please remember that I spent a lot of time listening to you sleep when we were in college, so I know what it sounds like."

"Have you been awake all along?" Jan asked, serious now.

"Yeah. I've been trying to decide about something. Can I turn on the light?"

"We can talk in the dark, can't we?" Jan asked, feeling a flicker of alarm.

"I know," Micky replied, "but I'd like to be looking at your face when we have this talk, so shield your eyes now. Here goes." And she switched on the bedside lamp.

"Oh, not now, please," Jan moaned, hoisting herself into a sitting position while she waited for her pupils to relax again. "Nothing serious in the middle of the night."

"It isn't the middle of the night," Micky said, unruffled. "And you know I have to take my opportunities when they find me."

"Is it about that 'brownie' business?" Jan asked.

"Indirectly." Micky was sitting now with her hands folded primly on the blanket in front of her. Her face and hair looked as tidy and unrumpled as when she'd first put them into the pillow. "It's time for us to go back to what we discussed at Christmas."

"Oh, no," Jan breathed. "Not up here. Not this week. This is supposed to be a vacation from all that. You made the rule yourself. While we're up here, you don't want to talk about it. You *said.*"

"I know," Micky went on relentlessly. "But I get to break my own rule. I need to ask you tonight if you've been thinking about what I want you to do for me."

"Of course I've been thinking about it," Jan cried. "How could I not think about it? I haven't been able to think about much else."

"Well then, you've had a chance to sort out what your answer is going to be. Are you going to help me end this 'long strange trip' when I say I'm ready?"

"I don't know why you have to pick right now to ask me this," Jan blustered, stalling. Her throat was constricting, her breathing starting to shorten.

"Simple," Micky said, her eyes narrowing as she searched Jan's face. "I saw the expression on everybody's face tonight over the 'brownie' mistake. That sort of thing is going to happen more and more from now on. And worse things."

"Why are you making such a big deal over this?" Jan flared, desperate, guilty. "It was just a little slip."

"Maybe. But it's only the beginning." She hadn't lifted her hands, hadn't raised her voice. Once again, apparently, she had planned pretty carefully what she would say. Lying there in the dark, she had rehearsed this. "Everybody is being so wonderful now. But nobody has a clue yet how bad it's going to be. Not you guys, not Peter, not my kids. Right now, it's just small allowances you have to make for me, little accommodations and compensations. But this is nothing compared to what's coming."

"But we aren't complaining," Jan said urgently. "We don't mind."

"But *I* mind," Micky said simply. "I mind that everybody feels sorry for me. And someday, not so far off, I'll feel too warm in a restaurant, and I'll just stand up and start taking my clothes off. And if Peter is with me, there will be horror in his face. And disgust."

"But you won't *know* that then," Jan insisted. "You won't be aware of it."

"Maybe I will be." Micky was almost whispering now. "Maybe somewhere in my brain, I'll know what the expression means. And I will mind that very much, indeed."

"I don't know what to say," Jan said helplessly, extending both hands toward Micky. "I don't know how to convince you."

"I'm not the one who needs convincing," Micky answered, and she didn't reach out for Jan's hands. "You are. You're my best hope. My only hope. If you say you'll help me, that you'll have everything ready for me when I can't take it anymore, I'll be able to relax. Then I can enjoy the good days I have left. There will be some good days—I know that. Today was a good day, mostly, and I had a wonderful time. But I must feel I have some control over what's going to happen to me as the good days get fewer and fewer. I'm counting on you, of all people, to understand how important it is for me to have some sense of control."

"You know what buttons to push, don't you?" Jan said, feeling a little rush of irritation.

"God, I hope so," Micky replied, and she was smiling. Then, after a small pause, she went on, her voice pleading. "Oh, Jan. I used to feel pretty good at running my life. I think I was pretty good at it. But it feels like I've lost the instructions. There are lots of separate pieces, and I sort of recognize most of them, but I don't know anymore how to find 'Tab A' or what's supposed to fit into 'Slot B.' And I hate it. I just want to kick everything to smithereens sometimes. If you say you'll help me, I might be able to hate it a little less."

"I can't!" Jan wailed, aware that she sounded like a petulant child, but unable to stop herself.

"You can't help?" Micky asked quietly. "Or you can't say you'll help? Which is it?"

Somehow this made Jan laugh, a high, hysterical laugh. "You always were jesuitical in your fine discriminations. And how many angels can dance on the head of a pin?"

"You're stalling," Micky said, her jaw setting at the stubborn angle Jan knew so well. "Which is it?"

"Oh, all right!" Jan cried, swinging back into a gust of irritation. "I can't say. Not now. I haven't decided yet."

"Well, I'm going to have to set a time then. Before we leave for home, you have to tell me your answer. If it's no, I'll have to make my own plans, so I have to know pretty soon."

"All right," Jan breathed, defeated. "Before we take off on Sunday, I'll tell you what I've decided. But don't bring it up again until then, do you hear?"

"I might forget," Micky said, and now Jan could see the old mischief in her eyes. "That's one blessing for us folks—we get to nag people to our heart's content, and when they complain, we get to say, 'Oh, did I tell you this before?'"

"Oh, yeah," Jan said, blinking fast to hide the beginning of tears. "Since when did you need an excuse to boss people around?"

When the light was out again, Jan lay there with her eyes wide open, listening to the rustle of the curtains in the slight breeze. For some reason, she was remembering Micky's twenty-second birthday in early March of 1968. They had been seniors at St. Augustine then, and Micky had been stewing for weeks because the Graduate Record Exams were scheduled for the very day of her birthday—no getting out of it.

"How many times in your life do you turn twenty-two?" she raved. "And I have to spend the whole bloody day grinding away at a test."

Her friends had, as usual, petted and soothed her: "We'll still celebrate. We'll have the whole weekend."

"It's not the same," she sulked. "I want a party on my birthday."

At ten on the night of her birthday, Micky announced that

she couldn't go to sleep unless she had at least one drink to celebrate. So Jan, exhausted from a day of anxiety and brain-busting, walked with her over to Bronco's, a grubby little bar near campus. They had both been "legal" since the year before, but were carded as usual; Bronco's had been in serious danger of losing its license over serving minors, and the employees were now careful. Micky insisted on ordering a boilermaker. She had apparently heard that this was a really "horrorshow" drink and declared herself in need of just such a beverage. When she was sipping her third one, some two hours later, a man in a dirty mechanic's overall nudged up to her and drawled, "Hey, little chicky, that's a man's drink. You'll need a man to handlé you if you keep downing those suckers."

Jan, who had been nursing one beer, was long accustomed by then to having males of all ages ignore her if she was in Micky's company. She just sighed and rolled her eyes up at the stained ceiling. Micky swiveled slowly on the barstool and gave the man a baleful stare.

"What did you say?" she asked. "I'm not sure I heard you right."

The man leaned in toward her face. Even on the other side of Micky, Jan could smell the blend of liquor, cigarette smoke, and bad dental hygiene that was pouring out of his mouth along with his words. "I said," he purred, "you're gonna need a good man to tuck you in tonight after all that booze."

"Well, then," Micky drawled back, flashing one of her radiant smiles, "if you should happen to see one of those, you be sure to send him here to me—from over there somewhere, please." And she raised a damp finger to gesture at the other end of the bar.

Jan watched the message register on the man's expression, saw his heavy brows knit into a scowl.

"You snotty little bitch," he growled. "You college cunts think you're hot stuff, don't you, but I'm betting a man's pecker would get froze into a Popsicle if he put it between your legs."

"Why don't you shut your foul mouth, you Neanderthal," Micky cried, and she actually tried to get up. Jan had a wild idea that Micky was going to try to fight the man. She grabbed one of the flailing arms, hauled her back down, and smiled ingratiatingly at the man.

"You'll have to excuse my friend," she said softly. "She isn't used to drinking, and she's had a bad day; her grandma died, and she's not taking it very well."

His face was instantly transformed; he looked confused, almost apologetic. After mumbling something unintelligible, he took himself off to the poolroom at the back of the bar. All the way back to the dorm, Micky loudly berated Jan, who would periodically catch her arm to keep her from stepping off the curb. "Why the hell did you have to talk nice to that creep? Maggots like that always think they're lords of light and any female should be thrilled to fall against their sweaty chests."

"I think you're mixing metaphors," Jan replied calmly. "And keep your voice down, please. If the Dragon Lady hears you, we'll both lose our jobs." They were resident assistants, responsible, Miss Sweetly said, for "setting a good example for the younger girls."

"Oh, yarbles," Micky crowed. "To hell with the Dragon Lady. I'll bet no pecker at all has ever been between her legs, frozen or not. You know, that was actually a pretty good line, that Popsicle crack. For a cretin, I mean." And she began to giggle, a snuffling sound she didn't try to mask. It was just like Micky to admire the wit of an opponent a few minutes after she had been furious enough with him to punch him out.

Jan managed somehow to quiet her as she used her key to let them into the dorm; it was after curfew. They were creeping across the darkened lobby when all the lights came on at once, a blinding dazzle that showed Jan just how bad Micky was looking: strands of long blond hair pasted against her cheek, a slack, openmouthed expression that only the most innocent observer would mistake for anything but drunkenness. The next thing it showed her was a lobby full of wide-eyed freshmen girls and a banner saying "Happy Birthday Micky!"

"Surprise!" the girls shouted, their high-pitched shrieks needling into Jan's frightened brain. Micky had staggered back against her at the first yell, and she had to hold her up with both arms.

When the shouts had subsided, Jan could see, past Micky's head, that confusion and apprehension had begun to replace the smiles on the young faces opposite her; God only knew what Micky must look like now. If even one of these girls went to Hilda Sweetly and reported that her R.A. had come in after curfew, staggering drunk, to a roomful of eighteen-year-olds who had gone to the trouble of trying to give her a nice birthday surprise, Micky was in real danger of being expelled before she could graduate.

"Mick," Jan hissed into her ear. "Close your mouth and stand up straight." She could feel that Micky was struggling to obey, but she knew that she must prevent her friend from even trying to speak.

"This is so lovely, you guys," Jan shouted, and Micky, whose ear was very close, made a moaning sound as if she had reinjured an old bruise. "But I'm afraid we'll have to do this tomorrow. I'm just bringing Mick back from the emergency room at St. Vincent's. She had a really bad reaction to something she ate in the caf tonight. I hope none of you had the meatloaf." Terrified glances flew among the assembled freshmen. "Anyway, she's had her stomach pumped—an ugly process—and she's not up to even talking yet. I've got to get her up to bed now."

Jan encircled Micky's waist with her left hand, lifted her slack arm up over her own shoulders with her right hand, and rushed toward the stairs, half carrying Micky along with her. A few minutes later, safe in their shared bathroom, Micky emptied her stomach without the help of a pump.

Wide awake in the cool darkness of the Sawtooth Bed and Breakfast, Jan wished with all her heart that she didn't always have to be the one Micky counted on. It would be so lovely to be the baby in just one group, to have decisions made and plans formulated by the big people, who would then simply tell her, "Oh, we're going to the beach" or "Donny looked, and there's no bogeyman in the hallway" or "Daddy's going to fix the dollhouse, so it will be all new when you wake up in the morning." And nobody at all would expect anything from her.

13 / Linda

"Wake up, you guys!" Linda became aware of the urgent hissing as she was dreaming that a toy train was carrying her makeup along a shelf, too high for her to reach, in a bathroom she didn't recognize. "Come on! You've got to see this."

Linda opened her eyes to find Sharon, her fine hair awry and her eyes bulging, hovering above her.

"Don't make too much noise," Sharon whispered. "Your room is closest to the back door, and you might scare him away."

"What are you talking about?" Mary said in a normal voice. Linda looked over to see that Mary was already sitting up.

"Will you please shut up?" Sharon hissed at her. "Just haul out and come with me. If somebody else doesn't see this, nobody will ever believe me."

"What the hell time is it, anyway?" Linda asked, whispering to humor Sharon, and pulling herself upright in the narrow bed.

"It's about six-thirty," Sharon answered. "You know I always get up with the roosters. It's that farm stuff in my blood. Now, come on."

Linda sighed and threw back the covers. Sharon had always been an early bird, she knew, but she couldn't help but be amazed that this woman could drink the way she had last night and then spring up out of bed at dawn the next day, looking like a twenty-five-year-old. There was no justice in the world, just as she'd always suspected. Mary groaned a little as she stood up and they both followed Sharon to the back door, whose glass inserts looked out onto the upstairs deck.

"Take a look," Sharon whispered. "I heard him when I was coming out of the john." She stepped back to let the other two women approach the door. Linda arrived first, looked out and then down. At the table on the lower deck, a medium-sized black bear was rummaging through the bags they had left there the night before after their return from Trail's End—half-empty sacks of trail mix, apple cores, and remnants of chocolate brownies. Even through the closed door, Linda could hear the crackle of paper, punctuated by a series of noises from the bear itself—sounds very like the snuffling grunts of a pig. Without making a noise, Linda gave way to Mary whose first glance produced a sharp cry; she clapped a hand over her mouth at once, but it was too late: the bear had heard, had stood up on his hind legs, and was staring up at the door. Instead of fleeing, he cocked his head first one way and then the other. Then, slowly, he dropped to all fours and started up the flight of stairs leading to the upper deck.

Sharon had already darted back down the hall after ushering the other two to the door and was now approaching with Peg in tow, literally dragging her along by the hand. Draped in a thin cotton nightie and groggy from sleep, Peg looked like someone being escorted to an execution. "What's wrong?" she kept mumbling.

Mary had moved from catatonia to panic in quick time. She dropped her hand from her mouth and shrieked, "He's coming up here! He's coming up the stairs." And she fled back into the room she and Linda had recently vacated.

"For heaven's sake, Mary," Linda said calmly, "the door's locked. He can't get in here."

"You tell that to *him,*" Mary called. "Somebody should get Steve."

Peg was next to Linda now, looking down. "Oh, it's a bear," she said sleepily. "We shouldn't have left that stuff outside."

By now Jan had appeared in the doorway of the room at the far end of the hall, and Micky was looking over her shoulder.

"Did somebody say 'bear'?" Jan called.

"Now look what you've done, Mimi," Sharon said peevishly. She had rejoined Linda at the door. "Your noise is scaring him away."

Sure enough. Linda looked out to see the bear moving off to the edge of the lower deck—not hurrying, just ambling along. Behind him he was leaving a trail of paw prints on the dew-covered boards.

"Somebody get a camera!" Sharon hissed. "We've got to have photographic evidence or our men are never going to believe we saw a bear. Hurry up before he gets down off the deck."

"I've got mine right here," Jan called, and she came scurrying along the hallway, her purple nightshirt swinging against her thighs.

"Oh, tell me you're not going to open that door," Mary moaned, running forward to close the door to her room.

"I think he's more scared of us than you are of him," Peg said soothingly.

"Hurry up!" Sharon cried, very loud this time, and Linda saw the bear hop down onto the grass and start a shambling trot for the woods. Sharon flipped the bolt and wrenched the door inward. "He's getting away," she cried, starting to laugh now. "Get a picture. Fast."

Jan stepped out onto the upper deck, raised her camera,

and then paused for a frozen couple of seconds. "Oh, shit!" she cried. "The lens cap!" And then she began fumbling with the front of the camera. From the back of the house, they could hear Duncan beginning to bark, and the bear broke into a run.

Just at the edge of the woods, the bear paused and turned back toward the house. It swung its pointed snout back and forth a few times and then went into an unmistakable squat.

"What's it doing now?" Micky asked, pushing past Linda and Sharon to stand next to Jan.

"I can't get a picture," Jan said. "The damned roof over-hang is in the way." And she started down the stairs to the lower deck, her bare feel slapping against the wood. The others bunched up into pairs to follow her.

"Why isn't he going into the woods?" Mary asked from the upstairs doorway.

"Because," Sharon called up to her, "he's busy giving us the definitive answer to a question that has troubled philoso-phers for centuries. And the answer, apparently, is no. Bears do *not* shit in the woods. They shit in clearings around bed-and-breakfast establishments."

Past Sharon's turned head, Linda saw the bear straighten up, turn, and trot into the first row of birches. In another sec-ond, the forest had swallowed him up.

"Oh, no," Jan moaned. "I didn't get a picture. Not even one."

"Well, take a picture of the tracks, then," Linda suggested. "There on the deck, before anybody steps on them."

"Okay," Jan said, game as always. "Somebody come down here and point to them. Peg, come on."

"Not on your life," Peg said. "Nobody's taking a picture of me in my nightgown at this hour of the morning."

"I'll do it," Sharon said, shouldering past them. Linda

watched Sharon stoop and extend one of her long arms. She was wearing a sleeveless, white gown—probably silk—which clung to every curve of her body as she bent, and once again, Linda marveled at how unchanged Sharon looked. No loose flesh hung from the extended arm, no middle-aged bulges spoiled the line of the shimmering fabric. How did she do it? Linda was painstakingly careful about what she ate and drank, exercised faithfully. And she knew that Sharon did none of that.

"Come on," Sharon said now, standing up straight again. "Let's go over and take a picture of the scat while it's still steaming. That should be good evidence that we witnessed the deed."

"I'm not going over there alone," Jan cried. "What if he's possessive about his waste matter and comes charging out of the woods at me?"

"We'll all go," Micky said cheerfully. "He won't dare take on all of us."

And true to form, they fell in with her suggestion. Just as they had always done, Linda thought. Even Mary came down and trailed along behind a few paces. Linda watched for a few minutes. Five women, barefoot, dressed for bed, were picking their way gingerly through the wet grass and hawks-weed, bunched up like kindergartners reluctant to come on stage for a school program. She chuckled a little and began to follow after them.

At breakfast, Kim Olson joined them for coffee before leaving for town. Linda admired the younger woman's style, a style only a lean, healthy girl like Kim could carry off. She was dressed in a gold silk blouse cinched at the waist by a wide patent-leather belt. Her granny skirt was a gold and black print, broomstick pleated, and she wore flat sandals, which tied, Grecian style, in a crisscross pattern up her slim ankles. Her jewelry especially attracted Linda's attention. It was almost certainly of her own design. Her masses of dark brown curls were held back above her ears by two spectacular combs, set with black and amber beads, and her blouse front supported a matching necklace of several strands. The earrings were simple amber beads set in gold. Linda thought she would definitely have to check out Kim's stand the next time she was in Grand Marais.

"Steve tells me you hoped to see the Witch Tree this year," Kim was saying. "I'm sorry to have to tell you that the Grand Portage band has closed the area to tourists. There are no tours any more."

"Oh, no," Peg cried, looking up from the last of the baked apple pancake on her plate. "I was so hoping we'd get to see it. What happened?"

"Vandalism," Kim said simply. "Some people actually tried to carve their initials into the trunk. That's sacred ground to the Indians, and tourists were leaving trash all over the place."

Steve, who had just come into the dining room with new pots of coffee, made a snorting sound of disgust as he overheard Kim's last words. "Pigs in human disguise," he said tightly. "They always spoil things for the rest of us."

Linda guessed that he would have liked to see the whole North Shore closed to tourists if only he could figure out a way to make a living without them. Yesterday morning, when she'd asked him if July was his busiest month at the B&B, he'd answered, "No, actually it's September and early October." "Why?" she'd asked, genuinely puzzled. "The fall colors," he explained. "We're overrun with leaf-peepers just as soon as the first golden tinge hits the birches." She had heard the derision in his voice, guessed that the term "leaf-peepers" was a standard local epithet not usually shared with outsiders.

"I'm so disappointed," Peg was saying now. "We were counting on going up tomorrow to the casino for a few hours and then out to see the tree."

Linda saw Steve and Kim exchange a glance; then Steve gave a small nod as he set down the coffee.

"I know somebody," Kim said slowly. "Somebody in the tribe. She might be able to fix it so she can take you out there. But you'd have to keep quiet about it. If other tourists got wind of it, there'd be hell to pay at the lodge."

"We'd be as silent as the tomb," Mary said. "And you know that six middle-aged yuppie females aren't going to make any mess."

Again, Linda saw the look that passed between the married couple. Perhaps they were thinking of the mess that had attracted a bear to their deck that very morning. Who had left that? Kim's dark eyes seemed to ask.

"I'll see what I can do," Kim said, looking now at Peg. "But it can't be tomorrow. Denise—that's my friend's name—works in town during the week. Maybe Saturday, though. Would that do?"

"Sure," Peg said eagerly. "We'll be happy to pay her."

"Oh," Kim said quietly, "that won't be necessary. She'll do it as a favor to us."

"We'd be so grateful," Peg breathed, speaking for all of them.

"Well, I have to get going," Kim said, lifting her lean wrist up to her eyes to check the time. "If I don't see you tonight, I'll tell Steve what I find out."

Linda watched the couple take leave of each other at the steps leading down the few feet to the front door. They didn't touch, and they said very few words, but their faces spoke volumes: knowing smiles, lifting of eyebrows, sidelong movement of eyes—all the subtly flirtatious gestures of people in love. Linda had long been observant about couples, people she knew and strangers alike, fascinated by the codes they developed to communicate with each other even when they were in crowds of other people.

She had become very much aware of Steve Olson during the past few days, the slow grin when someone spoke to him, the preoccupied way he served the food. When he reached past her face to pick up a coffeepot, the sight of his well-muscled forearm—covered in fine, sun-bleached hairs—sent a jolt of sexual excitement through her whole body. Just to the left of his mouth, there was a small, crescent-shaped scar, white inside the reddish beard stubble. She wondered how he'd got a wound there. When his face was close to her as it was when he set down her plate, she had to clench her hands to resist the impulse to reach out and caress that raised half-moon with the tips of her fingers. And the movement of his hips as he walked away made her feel a little dizzy.

She suspected that he was well aware of the effect he created, sometimes said things that he knew had double meanings, although he never leered or otherwise punctuated the remarks with his voice. Tuesday morning, after the distribution of the shirts and the picture taking, he had hung around in the dining room for a while until Sharon had said, "There's going to be a lot of girl talk going on in here, so you better cover your ears or escape to the kitchen. No offense." Steve had given one of those slow grins and replied, "No offense taken. I can slide out just as easily as I slid in." Peg had pinched her lips tight shut and turned scarlet. Sharon went into a coughing fit designed to hide her laughter, and Mary, standing behind Steve where he couldn't see her, opened her mouth in a distorted grimace of mock surprise. But Steve appeared not to notice any of it, ambled slowly out of the room after collecting the last empty coffeepot from the table.

But clearly, Kim Olson had no need to fear that her handsome husband would ever go beyond giving a few cheap thrills to his middle-aged guests by such harmless banter. Seeing them together today had convinced Linda of that in five minutes. More than five years had passed since her own split from Tom McDonald, and while she had not been entirely celibate since then, she had found no one she could consider as a likely substitute. And she missed Tom still. There were moments, even now, when the pain was so terrible that it almost doubled her over. She'd had such a moment this morning, barefoot out in the yard following her oldest friends to the edge of the woods to take a picture of bear scat.

A morning breeze had caught her, had rushed right through the thin nightgown to set her shivering all over—one of those North Shore chills that made people forget it was summer. And it brought back an image of Tom so sharp it was almost like a vision. He had always thrived in cold weather, loved the icy Chicago winds that made her shrink against him as they walked. He would push his face into the wind as if he meant to drink it, gobble it up, his thin hair lifting from his forehead to reveal a look of dreamy pleasure in the dark eyes. His stride would lengthen, all his gestures would quicken. He seemed almost to crackle with energy when it started to get cold. In heat and humidity—and Chicago could produce those conditions too—he was torpid, gloomy, so she hadn't always enjoyed being around him in July and August. And that, really, had been one of the chief advantages of the relationship—that they could pick and choose their times together, the frequency, the season. Marriage, of course, would have been quite a different thing.

In the long run though, he had preferred marriage. For most of their time together, he had told Linda that he would divorce his wife and marry her, that he wanted to do this. "I love you," he would say when she asked him why, "and I want to be married to the woman I love." But she had steadily refused, argued that she couldn't bear to be responsible for breaking up his family. It had taken years for him to see through that rationalization, to see that she just didn't want to be married. Even then, he didn't break it off; there was so much to hold them together by that time. They were both artists, both eager teachers and learners. From her, he had learned to appreciate the graphic arts, to delight in the subtle shadings of light in a black-and-white photograph. From him, she had come to love words, to savor them almost as much as she savored visual images. Some words she loved to roll around in her mouth like plump grapes; others she loved to chew slowly like exotic Eastern foods. When she could combine the verbal and the visual, her joy was tripled—a close-up picture of blue flowers against velvety green foliage was even more delicious when she could say that the flowers were called "Carpathian harebells," the words conjuring exotic places and foreign sounds to enrich the nuances of light falling across the fluted blossoms.

And with Tom, the sex had stayed exciting too. He would never admit that marriage would probably have made it less exciting, but she had a deep conviction that this was true, and she was determined not to risk testing it. But Tom was right, too, when he accused her of wanting to remain free of "entanglements" that would interfere with photography trips to Utah and to Brazil. "I can work at my art while being married, the father of two kids, and having a mistress," he would say. "Why can't you work if you're married? My kids are practically grown up already, and they'd live most of the time with

Nancy anyway. I'm assuming there's no question of us having children together, even if we *were* married. So what's the hang-up?"

That was an interesting question. What was the hang-up, anyway? Linda couldn't answer the question even in her own mind. Not even now that Tom was in her past. She should have kept her mouth shut when he made that remark about their not having kids together, but no, she had to start up with the usual rationalizations. Of course, she wasn't ever going to have children, she told him. There was chronic depression for three generations lurking in her recessive genes, just waiting to manifest in a new generation, especially if she yoked her genes with those of a man whose Scottish ancestors were hardly known for cheerfulness.

And then she went one step too far. That was why, she told him, she'd had the abortion in 1977. He stood straight up from the sofa in her apartment, staring down at her with his mouth agape.

"Nineteen seventy-seven?" he echoed. "You were pregnant in seventy-seven? Was it mine?"

"Of course it was yours," she cried. "I haven't had sex with anybody else since you first fell into my bed in nineteen seventy-five. What do you take me for?"

"You should have told me," he said, and his face had gone very pale. "Why didn't you tell me?"

She had launched into a stream of explanations, of re-assurance: it had been so early in their relationship, she wasn't sure of him then, she couldn't just trap him that way into leaving his wife. But all through it, he just kept staring at her, his expression beginning to set into one she'd never seen before—he was looking at her as if she were a stranger. Even in their first meeting, the expression on his face as he stared at her over his children's heads had said, "I know you.

I recognize you." So this cold stare was terrifying. It had taken another four months, but finally Tom had simply told her he was breaking it off, that he was, in effect, choosing Nancy.

"It's because of the abortion, isn't it?" she had asked coldly.

"I can't get past it," he replied. "You kept it from me—all these years. It's too *big* a thing. I can't put it out of my mind."

In the years since the breakup, Linda had faced the truth about the abortion; none of what she'd told Tom about it was true. She just didn't want a child—not then, not ever. When Peg had been talking yesterday in the canoes about how much she envied Jan's four boys, Linda had thought with a shudder of the emotional chaos that would be created by having *four* children clamoring for your attention—no, demanding your attention. She hardly remembered the abortion, had never regretted it. She liked living alone, craved solitude as her greatest emotional need. Maybe, she had been thinking lately, it wasn't just a "slip" that she'd finally told Tom about the abortion; maybe, at bottom, she knew it would drive him away, and she had unconsciously chosen to do just that.

When she looked in the mirror now and saw the line of gray roots, the sagging flesh under her jaw line, she would have flashes of alarm; she was getting old and she was alone. Maybe she would die alone. But then she would shake herself mentally and think, "Everybody dies alone," remind herself that she had chosen her life—always—and the choices hadn't been such bad ones after all. But she colored her hair, exercised at her gym until her thigh muscles screamed at her to stop, massaged expensive lotions into her throat and her forearms. For what? Was it just that an aesthetically pleasing appearance was an asset to her career? Her agent had told her that. Or was it that she herself couldn't bear to see the portrait in the mirror crumble into that sad, half-mad mask she saw whenever she looked at her mother. Could you light me so I look ten years younger? Could you find the camera angle that will guarantee that the glint of desire will never fade from men's eyes when they look my way?

"Linda, are you paying attention?" It was Mary, leaning in toward her at the table. "Jan's refused to make the list, so I'm elected."

"What list?" Linda said absently.

"We're having the massages today, remember?" Mary said. "And I'm making a list of who goes first, who goes second, and so on."

"Why is that necessary?" Linda asked, really curious.

"Well, each massage is an hour long," Mary explained, the mild exasperation in her voice indicating that they must have been discussing this already while Linda was woolgathering. "If we know about when our massage is scheduled, some of us can go off and do other things while the first ones are having theirs. Hiking maybe, or even into town if you're scheduled somewhere toward the end."

"Oh, I see," Linda said, smiling. "Well, who's signed up so far?"

"I'm first," Sharon said. "I'm having only half an hour. I don't think I could lie still any longer than that."

"And I'm second," Mary explained. "That's all we have so far."

"Okay," Linda said. "I'll go next, if that's okay with everybody."

They went on to fix the rest of the order. Jan had told Linda in June about this plan to bring a local massage therapist up to the Sawtooth for a whole day. He was a friend of Steve's, who had arranged everything at this end. Linda knew that the woman who had taken the group out last year to let them participate in the summer training of a dogsled team was also a friend of the Olsons. She found it both amusing and appealing that they seemed so eager to share their guests' traveler's checks with their friends. And certainly Linda had no objection to a massage. After paddling a canoe for three hours yesterday, her aching muscles could use a little pampering.

Now, the rota decided on, they were listening to Peg tell how she and Jerry had taken training in massage techniques after Jerry's surgery. "We both needed something to help us relax after that ordeal," she was saying. "And it really is quite wonderful. Have any of you had full-body massages before, with the oils and everything?"

"I have," Mary said. "It's a luxury I allow myself about every two months. There's a masseuse at the Y who's just marvelous."

"I have too," Jan said, "but not very often, and I don't know about this today. I'm a little queasy about it. I've never been done by a man."

It took two beats for the shrieks of laughter to explode. Linda wondered what Steve, out there stacking plates in the dishwasher, must think. Peg, already beet-red, pursed her little mouth, pulled her eyes into a sidelong glance, and said, "Well, Jerry and I do each other—but I'm not going to tell you how often." This time, the laughter was even louder, even more prolonged. Linda could see that Micky had tears leaking from her eyes as she rocked back and forth, her napkin caught up to her mouth. Only Jan seemed not to be enjoying the joke; she was looking at Micky with an expression that seemed both concerned and a little angry, as if she disapproved somehow of Micky having such a good time this morning.

14 / Mary

When Padraic—"Paddy"—O'Neill came up into the dining room carrying the folded massage table he would
install upstairs in the big bedroom, Mary could tell almost at
once that their fears of embarrassment were unfounded. He
was a tall, lean man of about forty, with ginger-colored hair
and wire-rimmed glasses. With his shy smile and gentle voice,
he seemed to radiate an almost saintly calm. He instructed
them to fill out a short questionnaire, prompting them
to include any aches and pains, any "areas" they thought
needed special attention. Mary dutifully recorded the
chronic bursitis she had in her right shoulder. Before he
was set up, they were confident that they were dealing with
an experienced professional.

"How does an Irishman come to be up here in the north
woods?" Jan asked him when he came back downstairs.
"We're usually city dwellers."

"Oh, are you Irish too?" he asked, lifting his pale eyebrows
above the glasses.

"I used to be," Jan sighed. "Before I got married and transformed into a German."

"I don't know," he said, smiling at her banter before
returning to her question. "I love the quiet, the peace. I'm
from Philadelphia originally, and I came here to meet my
girlfriend's family. That was all it took. When we got married,

she wanted to live somewhere else, but I talked her into coming back here."

"Well, you could both have done much worse," Mary assured him.

"Oh, I know," he said, his smile revealing large, uneven teeth. "And I couldn't have done better than my Susan. We're both cabinetmakers too. Nobody up here has just one job, you know."

"We're beginning to find that out," Peg laughed.

"Well, who's first then?" he asked, surveying them all.

"Me," Sharon said, bounding forward. "I get you while you're still fresh."

He ignored the innuendo, which Sharon delivered complete with broad wink, stepped back, and murmured, "This way, if you please," and let her go ahead of him up the stairs.

"Oh, he looks just like my brother Larry," Peg exclaimed when he was out of earshot. "He has a very different voice and manner, but that hair—even the shape of his hands. He's just the image of him."

"I haven't seen Larry in so many years," Mary said, flopping down onto the love seat. "But I suppose he would have grown up to look like this—maybe a bit thicker in the body." When Peg and Mary were high school classmates at St. Mary's Academy for Girls, they had spent time in each other's homes. Mary remembered Larry Ward as a loud, good-natured young man, several years their senior, whose teasing had offended her mightily, although she would never have said so to Peg.

"Larry's the brother closest to me in age," Peg was explaining to the others. "And I guess he's my favorite too. He lives in Phoenix now, and I miss him. What a clown he always was! When we were little, he would say the most outrageous things in such a calm voice that I almost always believed him, and he would introduce each one by saying, 'Of course you know,' which made it seem even more plausible. We would beg to go along whenever our dad went out, and sometimes Dad would make us stay in the car if he was just going inside somewhere for a few minutes. As soon as he would disappear inside some door, Larry would start: 'Of course you know he's not coming back. Bad guys in there are gonna catch him and tie him up.' By the time Dad got back to the car, I would be blubbering: 'Larry said—he said' and Dad would just sigh, 'Oh, for heaven's sake, Larry.' And once when we were in Grandma Ward's old attic, just the two of us, Larry closed the door, put his back against it, and said, 'Of course you know we're using up all the oxygen in here. You'll be able to feel it pretty soon.'"

And Peg put her head back and laughed her best and merriest laugh. Mary could feel her own cheeks flushing with anger and outrage. "That's not funny," she said, her voice louder than she'd intended, but some of the others were laughing, too, and that made her even more upset. "Why are you laughing at that as if it were some big joke?" she went on, standing up from the love seat and beginning to pace. "It's abusive behavior. How old were you? You must have been terrified."

Peg had been staring at her throughout this series of exclamations, a wide-eyed expression on her round face. Linda and Jan were exchanging glances, and Micky looked a little alarmed at the sudden change in the tone of the conversation.

"I must have been about six or seven," Peg replied, "and no, I don't think I *was* really terrified. It was a game we had— he would tease, and I would whine to our parents about it; we both knew our parts. I knew quite well that he wouldn't really be allowed to hurt me, that my father always did come back to the car."

"Well, I still think it's awful," Mary huffed, beginning to feel a bit foolish now. "And maybe you just see it differently after all these years. I'll bet your tears were genuine at the time."

"Maybe," Peg shrugged, always willing to make peace. "But I suppose I made his life crazy, too, by tagging along behind him every move he made. I don't see why you think it was such a big deal."

Someone changed the subject, and equilibrium was restored, but Mary still felt sore, "corrected," as if she were some child. And at the same time, she realized that the others were genuinely complacent about the torments Larry Ward had visited on his little sister—to them it really was no "big deal." So why was it to her? Perhaps, she reflected as she sat down again and began thumbing through a magazine, the key to the difference was in something Peg had just said: "I knew he wouldn't really be allowed to hurt me." Margaret Ann Ward had grown up in a family where the big people kept vigilant eyes on the little ones, where boundaries were clear, where children could feel essentially safe. Mary Victoria Cavallo had not enjoyed the same kind of privileged childhood. She could not even remember a time when her family had been intact, could not remember her mother at all.

Teresa Quinn Cavallo had died at thirty-one of pneumonia, leaving her bewildered husband with two sons, ages nine and seven, and one three-year-old daughter. Tony Cavallo, who worked for the railroad in those years, could not be home in Green Bay enough to raise his children alone, so they were "farmed out"—that is, the boys were. Mary's brothers had gone to live with their father's brother, John, whose family size was relatively small—only two girls—and whose ambition for sons could be filled vicariously by taking in his brother's boys. Mary, on the other hand, was "passed around"—living for four-or-five-month periods at a time in the crowded homes of her father's four sisters. In every household, she was a burden, an extra mouth to feed. The Quinns, her mother's people, lived in Milwaukee, and Tony wouldn't hear of having her sent so far away. Only much later did Mary learn that he found his wife's relatives so daunting that he never saw much of them even when Teresa was alive.

In the homes of her aunts, Mary had been fair game for the childish cruelties of her cousins, most of them boys. They would shove her down on the broken sidewalks of their working-class neighborhoods, kneel on her chest, and shout things like, "Stupid girl!" and "Your mother gave you an ugly face, and that's all she ever gave you." They would stick broken pieces of their parents' cigarettes into her food. They would trip her when she was running and then jeer at her if she cried. Her aunts and uncles, no doubt harboring resentment over having to stretch their meager resources to include yet another child, did little to intervene, seldom punished their own children for mistreating her. Able to read long before she went to school, little Mary always outshone her cousins in the classroom. Her aunts never lost an opportunity to belittle her academic accomplishments. Aunt Louisa, especially, would jeer, "Nobody likes a smart-aleck girl, little Miss Straight-A. Maybe you should go live with those east-side doctors' kids—see if they'll feed you for a change."

When she told her father on his infrequent visits about any of this treatment, he would grow quiet, look even sadder, "You have to try to be a better girl" was all he would say. So she grew up swallowing her rage, learned how to endure abuse without crying—her cousins seemed to be impressed by stoicism. She never lost her deep sense of outrage at injustice, whether aimed at her or at other kids. But she did gradually adopt the Cavallo family disdain for "snobs," for any form of social climbing, including academic achievement. By junior high, she was just coasting in school. She loved to watch television, soaked in every program that depicted families as they should be: "Ozzie and Harriet," "Father Knows Best," the "Donna Reed Show." Someday she would have a family like that—she would make it happen. And when she had it, she would never, never let anything take it away from her.

In 1960, when Mary was fourteen, her father got a job at one of the paper mills in town and quit the railroad for good. Both of her brothers had already graduated from high school, and the elder one was about to get married. The younger brother, Tony junior, elected to remain with Uncle John, so Mary went alone to live in a small upstairs apartment with a father she hardly knew. He had never remarried, had become a silent, rather crotchety man. But he now made it clear that he intended to make up to his daughter for the years of hardship and neglect. He enrolled her in St. Mary's Academy for Girls, insisted on several hours of homework every night—no television until that was done. She hated it, hated him. But gradually the lure of learning began to pull her in, and by the time she was a senior, she had pulled her grades back up so that she was being courted by St. Augustine College, having scholarships dangled before her.

She understood now what sacrifices her father had to make to send her there—and not just financial sacrifices. His relatives were aghast at the "waste" of a college education for a girl. But she had never been able to wholly forgive him for the abandonment she had experienced as a child, had never been able to feel she really got to know him. He lived now on his pension in a single room of a boardinghouse for the elderly. He could have afforded a small apartment, but he preferred having someone else cook and clean and make his bed. Every afternoon, he played cards in an Italian café frequented by other aging men who were almost as silent and unconnected as he was. Mary saw him about twice a year, and that was only because Christopher insisted on making the trip. She never saw any of the other Cavallos.

After her divorce from David Schneider, Mary had recoiled in revulsion from every version of family she had ever experienced. She had chosen her mother's maiden name as her own last name, would have changed her daughters' name to Quinn, too, if David hadn't blocked it legally, and she had gone in search of the Quinns themselves—her mother's sisters—of whom she had heard almost nothing in fifteen years, not since Grandma Quinn had died. But most of that branch of the family no longer lived in Milwaukee. The only one she found there was her grandfather's youngest sister, Laura Quinn, a crusty, lively old woman with glorious silver hair. Laura had never married and now lived alone in the Quinn's original home. She was seventy-five years old when Mary first contacted her in 1983. And most important for Mary, she had known Teresa Quinn very well, had doted on her niece until the day she moved to Green Bay as a young bride.

Once established in Kenosha, Mary had "courted" Laura Quinn, had made it a point to drive up to Milwaukee to see her often, had invited her down to Kenosha for holidays, had forced her daughters to write long notes whenever they received any little token from their great-great-aunt. There *would* be an extended family, only this time it would be only Quinns, only women. Eventually, as their teenage rebellion began to subside, Angela and Carol warmed up on their own to "Auntie Quinn," as they all called her, came to enjoy her visits, liked to question her about their grandmother and the life she had lived before a handsome young Italian-American railroad worker came into her life.

Then last Thanksgiving, only three months after Peg had called to tell Mary about Micky's diagnosis, there had been an upsetting episode. Mary had prearranged it with Aunt Quinn that Angela and her husband, Jim, and baby, Austin, would collect the old woman and drive her down to Kenosha on Wednesday evening, and all of them would spend Thanksgiving weekend together—four generations under one roof. Carol was in the Philippines in the Peace Corps and wouldn't be with them, but it would be a family celebration anyway. At seven-thirty, Angela had called from a pay phone to say that the old Quinn house was locked and darkened— apparently no one at home. Mary had flown into an instant panic, and even Christopher, usually so calm, had looked troubled as he took the phone from her trembling hand. "You'd better dial 911," he said to Angela. "Something must have happened to her. Call us as soon as you know anything."

Forty-five minutes later, Angela called back to say that, instead of calling the police, she and Jim had secured a key from the next-door neighbor and had let themselves into the house. A thorough search had revealed that the house was, indeed, empty—nothing disturbed. What should they do now? Chris had told them to alert the Milwaukee police before leaving the city—leave phone numbers where the family could be reached—and then come down to Kenosha. It was almost midnight when the police called. An elderly woman matching the description they had given was at the Milwaukee bus depot. She was disoriented and couldn't tell anyone whether she was going to take a bus out of the city or was supposed to meet someone arriving in Milwaukee—all she kept saying was, "I'm supposed to have Thanksgiving with my niece." Asked what her niece's name might be, she kept saying, "Teresa Quinn," but could give no address or phone number. Chris and Mary had left at once for Milwaukee. When they arrived at the bus depot, they had found Auntie Quinn distraught and raving.

"You said I was coming to your house," she screamed at Mary as soon as she spotted her. "Why didn't you come to meet the bus? I've been waiting and waiting."

"Oh, Auntie," Mary cried, trying to put her arms around her. "I told you Angela was coming to pick you up. What made you think you were supposed to take a bus?"

The old woman shook off Mary's embrace, glared at her. "You said you would get me. You said to take a bus." Her voice was high and strident, echoing in the big room. People were gathering to watch the scene.

"No, no, my dear, " Mary said soothingly. "I never said anything about a bus. Try to be calm. We'll go right now to the car."

"Don't you lie to me, you wicked, wicked girl!" Aunt Quinn was shrieking now, her rheumy old eyes flaring. "You left me here, among strangers, for days and days. I want to go home right now."

Somehow they had got her out to the car, calmed her enough to get her inside. Mary argued for taking her to a hospital, but Chris talked her out of it; Aunt Quinn wasn't in any apparent physical distress, and a hospital would only warehouse her anyway until after the holiday weekend. They should take her home with them and let her rest, decide what to do tomorrow. On the drive to Kenosha, the old woman fell asleep almost immediately, snoring noisily in the backseat.

"This is just awful," Mary said, near tears. "I was counting on such a lovely Thanksgiving. How could she round on me like that? I've never been anything but kind to her."

"She's eighty-nine," Chris said soothingly. "She's just confused and exhausted, that's all. Probably she won't even
remember most of this tomorrow."

"What if she doesn't remember *anything* tomorrow?" Mary
wailed. "What if she's had a breakdown? Senile dementia or
something? What are we supposed to do then? I'm telling
you, Chris, I didn't sign on for this."

He drove for a few minutes without speaking. Only the
snorting sounds from the rear seat broke the silence.

"But you *did* sign on for it," Chris said finally. "As I recall,
you told me that you're the one who sought *her* out. You're
the one who wanted to reconnect to your mother's family,
to give the girls a sense of family beyond fragmented units.
Did you think it would be just for cute and cuddly times?
That she would always be the twinkly, spry old character
you found in 1983? People get old, Mary. They lose their
tempers, sometimes inappropriately. They say things they
wouldn't otherwise dream of saying. Family is bad along with
good."

Mary had made the rest of the trip without speaking. And,
indeed, the next day, Aunt Quinn seemed her old self, acted
as if the day before hadn't happened at all, although Mary
could tell from a faintly guilty look in her eyes that the old
woman remembered at least some of it. Since then, Mary
could not shake free of the dread that something of the kind
might happen again, and she couldn't stop feeling angry
with Aunt Quinn for "spoiling Thanksgiving," as she said in a
letter to Carol. At Christmas, she made an excuse about the
risk of bad weather to explain why they were not coming up
to Milwaukee, and at Easter she and Chris had stopped in for
only an hour at the Quinn house after spending the day with
Angela, Jim, and the baby. Chris didn't say a word about it,
but Mary sometimes thought that his glance was reproachful

whenever he heard her end of the conversation on those occasions when Aunt Quinn phoned.

And it had been the timing of it, too, she supposed that made it so upsetting. Her shock about Micky hadn't even had a chance to wear off when she'd been confronted by the reality of Aunt Quinn's growing debility. Why the hell was life like this? Why were people always leaving? She looked up from her magazine now, scanned the dining room where the others were talking. In college, these women had become her substitute family, the sisters she'd never had, but marriage had taken her away from them. The round-robin and the occasional phone call had been a poor substitute for their daily support. Then, after a few years, she was rather grateful that they couldn't witness the shame and humiliation that went along with tolerating David's affairs while she was sinking into mindless housewifery. She felt relieved when the annual letter began to sputter, once stopped it cold by not sending it along. How could she write, "Carol got three stars on her spelling test" without sounding like every cliché of the mothers they had formerly mocked?

But, at the same time, she was really enjoying motherhood, happy to be able to stay home with the girls instead of going off to some other job every day. She would have been unable to find the words to convey to her college friends the secret joy she felt when Angela turned to wink at her right in the middle of the Christmas pageant—a joy that made the daily grind tolerable, that even made it possible to pretend that David's "chickie parade" was meaningless by comparison with this pride, this bursting sensation around her heart. Once when she was sitting next to Carol's bed in the middle of the night, she had seen the child stir, stretch like a cat, arching her back and pushing her fingers out into the air as if they might grow claws, and suddenly the misery she'd been feeling because it was 3 A.M. and she didn't know where her husband was fell away in a blinding rush of love and tenderness for the sleeping child.

Yet she couldn't pick up a phone to tell such things to her old friends. She imagined that their lives had become very different from hers, that their daily experience was on a higher plane where their children were somehow tangential—a place where they dined on some constant gourmet feast to which their mother-pride was only a sweet sorbet to cleanse the palate for the next exotic course. Perhaps that was wrong. Maybe, the whole time, they had been enjoying tuna casseroles and s'mores. And maybe they, too, had been gagging on some of what life was putting on their plates.

When she finally left her marriage behind in pain and rage, her "girlfriends" rallied to her aid, Micky providing financial help, and Peg mothering her again as she had in high school and college. Yet not one of them could understand why she found Larry Ward's teasing of his sister so sinister. Not one of them had shared her childhood. She sighed and stood up, wandered over to the buffet table, and picked up a deck of cards.

"If we're going up to the casino," she said, "maybe we should get in some practice gambling first. Anybody up for a little poker?"

Micky was still seated at her place at the dining table and Jan, standing behind her at the windows, snapped to attention, her eyes flaring and her mouth forming the word *no*. She nodded down at Micky. But of course it was too late. Peg had already said okay, and Linda had said, "Sounds like fun." Micky lifted her head slowly and said, "Yes, I'll play. Should we play for money?"

Mary could feel her cheeks burning. She had blundered again. Jan must know something she didn't know. Could it be that Micky had forgotten how to play cards? That didn't seem possible because her long-term memory seemed fine. Both Peg and Linda were reacting now to Jan's signal, were uneasy and silent. Micky turned first one way and then the other. "Well, come on, you slowpokes," she said finally and everyone moved forward to take a seat, Jan making a point of sitting immediately next to Micky. Mary sat on the opposite side of the table, where Linda joined her, and Peg sat at the end.

"We'll just play a few hands for fun," Mary said, aware that her voice sounded a little strained. "We don't have to bet." She was searching her mind for the simplest form of poker she could remember. Micky had been the great cardsharp among them—poker, canasta, bridge. At St. Augustine, she and Peter had made a formidable team in the informal bridge tournaments that were always going on. Mary, living at home and working part-time in those days, had little leisure for games. Seven-card stud. That was a simple game. Nothing wild. She announced the game and began to deal.

"You'll have to remind me about what beats what," Peg said now, putting her fingers down on her hole cards once she'd glanced at them. Mary wondered if this was true or if Peg was simply trying to set up an atmosphere where any slips on Micky's part could be passed off as being "rusty" about the rules. Either way, it gave Mary the chance to keep up a reinforcing patter every time she dealt a card face up: "Two of clubs, no help. Pair of tens—that's high on the table so far. Oh, oh, pair of kings beats your tens, Jan." Before she got halfway through the deal, Micky turned over her hole cards and placed them next to the other cards that were already face up in front of her. Jan reached over and picked up the two cards, murmuring, "Keep these two face down," and handed them back to Micky. Mary could see a dull color coming up into Micky's face, spreading under her eyes; she didn't look at any of the others while she placed the cards face down in front of herself.

Mary distributed the third up-card, her monologue sounding almost desperate in her own ears: "Nobody's got three of a kind showing, but of course you might have it in the hole. Three of a kind beats two pair, as I recall." And Micky reached down and turned over her hole cards for the second time, arranging them neatly next to the up-cards: she had a pair of eights, a queen, a seven, and a jack. There was a frozen pause before Linda wordlessly turned over her own hole cards and lined them up. Peg and Jan immediately followed suit, and Mary hid her own face by bending low over her cards as she did the same. Mary dealt the last two cards faceup, revealing that Peg had won the hand with three kings.

Linda took the deck from Mary's fingers and said, "Five-card draw." She dealt fast, her face set in a mask that revealed no emotion at all. Micky watched as the others picked up and held their cards, and then she did the same. When all five cards had been dealt, Jan dropped her cards and exclaimed, "All I have is crap. I'm not even going to bother to draw. You and I will play your hand together, Mick." She leaned in to take a look at Micky's cards, pointed at two, and helped Micky to isolate the three cards she would reject. Micky kept glancing at Jan's face, nodding at anything she said, following instructions like a child. Mary could feel a tightening in her stomach, a wave of mild nausea. Jan whispered something into Micky's ear.

"I'll take three cards," Micky said meekly. Linda dealt the cards, smacking them onto the table—one, two, three. Once again Jan leaned in as Micky picked up the cards and added them to the two in her hand. But Mary could see that Micky wasn't even looking at the cards now. She was looking across the table, straight into Mary's eyes. And the look on her face said more clearly than words could have said, "Do you see this? Do you see what's happening to me?"

Mary's throat was beginning to spasm now; saliva was flooding her mouth and it had a sharp, unpleasant sting. She began to swallow. "Oh, God! Let me make it to the end of this hand," she thought, focusing hard on her own cards. "I'll play these," she murmured when Linda said, "Mary?" in a sharp, angry-sounding voice. Mary had nothing, not even a pair, but she couldn't bear to contribute to making this hand last even a few seconds longer than it had to. When it was over—she had the impression that Linda had won—she sprang up.

"Deal me out," she managed to say. "I need a cig." And she fled, remembering at the last moment to snatch up her purse, to reinforce the fiction of why she was running outside. She made it off the deck before the sobs hit her, ran almost blind for the bench at the front of the house. It was there that Jan found her some fifteen minutes later. She had cried herself into hiccups by then, had lit a cigarette and was taking long drags between the violent twitches of her diaphragm. Jan sat next to her and put an arm around her shoulders.

"It's so awful," Mary said, gasping as a new sob came up along with the words. "I wanted to believe it was just a little forgetting, like absentmindedness over where you put your glasses. But she has the mind of a child." And she wept again, putting the hand with the cigarette against her face.

"Not all the time," Jan said, squeezing her a little. "And not about everything. Her sequential reasoning skills are pretty much shot, and numbers mean almost nothing to her anymore, so card games are impossible—even ones she used to know quite well how to play. Other things are still functioning at a higher level. Her emotional life is still that of an adult."

"But for how long?" Mary wailed. She could hear that she sounded like a petulant child herself. "Oh, I was so determined I wasn't going to do this! I made up my mind I wasn't going to blubber while we were up here. Micky asked us not to talk about it. She just wants to have a good time with her friends while she still can, and I vowed I was going to have a good time with her. Did she notice I was upset?"

"She suspects, I suppose," Jan sighed. "She's always had that radar about other people's feelings and that seems to still be in full operation. In fact, it may be hyperactive these days. She's afraid of pity, watchful for signs of it."

"I suppose there'll be a time when she doesn't see it any more," Mary said, taking a long pull on the cigarette before grinding it out under her foot. "When will that be?"

Jan didn't answer at once, removed her arm and folded her hands into her lap. "Nobody knows the answer to that," she said, and now she sounded as if she might cry herself. "Maybe not for a while yet. Maybe she'll go on minding for a long time."

"But she knows now what's going on," Mary said, drawing a ragged breath. "I could see it in there. She knows, every minute, what's happening to her."

"Oh, yes," Jan answered, looking away at the pines. "Just before, when we were filling out those forms for Paddy, she wrote 'I'm under a lot of stress' under the question about whether there was any other condition Paddy should know about. I saw it before she turned it over to the front again."

Mary bent over and began to sob again. This time Jan didn't try to stop her.

"I'm sorry to be such a baby," Mary said when she'd got control of herself again. "I'll get it out of my system out here. I promise you I won't let her see me blubbering."

Now Jan was silent for so long that Mary turned to stare at her face. Jan looked pale, tired.

"I don't know about that," she said finally. "Maybe we shouldn't hide our feelings from Micky. Maybe we *should* cry with her over this, let her know how much she means to us."

"But you said," Mary protested, "that she hates it when people cry, that she fears pity."

"I know what I said," Jan replied, and she sounded a little angry now. "But that's only a way of denying what's going on—for her and for us. Brave faces. Lies, really."

"But she said she didn't want to talk about it while we were here, and I don't think we should go against her wishes."

"Oh, sure," Jan said, a gust of irritation breaking through as she stood up. "As usual, she gets to boss us all around, to tell us how and when we get to express our feelings."

Now Mary was silent for a moment, watching Jan pace. Of all the reactions she might have predicted when Jan came outside, this was not one of them.

"That seems a little harsh, under the circumstances," Mary said quietly.

"Oh, you know it's true," Jan cried, wheeling to look at her; there were tears on her face now. "She always bullied us. Maybe not Lindy, who's never moved by what people want, but all the rest of us. She's always had her own way, ever since we were in college and she first started 'managing' us. Now she's sick and that means we're not even allowed to feel our feelings."

"Where the hell is this coming from, Jan?" Mary asked, getting up from the bench. "What are you so damned angry about?"

Jan stood her ground for a moment, bent slightly forward at the waist, her thin arms wrapped into a tight fold, as if she were trying to hold herself in, to keep something from spilling out of her abdomen. On her face was a pageant of emotions—anger, uncertainty, and something else, something in the hazel eyes; she looked as if she were trying to make up her mind about whether to speak or not. But finally her face sagged, her mouth contorted into a silent wail, and her body began to shake with suppressed sobs.

Mary ran to her, folded her own short arms around Jan's middle, patted the heaving back.

"I know," she murmured. "You're mad at the world, at the unfairness of it all. I am too. But we've got to hold it together, for *her* sake. If it's this hard on us, think what it must be for her. I say we've got to honor her wishes, handle it the way she says she wants us to handle it."

Jan moaned—a long, wrenching sound that made her thin body shake as if she were having convulsions. Mary closed her own arms a little tighter, rocked her friend back and forth. How odd it was—Jan had come outside to comfort her and had ended up needing even more comforting herself.

15 / Sharon

Sharon was lying on her stomach and staring straight
down at the floor, her face supported on its outer rim by
the padded, doughnut-shaped extension that jutted out
from one end of the massage table. Her head was throbbing
slightly. Hangover. Even after they got back from Trail's End
last night, she had poured herself a big scotch before bed.
Steve kept an ice bucket ready for their use during the
evening hours, and they had brought along their own bottles
of liquor. And, as usual, when she'd had too much to drink,
she'd slept only a few hours. The headache had waked her
even before she heard the bear. Now she could hear the soft
strains of "Great Lakes Suite" coming from the boom box
Paddy O'Neill had brought with him, and she could smell
the lavender-scented oil he would be using on her back and
shoulders. "I just want you to concentrate on my upper back,
shoulders, and neck," she'd told him. "That's about all you'll
be able to handle in a half hour, I guess." What she didn't say
was that she had deliberately requested only a half hour
because that would prevent his doing a full-body massage.

"Remove as much clothing as you feel comfortable removing," he'd said in his reassuring voice. "And cover yourself
with this towel once you're on the table. I'll wait outside until
you say you're ready."

She had watched him leave, thinking desperately, "How

about if I remove none of my clothes? What would you think of that?" In the end, she'd elected to leave on her panties and shorts, had arranged herself carefully face down on the table, so that her breasts were completely flattened beneath her body, her arms tight against her sides. "Okay," she'd called in a weak voice, grateful that the position of her face made it impossible to see him except for his lower legs and feet. She had noticed almost immediately that, below the legs of his khaki-colored, twill pants, he was barefoot, and even *that* had sent a fresh wave of embarrassment through her. She wondered if your back could blush.

But luckily for her, blushing had never been one of her reactions—not like poor Peg, who couldn't stop herself from reddening at any little thing. But Sharon Gill Kazmerinski did not blush easily. Oh, no. So as long as she could keep up the bluster, the patter, the succession of nudges and winks, nobody could guess how queasy she felt about all of this. And she would do anything she had to do to keep them from guessing. From the moment Jan had told her about the plan to hire a massage therapist for this vacation, she had been dreading the actual moment. She had volunteered to be first only because she knew that having to wait while the others were being massaged, having to imagine it, would make her lose her nerve completely. And it would be pretty hard to make up a plausible excuse to back out at the last minute— not after she'd gone through her usual antics: "Oh, boy! What all do you suppose he's going to massage?" Leer, wink.

Sometimes, Sharon had a feeling of having a separate per-son inside herself who watched the outer Sharon posturing and guffawing—watched with cold disdain. What a phony! What a vulgar poseur. And yet that person could never *stop* the outer Sharon, could never win out over the terror of exposure that had dogged her most of her life. If people, even her closest friends, knew the truth, they would laugh at her, dismiss her, and—worst of all—pity her. When Peg started to cry in the canoe yesterday, Sharon had seen the others looking at each other; they would never again be able to think of Peg in exactly the same way, would ever after regard her as "Poor Peg who's sad inside because of her hysterectomy." When Jan got all serious about Doug's scar, everybody in those boats was thinking, "Poor Jan who can't stop worrying because her son is gay." No, no. Once you let your guard down, people *had* something over you, could feel superior whenever they looked at you.

Luckily, the massage required no talking at all on her part. And Paddy O'Neill went about his work in blessed silence too. Once, at the beginning, he'd murmured, "Oh, yes. You're carrying a lot of tension in these muscles." But he'd said nothing since, had simply gone about the kneading and rubbing of her back and shoulders, sometimes pausing to apply pressure—a steady, pointed gouging that she suspected was done with the thumbs—to certain places on her scapula and along her upper shoulders. Indeed, those spots felt sore as soon as he touched them. Was that what he meant by "carrying tension"? Funny that she hadn't noticed the soreness until he touched the places. In any case, she could keep on telling herself that there was nothing sexual in his touching, no demands being made on her in that way. No exploitation either.

For as long as she could remember, she'd thought of sex as exploitation, as someone—almost always a man—using someone else—almost always a woman—to "get off," without any feeling for that other person. In fact, the only feeling the exploiter had afterward, she thought, was contempt for the exploited. She knew quite well that, if she ever told this to anyone—anyone at all—that person would immediately assume that she must have been sexually abused as a child; that person would never believe her denials, might even suspect that she had "repressed" the memory of the abuse. But all of that was nonsense. No one had *ever* touched her in her childhood and early adolescence. In fact, she had grown up in a family where touch of any kind was almost nonexistent.

No, it wasn't anything that most people would think of as sinister at all. Just a pattern of instruction—from her mother, from the nuns, from the whole of Roman Catholic dogma—that the desires of the flesh were disgusting. Fasting was one of her mother's settled habits, imposed on her children, even when it *wasn't* absolutely required by Church imperatives such as Lent. The Gills fasted between meals as a matter of course. Snacking, like taking naps in the middle of the day, was considered a moral failing, a weakness. Boys, her mother told the Gill girls, couldn't be expected to control their nasty desires, so it was the responsibility of girls to be ever cautious. Boys wanted only one thing, and girls foolish enough to let them have it would be universally laughed at as "easy," would never attain the respected position of madonna/wife. That girls might feel sexual desire of their own was never presented as a possibility.

At Holy Martyrs Elementary School, Sharon's seventh-grade class had been divided up one spring morning; the boys were sent to the cafeteria for a talk from Father Marx, and the girls remained in the classroom where, for almost an hour, Sister Cherubina spoke cryptically of "sensations and feelings" that Satan used to entrap young people into sins of the flesh. She warned them about something she kept calling "self-abuse," but she never explained or defined the term. Sharon, seated in her back-row desk—tall children always sat in the back rows at Holy Martyrs—tried to imagine what "self-abuse" could mean. Was it like putting cigarettes out against your arm? Hitting your own back with those multistrand whips she'd seen in religious paintings? But surely it wasn't necessary to warn people not to do such things. Only crazy people or olden-days martyrs ever got up to such nonsense.

And then Sharon's older sister, Rosemary, proved everybody right by getting pregnant at seventeen. Their parents reacted with a blood-freezing rage—father—and terrible rejecting silence—mother. The boyfriend, upon being confronted, began by denying responsibility and ended by loudly denouncing the "slut" who was trying to trap him. His parents, who operated the drugstore in the village, sent a lawyer to the farm to "negotiate" what would happen next. Rosemary was sent away to a home—at the druggist's expense—and gave the baby, a girl, up for adoption without ever seeing her. Sharon's first date in high school had begun pawing her as soon as they were alone in his car. When she fought him off, he got angry, told her that he'd heard she was "a roundheels like your sister." She had hit him with her fist, a wide-swinging punch in the face. He was still holding his hands to his bleeding nose as she walked away from the drive-in. And she'd walked the whole three miles home.

There were other dates, less dramatic but no more reassuring. She couldn't relax, couldn't enjoy the movie or the ball game or the pizza because she was always anticipating the time when she would have to fend off the fumbling hands, the effort to pull her blouse out of her skirt, the sudden grab for her breasts. It was the urgency of these gestures that bewildered her, the persistence of the boys in making them that puzzled her. Why, if someone made it clear to her that a *handshake* wasn't wanted, she would never have tried to shake that person's hand again.

In college, she had dated very little. Very few St. Augustine boys had cars, so it was hard for them to date a girl who didn't live on campus. Sharon's need to go almost thirty miles away at the end of every school day provided a convenient excuse for her to refuse most of the invitations that came her way. And there had been quite a few such invitations during her freshman year. There was one boy in her sophomore botany class that she rather liked—a quiet, skinny kid named Joe. They went to several campus dances together—she was allowed to stay over in the dorm—but he never tried anything more than a few chaste kisses. During her junior year, she had developed a full-blown crush on another history major, Donald Bolger. He was handsome, in a pale, Nordic sort of way, and a wonderful talker; she had noticed *that* about him first, the way he could talk in class with ease and intelligence. And he had a car.

By their fourth date, she ran out of excuses for denying him what he wanted. Her friends in the honors program talked openly about sex, acted as if it was no big deal, made it seem as if virginity was something to be embarrassed about once you were over twenty. And Sharon had already developed her wisecracking persona, had learned that making jokes about sex was one way to avoid the necessity of ever talking seriously about it. So now, it was time to put up or shut up. Or put out. After the first searing physical pain, she had never felt anything at all while having sex with Don. He seemed not to either notice or care that she was wholly passive during their encounters, most of which took place in his car. Sharon watched his frantic pumping, listened to his pants and moans, with a bewildered detachment. This was certainly not what she had read about in romantic novels. It seemed sordid and undignified, and she was always grateful that he never wanted to talk about it afterward—in fact, he always acted as if it hadn't happened at all.

Remembering this now as Paddy began a series of

slow, deep strokes from the small of her back up to her shoulders—first on one side of her spine and then on the other—it occurred to Sharon that anyone reading her thoughts might think that she was gay, that she couldn't enjoy sex with Don Bolger because she was secretly attracted to females. But this was simply not the case. The necessity of disrobing in the presence of other girls, of showering after gym class in the big room that allowed for no privacy, filled her with the same agonizing embarrassment that she felt in exposing herself to men. In fact, she had regularly refused Donald's request to see her completely naked. She did not look at the bodies of other girls, did not feel any curiosity about their sexuality. What she was attracted to was the romance of male/female love, the version of sex that was presented in the films of the era, where the cameras panned discreetly away from lovers after the initial embrace. She had crushes on movie and television stars, on professional football players. She was warmed by any chivalrous display, by the tokens of respect and adoration men were always lavishing on women in the novels she devoured. She longed to have a man fight a duel for her, give up a brilliant New York career in order to join her in an African medical clinic, score six touchdowns in one game, and then say on national television, "I do it all for my precious Sharon, so she will be proud of me."

In their senior year, Donald had suddenly begun to date Martha Rawlings—no breakup, not even an explanation. Sharon had told her friends, "I just got so bored with him. I hope poor old Martha has lower standards than mine where manhood is concerned." In fact, she didn't miss him at all, felt surprised and even a little frightened that his departure from her life had so little impact on her. As a new high school teacher in Oconto, Sharon had little time or opportunity to consider the men around her. Most of the male teachers were married, and those who were not seemed decidedly uninterested in her. She had been on the job for four years, just long enough to thoroughly hate it, when she met Bob Kazmerinski. He played shortstop on a local base-ball team, and she had gone to the game with another single teacher, Ann Schact, who clearly saw it as an opportunity to troll for men. Sharon had already noticed that Ann didn't care too much whether her dates were married or single. When the balding shortstop with the funny nose followed them to Ann's car after the game, Sharon had felt sure he was pursuing Ann—perhaps he had heard about her reputa-tion and was hopeful despite his unprepossessing looks. But no, he wanted to talk to Sharon, had asked her if she "would like to take in a movie some time." All the time he spoke to her, he looked at his baseball cap, which he was holding in his big, square hands. She said yes mainly to impress Ann.

For the next six months Kaz had taken her to movies, to dances, to Packer games, to the Ice Follies when the show came to Green Bay. He bought her flowers, candy, even Christmas ornaments—she had no tree that year, and he had been embarrassed when she said so. "I'll get you something else," he'd said, trying to retrieve the box from her hands. But she wouldn't let him take it, still had those ornaments. In all that time, he was humble and respectful, kissed her at the door of her apartment when he took her home, held her elbow when they crossed streets, took her hand after the lights had dimmed in the movie theater. Finally, she had simply asked him if he wanted to go to bed. "God, yes," he breathed. "Do you want to?" She had said, "Well, of course," even though that wasn't true. But he had been so obviously adoring that she thought she owed him the lie. And after-ward he had been almost pathetically grateful, tender and gentle. He had proposed to her that night. "You will make me the happiest man on earth if you say yes."

In twenty-two years of marriage, Sharon had never been able to enjoy the act of sex. She had no idea what a female orgasm was supposed to feel like, but she was pretty sure she'd never had one. In the early days of her marriage, she had no idea there *was* such a thing, could not have faked one if she had felt disposed to do so. Kaz didn't seem to expect much reaction from her beyond cooperation, and that she was always ready to give; she never pleaded headache or made up other excuses the way women in books sometimes did. Years later, when she'd seen more explicit movies and read some "racy" novels, she might have been able to fake orgasm pretty convincingly, but it seemed a little silly to start at that point in her marriage when Kaz had not seemed to expect any such reaction up to that point.

What she did enjoy, very much, was cuddling—being held, having Kaz stroke her hair, having him rub her feet at the end of a long day of shopping, having him come up behind her at the stove and just kiss the back of her head. It would have been impossible for her to tell anybody—even him— how much she loved this man, how her heart would swell and spill over sometimes when she looked across a room at him, how fiercely protective she felt about what she knew to be the tender feelings he harbored beneath that rough exterior. Because what she got from her husband was exactly what she had always imagined sexual love to be—chivalrous care, respect, tenderness, even adoration. In his eyes, she could do nothing wrong.

And of course that made everything worse. Because she would so much have liked to do everything right for him, to feel and show for him the desire she read about in books.

But she couldn't, and that made her feel guilty. And she couldn't give him children, and that made her feel guiltiest of all. Kaz loved children, was able to play with his nieces and nephews as if he were an overgrown child himself—family picnics among the Kazmerinskis meant lots of children, herds of children, for this was a fertile clan. Kaz would romp with the little ones, organize volleyball games with the older ones, play referee when toddlers quarreled and screamed over toys their parents had lugged along to the park. He was less adept at quiet times—reading to children, holding a sleepy child in his lap just before bedtime—but when they baby-sat the family's children in their own home, Sharon herself took over at such moments.

For years and years, Sharon secretly feared that her infertility was caused by her inability to enjoy sex; she imagined her womb as closed, locked down, inert. Life couldn't take hold in such a place, she thought. She remembered with growing panic that Donald Bolger had never used condoms in all those awkward encounters in the backseat of his car. At the time, she had no clue what contraceptives she might have used herself. She marveled at her own innocence in those days. What was she thinking? Her own sister had given her a powerful example of what *not* to do where sex was concerned, yet she had considered no precautions against pregnancy.

Now in the middle of her life, she realized that this "innocence" had really been rebellion, an unconscious desire to defy all the norms foisted on her by Church and family. She was still living at home at twenty-one, for God's sake, still being grilled and suspected by her mother whenever she stayed over in the dorms with Jan and Micky. So she had unconsciously courted pregnancy and disgrace as a way to punish them. That's what Jan would say, probably, if she knew. But in the first ten years of her marriage, the fact that she had never become pregnant in college had seemed like certain proof that the "problem" was with her. It wasn't Kaz who was infertile. No, no. Sharon Gill couldn't conceive a child no matter what man was sending his little emissaries up there to get one started.

She read every book she could find about infertility, too embarrassed to ask a doctor about the cause. The books suggested that pregnancy could occur—often *did* occur—even when a woman was violently resisting intercourse, as in rape. Female orgasm was apparently unnecessary for conception. Another of those species-survival adaptations that gave all the perks to the men while turning the women into incubators, she'd thought at the time, like the holsteins on the farm who never even met the bull whose expensive semen was injected into them with big turkey basters. But as soon as she thought it, she recognized that this attitude was part of her brainwashing—men use women. Only she couldn't stop the feelings, even though she knew that *she* had found a completely non-exploitive man. And she couldn't shake the feeling that her frigidity was preventing them from having a child.

At last, when she was thirty-six, she worked up the courage to go to a gynecologist. After a series of embarrassing examinations and painful tests—she had always dreaded needles—this grandfatherly doctor had told her that she had a tipped uterus which made conception more difficult, but certainly not impossible. Nothing else was wrong with her. He suggested that Mr. Kazmerinski should have some tests, too, but Sharon never told her husband about that suggestion. She did tell him about the tipped uterus, exaggerated what the doctor had said about the difficulties this presented. Kaz was full of generous sympathy, folding her against his chest and murmuring, "That's all right, sweetie. We're all right the way we are. We're so used to having just each other that we'd probably go nuts if we had kids around now." They had never talked about adoption, not even once in all their married life. Now, lying here on this table with another man's hands stroking and kneading her back, Sharon wondered why. Could it be that adoption would have meant failure to Kaz, too, the same way it did to her?

She blamed the Church. Both directly and indirectly. The nuns had taught her that repression was a virtue, and the Church had taught her parents that pleasure was a sin, had taught it to her grandparents and their parents before them in Poland and in Germany. She had been maimed, crippled, and taught that her crippling was loved by God. Unfortunately, knowing you were maimed couldn't cure you. You couldn't regenerate the lopped-off limb. But you could reject and despise what had crippled you. She had stopped going to church in 1982. Kaz, who had never been very devout, was rather relieved that he didn't have to get up on Sunday mornings anymore. He went with his family to Midnight Mass on Christmas and would go on Easter Sunday if he was with his parents. "Wanna come with?" he would say to her casually, and she would always say, "No, thank you." Never more than that. Never an explanation or an excuse.

But she drank too much. She knew that. Kaz never criticized her drinking. When she had been especially obnoxious in public, she would sometimes ask him, "Did you think I made a scene?" And he would answer, his pudding of a face beaming as usual, "No, no, honey. You're just lively. Everybody knows what a card you are." Yes indeed, what a card. And nobody she could confide in, nobody to whom she could say, "I'm scared I might be turning into an alcoholic." Last night at Trail's End, she had caught Micky looking at her when she'd ordered the third Tom Collins. There was a little frown between her blue eyes, a slight pursing of her lips. Not disapproval, no, but concern. As if she might be thinking, "What's this, girl? What's going on?" Sharon thought for a few seconds that she would like to take Micky outside, away from the noise and the bustle, sit with her at the edge of the little lake at Trail's End, the lake that lapped almost to the parking lot, and just tell her everything. See what she had to say. She would forget it all, anyway, forget it along with the canoe trip and the little bunch of wildflowers. But no. The habit of silence was too old, too strong.

Paddy O'Neill was increasing the pressure now, each time his hands moved up her back. It felt as if they were in tandem, one following the other. She could feel the breath was actually being forced out of her lungs. Suddenly she felt, on the left side where he was working, an odd sensation—it was as if a whole group of muscles, extending from her shoulder down to her lower back, had decided together to give up all resistance and release their contracted tension. She said, "Oh," in soft surprise and Paddy answered, "Yes, that's much better, isn't it?" And he went over to the other side, his strong palms bearing down against the oiled skin and sliding upward. She concentrated now, focused on the right-side muscles that corresponded to those she had felt relaxing on her left side. She was certainly not aware of any contraction, any tension or resistance there. But, sure enough, in two more passes, she felt those muscles surrender to the touch, let go all in a rush of relaxation. It felt wonderful, delicious. "There," Paddy said and began to knead the muscles that connected her neck to her right shoulder.

Sharon closed her eyes now, forgot that a man she didn't know was touching her naked body, let herself feel only the lovely sensations in her skin and muscles. This must be close, she thought, to what she'd been missing, her body reacting to external stimuli, separate from her will, from her terrors, as if it had a mind of its own. He moved on to the left shoulder, his skilled fingers forcing a knot there to open, to release. Then he lifted her left hand, pulling the arm away from her body, and held her forearm against his chest so that she felt her fingers must be just below his chin. Slowly he began stroking the forearm from the elbow to the wrist, pulling her muscles and tendons and then releasing them. And last, he massaged her hand, rolling and pulling each finger, pressing his thumbs into her palms. It was lovely, unexpectedly lovely. Tears were slipping from beneath her closed eyelids and falling away from her, straight down, so that they didn't stay on her face. Lovely, lovely. Why had she been robbed of this bliss for all her years? Why had she let herself stay untouched for all this time?

16 / Peg

They were on their best behavior, Peg was thinking, freshly showered and dressed up, but mostly awed by the atmosphere in the solarium of Naniboujou Lodge where they had come for afternoon tea. This had been Linda's idea, something she'd read about before coming up to Grand Marais, so it was a "first time" for all of them. After Paddy O'Neill had left the B&B, a tired but far richer man, they had been sitting around downstairs, smiling a lot, but fairly quiet—still enjoying the aftereffects of the massage. Steve popped in for a few minutes and asked if they were "in the noodle zone." To their puzzled stares, he responded, "It's what we say when we've been cross-country skiing all day and our muscles feel like wet noodles." And so, of course, the phrase immediately became part of their vocabulary. After Steve went into town, leaving a key with Jan, Linda had proposed the short drive up the shore to Naniboujou. "They serve an English cream tea every afternoon from three to five," she said. "And the architecture of the place is supposed to be quite fabulous. It's only a little after three now, so we could easily make it there before four. It's only about fifteen miles."

Of course, Peg had heard about Naniboujou on the other occasions when she'd been up to the North Shore; it was a favorite topic among the locals. In 1929, some spectacularly

famous Americans had become members of the Naniboujou
Club, conceived as an exotic getaway for the sports-minded
elite: Jack Dempsey, Babe Ruth, Ring Lardner, Clark Gable.
The developers had acquired more than three thousand
acres of land along the Brule River and built a lodge at the
edge of Lake Superior with a private dock for the unloading
of their famous guests from the steamer *America*. They
planned to add riding stables, tennis courts, and cottages,
but the stock market crash in October put an end to their
grandiose dreams. The lodge itself soldiered on through
various owners with only a few changes and modernizations.
It was now on the National Historic Registry.

The club and lodge had been named for the Cree Indian
god, Naniboujou, who was revered as a friend to mankind.
The legend said that a wicked spirit had come to the North
Shore loaded down with sacks containing creatures that
would devil human beings; he had already dumped his sack
of no-see-ums, the tiny and maddening gnats that still plagued
the woods up here and was just opening the sack of snakes
when Naniboujou appeared and drove him off. This was the
explanation offered for the mysterious absence of snakes in
the Arrowhead region. The lodge was designed to incorpo-
rate the motifs of Cree art, sided in cypress with the trim
painted in the bright oranges and yellows favored by the Cree.
The vaulted dining room with its massive fireplace was, according to Linda, famous in design circles.

Tea was served in the solarium, which, according to the
little brochure they picked up in the lobby, was a later addition built over what had once been the shuffleboard court.
Its windows looked out on a shallow beach leading down to
Lake Superior. The room was furnished like a lounge—
upholstered furniture in various groupings around low
tables. Peg could understand the attraction of this place for

Linda and not just the chance to photograph an historic building. Lindy was an Anglophile, a lover of all things British, so an authentic cream tea was irresistible to her. The table they were seated around had disappeared under trays of cucumber sandwiches, sweet cakes, and scones. Nestled among the trays were bowls of raspberry jam and whipped cream for the scones. The tea was poured into china cups, no two the same. Victorian silver spoons were provided to stir in the warm milk and sugar. Everything exuded elegance and decorum. The atmosphere seemed to have subdued even Sharon, who had said almost nothing since their arrival. In fact, as Peg thought about it, Sharon had been pretty quiet ever since her massage.

"God, this is like a movie," Mary said. "Cary Grant should come strolling along at any moment now."

"It is lovely, isn't it?" Linda said, crossing her legs under her long skirt and leaning back into the winged chair. "Squint your eyes a little, and you'd almost think you were on the Cornish coast."

"You know," Peg said to her, leaning forward over her plate of little sandwiches and shortbread cookies, *"you* should have been the one to win that foreign studies scholarship when we were juniors. You would have got so much more out of going to England than Susan Emory got out of going to France. She only got the scholarship because she was active in clubs and a sorority."

"Oh, it's not a big deal," Linda said quietly. "I got what I wanted out of my junior year. And I've been to England since, when I could appreciate it better. Poor Sue probably hasn't left Green Bay since."

"Old Adenoid Annie," Mary said, and Peg remembered that the nickname had come from Susan's performance in a St. Augustine production of *Annie Get Your Gun.* "I saw her at the reunion. And you're right, Lindy. She's gone country-club-matron just as we knew she would. She's got six ade-noidal kids."

"How do you know they're adenoidal?" Jan asked, laughing. "*They* weren't at the reunion."

"Oh, how could they help but be?" Mary replied. "She married Mark Lawler. Remember what he sounded like? They were a perfect match, those two. Homecoming king and prom queen. Frat Boy and Sorority Sue."

"Oh, to hell with them," Jan said. She was poised at the edge of her sofa cushion, holding her teacup and saucer in her narrow lap. "We had much more fun as GDIs than we would ever have had in those snob clubs. Well, didn't we?"

"Remember our dinner dance, senior year?" Micky asked, sitting forward suddenly next to Jan. Until this moment, Peg would have said Micky wasn't following the conversation. "I'll bet those carhops are telling their children about that to this day."

"Maybe their grandchildren by this time," Peg laughed. They were quiet for a moment, faces dreamy with the memory. As independents, the honors program crowd felt obliged to mock every ceremony of the Greek scene at St. Augustine. When the fraternities sponsored candidates for homecoming queen or military ball queen, they would put up signs around the campus for their own candidate—George Dailey, a hulking pre-med student who allowed Linda to photograph him in crown and scepter for the posters. Always the same candidate, for any such contest, year after year. When they were seniors, George got almost ten percent of the votes cast for snowball queen. The biggest events of the spring social season, however, were the dinner dances sponsored by each of the frats. These were elaborate, catered meals to which the girls lucky enough to be asked wore cocktail dresses. They would then go back to the dorms to change into floor-length gowns, purchased on Easter-break trips to Milwaukee and Chicago, in order to walk back across campus for the dances at the student union. A sorority girl not invited to one of these affairs felt the disgrace keenly.

It was a tradition too ludicrous to escape parody. The GDIs huddled in the Honors Lounge to plan. Every detail was discussed. The girls voted to wear old prom dresses from high school, but no one could wear her own dress; they would have to swap so that every girl was wearing a borrowed formal. The boys decided to pool their loudest trousers and sports jackets and then mix them so that each would be wearing the most hideously mismatched clothes he could create from the pile, and they agreed to wear the checkered bow ties David Schneider found at a novelty shop. Peg remembered that many of the crowd were already paired up in "steady" relationships—she and Jerry, for instance—but the consensus of the group was that having an actual "date" would defeat the spirit of independence. They would just rendezvous at the chosen site, getting there however they could.

The site was the topic of longest debate. It couldn't be on campus—that could get them into real trouble—but it must be near enough to campus so that the targets of the parody would know about it. Finally they settled on Henry's Diner, a hamburger joint just two blocks east of the campus. Long demolished now, it had been in those days one of the last of the outdoor diners, where carhops came out to take orders and to deliver food on trays that attached to car windows. On a Saturday evening in early May, they arrived at 6:30 P.M. in whatever cars they had been able to scrounge. Peg's father had looked black as she left the house—she was wearing a bright pink, strapless formal borrowed from Paula Engels who was a size smaller than she was—but he didn't rescind permission to use the family car. She collected Mary from her father's apartment and then went to campus to pick up Jan, Micky, and Linda. Jerry, resplendent in paisley trousers and a plaid jacket, had his father's car, the one with the best radio, and he had driven into the country to get Sharon. They ordered their burgers, fries, and sodas from the startled carhops, ate and drank while yelling at each other from inside their cars—dinner conversation. Then Jerry cranked up the sound on his radio, and they all clambered out to dance in the parking lot. The carhops brought them two more rounds of Cokes when they ordered them, but they were beginning to look pretty grim. Both David and Mike had bottles of vodka in their jackets so they could spike the drinks. Finally, one of the carhops—a nice kid about their age—came up to Peg and said, "Look, you guys better get going. I heard the manager say he's gonna call the cops." The next day, to their intense satisfaction, the story of their dinner dance was all over campus.

"God that was fun," Sharon said now, setting down her teacup on a lamp table next to her chair. "Do you still have that yellow prom dress I borrowed from you, Jan?"

"Hell, yes," Jan said. "I wore it for a costume party one Halloween a few years ago."

"Oh, sure," Mary said. "Rub it in that you can still get into a dress you wore in high school. You, too, Sharon. You're still the same size you were in college, aren't you?"

"I guess," Sharon said. "But nothing is sized the way it used to be. I think the people who decide that stuff are just trying to suck up to us Boomers. Women who gain thirty pounds can say they wear the same size they wore in college because those fashion folks are putting smaller numbers on bigger clothes."

"My God," Peg breathed. "I think you're right. Are we that vain? We used to say we were never going to be like that."

"Oh, we used to say a lot of things," Jan sighed and her voice was suddenly serious. "We were going to get smart in other ways. Let other women care about fashion and hairdos and achieving suburbia. Oh yes. We would stop the war and secure civil rights for every American. And when we were done with that, we were going to go off to Latin America and help the Indians throw off the injustice of colonial rule and capitalist greed. Remember when we were hot for 'liberation theology'?"

"Listen," Mary said with an emphatic shake of her ponytail. "If it hadn't been for liberation theology, I would have left the Church way sooner than I did. I believed, after Vatican II, that our religion was actually going to lurch into the nineteenth century, that it was going to become relevant."

"Oh, Lord," Linda said, a little smile playing around her full mouth. "There's the *r*-word. We start talking about the sixties, and we fall right back into the jargon."

"Don't mock," Mary said, shifting restlessly in her seat as she always did when a topic engaged her considerable energy. "If I thought any religion was serious about working for social justice, I'd still be going to church."

"But you don't need a church to work for social justice," Jan said. "We could be doing that in other ways. But are we? What happened to the passion we had when we were that age? Hell, we were going to save the world. And look at us. We're all yuppies. Here we sit having cream tea in a rich man's lodge, and everyone of us is wearing Birkenstock sandals, for God's sake, at ninety-five bucks a pair. How would we have reacted then if anybody had told us we'd someday pay that much for *sandals*?"

"Mine only cost sixty-five," Linda said smugly. "I got them

on sale." Everyone else laughed, but Peg could see that Jan was not going to be jollied out of her serious mood.

"No, I mean it," Jan said. "I sometimes feel so damned guilty about what I've done with the advantages I was given. We were the women who were not going to follow, remember? We were going to lead. And sometimes I think I've just sold out for creature comforts. You said earlier, Mary, that Susan Emory had become a country-club matron. Well, what are *we*? I live in suburbia, with a vengeance. And at the St. Paul school where Doug and Kevin used to go before we moved, the teachers wear whistles on the playground now. Three short blasts mean 'Run like hell for the school' and one long blast means 'Hit the dirt.' They started doing that last year after some neighborhood gangs shot at each other across the playground at two-thirty in the afternoon. And I'm not doing anything about that. I just ran away from that."

Peg shifted uneasily in her own chair, set her plate down. Her usual impulse to smooth things, to soothe ruffled feelings, was rising in her bosom. Sometimes Jerry would say, "It's not your job to fix everything, Peggy." Yet she couldn't help herself. She was poised to speak when Micky beat her to it. She had been listening intently, watching Jan's face all the while she was speaking. Now she sat back and said with quiet intensity, "Yarbles. Great big yarblockos, Jan. Who do we know who does more to fix people than you? Since you got to be a—." Here she paused, groping for the right word. Peg had been noticing that Micky did that often now. "A doctor," Micky said finally, having failed to find the words *clinical psychologist*. Then she started the phrase over. "Since you became a doctor, you spend your whole life helping screwed-up people so they *won't* shoot at each other."

"And I make a great deal of money doing it," Jan said, turning to face Micky. "They're not the people who need help the most either. The poorest people don't have sessions with psychologists to help them solve their despair and their anger."

"Why is it bad to make money by doing good?" Linda put in. "That's something of the liberal philosophy I never *did* buy into—that you can't help the poor and the downtrodden unless you're poor and downtrodden yourself. That's bullshit. How much money do you and Mike give to good causes every year? I'll bet it's a packet."

"It's not the same thing," Jan wailed. "I listen to people my own age talk about retirement already, planning it so they'll be able to afford the leisure they seem to think is the highest good they have to look forward to. But I don't feel that way. I look in the mirror, and I see some wrinkles and some gray hairs, but on the inside I don't *feel* any different than I did at thirty. I don't think of myself as 'over,' in terms of what I might do in the world. I still think I have something important to do. If only I could figure out what that is."

"Well, I think Micky is right." Peg finally managed to find an opening in the dialogue. "You've already *got* something important to do. We all do. I sometimes feel worn out counseling in the schools and things are tougher there than they were when I started—even in little Menominee. But I know what I do is a positive thing, that it changes the lives of some of those kids for the better. Maybe it's not on a grand scale, but it's important. And Linda—"

Here Peg was startled into silence by having Sharon spring upright from the chair next to her. "I have to pee," Sharon announced, her voice louder than any of the other talk had been. "Where do you suppose they hide the johns in this place?"

A group of elderly people sitting around a nearby table stopped their own conversation to stare at Sharon, and a waitress who was just approaching with a tray of chocolates looked somewhat alarmed. "The rest rooms are just off the lobby where you came in, madam," she said softly. Peg thought she heard disapproval in the woman's tone. Sharon loped off without a backward glance.

"Well, that was a conversation stopper," Mary said wryly.

"As I was starting to say," Peg went on, aware that she must be blushing for Sharon. "Linda's Brazil photographs are helping people to raise buckets of money to save the rainforests. That's pretty important."

"But that's not why I took the pictures," Linda said calmly, leaning back and lacing her fingers together. "I took them because I read that development was wrecking the flora and fauna of the *selvas* inland from Monte Alegre, and I wanted to get some of it on film before it disappeared. The monkeys especially, because I thought they had such interesting faces, and I was tired of seeing them photographed in zoos. I was after the faces in their natural settings. That's all." She paused to take note that they were all looking at her. She tapped her steepled forefingers against her chin before going on. "I don't accept that any of us has a duty to 'save the world,' as you put it, Jan. We have a primary duty to find out what we're good at doing and then to do it with all our might. I make images. If those images cheer or inspire others, give pleasure or help to save rainforests, that's a nice bonus, but I don't think about it when I have the camera in front of my face. That extra stuff is none of my business."

"Well," Peg said, flustered, feeling that she had been corrected and wanting to recover what she believed was the high ground, "You're doing good in any case. And I'm sure you wouldn't argue that *everything* a person is good at doing should be done—some people are good at assassination, after all. Hit men for the mob, for instance." Linda shrugged and looked out at the lake. "I still think it's important to try to be on the right side," Peg went on, as if the shrug had been a rebuke, "and to realize that we can't do everything. Maybe our gardens are small, but we can grow good things there—some are veggies to feed people and, yes, some are for beauty alone, but they're all good things. And we have a right to be satisfied about growing them."

"You're a poet, Peggy," Mary said, reaching out to pat her knee. "I don't sell bric-a-brac to save the world, but I'm not ashamed of doing it well. And we've got nine kids among us, too, don't forget that, Jan. We've raised them with good values, I think. We've produced teachers and social workers and an almost-doctor. Not a bum or a gang member in the lot. I was once going to join the Peace Corps, remember? And I didn't. So what? My Carol is in the Peace Corps right now."

Jan had sunk against the back of the sofa she was sharing with Micky, and Peg could see that she was absorbing this onslaught but was still troubled. "I don't know," she sighed. "Maybe it's just all that Roman Catholic guilt I'm still saddled with. You know, all that 'from those to whom much is given, much is expected.'"

"I think that's Plato," Linda observed dryly, "not Catholicism."

"Well," Peg said with a chuckle, "why do you think the Renaissance Church was so eager to embrace Plato? Because they already agreed with him, that's why."

"Oh, hell," Mary said with a little smile, "we can't blame the Church for everything. We were idealists when we were young. Well, that's what it means to be young. But we're still sort of idealists, aren't we? We're just idealists with money. If it makes you feel better, Jan, I read somewhere that Bobby Seale recently wrote a book of barbecue recipes."

"Are you kidding me?" Jan said, sitting forward again. *"The* Bobby Seale?"

"That's right," Mary answered. "The article identified him as 'sixties radical Bobby Seale, founder of the Black Panthers.' A book of barbecue recipes, I'm telling you. So maybe we can relax a bit about how our lives have turned out."

They thought that over for a moment in silence.

"Maybe they're *good* barbecue recipes," Micky said at last. The others turned to stare at her, and Peg could see that everyone was trying to gauge how aware Micky was of the joke she had made; no one wanted a repeat of the "brownie" gaffe of the night before. For a few seconds, Micky's face was blank, the picture of innocence. Then Peg saw the corners of her mouth beginning to twitch. Finally, the merriment spread to her eyes.

"You stinker," Peg laughed, reaching out to give her a little poke. "I think you got that just right."

"And I think we should let that be the last word," Jan said, joining in the general laughter. "Whenever we start brooding about how we might be wasting our talents, we can just say, 'Maybe they're *good* barbecue recipes.'"

Sharon was picking her way through the tables on her way back to them. Peg thought she looked pale. Could she be hung over still from last night? Surely not. Sometimes Peg wondered if the others noticed how much Sharon drank. She had the impression that this drinking thing began after Sharon left the Church in 1982—she had announced it in the round-robin letter that year. Maybe it had been going on before that and she, Peg, had only noticed it when the Brunners' move to Menominee in 1983 put them into more frequent contact with the Kazmerinskis. Peg didn't feel she could discuss religion with any of these old friends any more—in college, they'd had long debates about theology—

because she was in a different category from them now. They were all so hostile to religion in general and Catholicism in particular that she felt sure they would mock her continued allegiance if the subject came up.

Besides, she didn't know if she *could* explain that allegiance, her continuing need for her faith. She had quietly rejected many of the doctrines of Catholicism over the years, as had many of her contemporaries. Indeed, the Church itself had abandoned some of the tenets she had learned as a child; nobody talked about limbo anymore, she'd noticed. She was what the bishop of her diocese referred to disdainfully as "a smorgasbord Catholic." But she was not temperamentally one of those all-or-nothing people. She wasn't going to dump an old friend just because she had a drinking problem and said "I have to pee" very loudly in public places. And she couldn't leave the faith that had comforted her all her life either. To her, Catholic theology could be boiled down into a few simple principles: if you apologize, you'll be forgiven; if you try hard, you'll be rewarded; if you're nice to other people, God is pleased; when you die, you'll go to a nice place where you'll still be you and everybody you loved in your whole life will be with you. When Jerry was in the hospital, the simple faith of her childhood had given her a sense of calm and peace about the surgery.

But there was more to it than that too. Peg would never have said the "more" out loud to her friends because she was afraid it would sound pretentious. But her faith answered some need in her for transcendence, a need to be more than flesh and earthbound, a need to give over her dailiness and her niggling fussing to something bigger, something with more coherence, more dignity, more nobility than she had found in the world of blood and bone. She called that something God.

Sometimes it occurred to her, as it did now in this room among the cakes and the china, that these friends of hers hadn't given up religion at all. They had merely substituted new faiths for the discarded one. And they sought their transcendence in the new faiths with the fervor of zealots. Linda found transcendence in art, in the pure distillation of image that gave to life an order and a permanence it didn't have on its own. Jan had found a new mission in saving minds. Micky had taken her political and social passion into the classroom, and what a firebrand of a preacher she must have been there. Mary had embraced feminism with an almost comic ferocity and had only recently begun to moderate her new faith, to pick and choose among its doctrines to make the right fit with her daily reality. And Sharon—

Ah, maybe she'd found the key to the problem. Perhaps Sharon had never found a new faith. But Peg had to admit to herself that she didn't really have a strong sense of what Sharon's inner life might be like. Did she like helping Kaz run his business? Did she regret any of her life's choices? Peg watched Sharon now as she picked up a chocolate, examined it, and then popped it into her mouth. Why, Peg wondered, was this old friend so opaque to her? Was it that Sharon chose to project only surface? Or was it that she, Peg, had never done much probing? Maybe she and the others had just assumed that funny was the same thing as happy.

17 / Jan

Jan had been watching Micky sleep. Propped up in her own half of the big bed with the lamp on that side illuminating the book in her hands, she marveled at how fast Micky had fallen asleep; less than five minutes had elapsed from the time her head made contact with the pillow and the time her regular, deep breathing signaled sleep. Easy for her! Jan was thinking. Present your lifelong pal with an ultimatum that will make it impossible for *her* to sleep well for the rest of this vacation, and then zonk out like a well-fed baby. But she knew that was unfair; the Alzheimer's was sapping Micky's energy so that she needed more sleep. Peter had told her last month that Micky regularly went to sleep before ten o'clock now. How different from the time when Micky had worn out the rest of them with late night card games and conversation.

But today she had begun to fade by about five. After Naniboujou, they had come back into Grand Marais for a visit to the Sivertson Gallery, a shoreside shop that sold paintings and prints produced by local and regional artists, many of whom made Grand Marais their studio-of-choice during the summer months. Mary bought a print called *Grandmother* by Betsy Bowen, whose gorgeously illustrated children's books had gained a national reputation, and Linda splurged on one of Craig Blacklock's Lake Superior photographs.

Micky trailed along with them, but she spoke only in mono-syllables or fell back on formula phrases. Jan had noticed lately how Micky would sometimes misspeak even these phrases, as if she were a foreign speaker who had failed to catch the true idiom.

They had a late supper at the Angry Trout, a restaurant on the inside curve of the harbor, and had asked to sit at one of the tables outside. It had been an unusually warm day for the North Shore—temperatures in the low eighties—and even at eight-thirty the light and the warmth were holding. But before the meal was over, Micky sat huddled inside the sweater she'd brought along and was staring blankly at the wheeling gulls. "What's the matter, Mick?" Jan had whispered to her. "Nothing," Micky said, and she sounded annoyed. "I'm just cold." It was only a little after nine-thirty when they got back to the B&B, but Micky had said at once that she was going to bed. "You want me to come up with you?" Jan had asked. "Suit yourself," Micky had answered. When they got to the room, Jan realized that Micky couldn't locate her night-gown and couldn't find the word *nightgown* to ask for it. Jan had to steer her through the bedtime rituals of washing and toothbrushing the way she would have done for a four-year-old, had to see to it that Micky took her medications.

The others were downstairs, and occasionally, through the closed door, she could catch the sound of a voice—not words, just a voice, and sometimes a laugh. She wished she could just go down there and say to them, "Micky wants me to help her kill herself, and I don't know what to do." She had almost told Mary this morning, there on the bench out-side the B&B. But that would be cowardly, she knew, a way of shifting the burden onto their shoulders. And it would be a betrayal too. Micky had not released her from holding in confidence the pact she was asking for. Jan knew that she should be spending this sort of time thinking about what answer to give Micky before they left for home on Sunday, but she couldn't focus. Her mind veered off, bounced instead to an image of Douglas reaching out for the basket of rolls that Ryan was passing him at the Easter meal.

Whenever Doug was home now, she watched him, ran her eyes over the slim torso, the long neck—so like her own. He had always been thin, she kept reminding herself, delicate among his beefier brothers—a gazelle among the wildebeests. But her heart twitched at the sight of a protruding wrist bone. *Was* he thinner now? When his plate was empty, she urged more food on him, actually stood up to carry the bowl of potatoes over to his side of the table.

Adam, always quick to observe and resent, said to her in the kitchen later, "For God's sake, Mom! He's not an invalid. Why do you need to hover over him like that?" And she'd wanted to slap him. Couldn't he see that her urge to protect Doug was a natural response to a whole range of threats that lurked just out of sight beyond their middle-class, triple-glazed windows? Homophobic louts could fall on his brother on any street corner, beat him bloody, even kill him. And sub-microscopic organisms, transferred unwittingly by some ado-lescent lover, might even now be gathering strength inside the veins that showed so prominently in those pale, thin arms. She wanted to tell her scowling third son that every time she thought of her firstborn, she could feel her hands closing into fists, feel herself rising onto the balls of her feet, poised to do battle with any sinister bully who might dare approach her son—just as she would do if she thought that he, Adam, were in any danger.

Why had she begun to think about Doug just now? Why here? Maybe the connection was inevitable. What if Doug *did* have AIDS? What if he someday asked her to help him check out before the full horror of that cruel disease robbed him of his mind, his dignity? Could she mix the drugs into some drink that he would still be able to swallow, lift it to his cracked lips so that he could sip through the bent straw, watch his throat move as he swallowed? Or would she snatch it back, screaming, "I can't! I can't!"

It was so easy to be wise and objective when death was stalking someone's else's son, or mother, or sister. How smoothly she'd said to one of her clients just last month, "Your father has had a long, good life, and he's suffering now, isn't he? If you try to talk him into a new round of chemo, are you doing it for him, or just to keep yourself from feeling guilty afterwards?" But when her own mother was dying, had already chosen to leave the hospital, Jan had raged at the doctors, *"Do* something! There must be something that can stop this damned cancer." And when they said gently, "There's nothing. You've got to let her go," she'd cried "No, no, no, no," wailing the single syllable over and over like a lost child.

She had to stop thinking about this, about Doug, about her mother, about Micky. Waking nightmares of this sort were bad enough in daylight, intolerable in the dark. She closed the unread book, slipped quietly out of the bed, and reached for her bathrobe.

When Jan came walking into the little lounge area where the others were seated, Mary was saying, "Does that stuff really have sunblock in it? Does it work?" as Peg rubbed lotion into her hands and forearms.

"That's what it says on the label," Peg answered. "And I always use it as a night lotion anyway, so I figured I'd buy it as a twofer."

"What lotion are you talking about?" Jan asked, dragging

over the wooden rocker so she could join the circle around the stove.

"This," Peg said simply, holding up the familiar bottle; it was Oil of Olay.

Jan chuckled as she sat down. "When he was a kid, Ryan called it 'Oil of Old Lady,'" she said. "So, of course, the other boys picked it up, and now I have to think a second before I can even say it correctly."

"Is Mick sleeping?" Sharon asked. She was curled on one side of the love seat.

"Out like a light," Jan answered, forcing cheerfulness into her voice.

"You know," Mary said, "that's a good one about the lotion. Most of the crap we buy should be called 'Oil of Old Lady.' That's the point, isn't it, to keep us from looking or feeling like old ladies?"

"Speaking of which," Jan said, settling herself and folding her robe over her knees, "have any of you started hormone replacement therapy? I've been doing some reading about it and trying to decide if it's for me."

"Well," Peg said, "I've been on hormone replacement for twenty-five years, ever since my surgery, but I didn't have much of a choice."

"I'm on it for six months now," Mary said cheerfully. "I couldn't take the hot flashes anymore, especially the night sweats. And my doctor advised me to go on vitamin E, too—the big ones."

"I've taken E tablets every day for years now," Linda said. "Ever since the scientists decided it's an antioxidant, people have been clearing it off the shelves in my grocery store. I sometimes can't find it."

"Have your hot flashes gone away?" Jan asked, leaning in toward Mary. What a relief to be discussing hot flashes, something normal and ordinary, instead of thinking about terminal illness, the death of the mind, suicide.

"Yup," Mary said. "And I don't think that's a very good name for them either. They're more like hot waves. Some of mine lasted for ten minutes. But you know, I've been noticing another bonus from the premarin—or maybe it's the combination with the vitamin E." Here she leaned forward herself, lowered her voice. "I've been feeling really horny lately. I'm having the sexiest dreams, and I even have orgasms during them. It wakes me up."

"Well, I suppose that beats the hell out of waking up to night sweats," Jan laughed. She could see that Peg was blushing, as usual, but the expected lewd comment from Sharon didn't materialize. She just looked away into the night that was pressing up against the window next to her head. Jan had noticed that she'd been quiet at the Angry Trout and that she hadn't had a drink—not even a beer.

"I suppose that must be a nice bonus for Christopher too," Linda said with one of her small, ironic smiles.

"He's not complaining, I can tell you," Mary said smugly.

"What about you, Sharon?" Jan asked. "Are you considering hormones?"

"Sorry," Sharon said, looking full at Jan. The skin seemed pulled especially tight over her cheekbones. "I don't feel much like playing 'Can you top this?'"

There was an uncomfortable silence. "What's the matter with you?" Jan asked finally. "You don't seem like yourself tonight."

Sharon made a snorting sound. "Yeah, right," she said, looking away at the window again. "Not myself."

"That's right," Peg said. "I noticed it at Naniboujou. You've been awfully quiet all day. And I think you look pale."

"Really?" Sharon said, looking back at them now, turning

her gray eyes on each of them in turn. "I'm amazed that any of you would notice."

"Okay," Jan said, "what bee is crawling up *your* butt, Sharon? Get it out here where we can see it, please." She was too impatient at the moment to try her therapy methods. Besides, the thought of one more needy friend making demands on her emotional attention on this trip made her simmer with resentment. If only they knew what she already had on her plate!

"Never mind," Sharon said, after a moment of staring at Jan.

"No fair," Mary pronounced sharply. "You can't start something like that and then run away from it. Apparently *all* of us are being accused of not noticing something. So, come on, give."

"Okay," Sharon said, and Jan noticed that she was clutching the edge of the love seat with both hands, one on each side of her knees, as if she were trying to prevent herself from levitating. "None of you ever seem to consider how the things you say are being heard by others in the group. At Naniboujou, you got carried away with how your lives haven't turned out the way you thought they would and maybe there's still something big you can do with your lives. And the whole time Micky's sitting right there. She has almost no life left, and pretty soon she won't even be able to make a cup of coffee. How do you think she feels when she hears you bitching like that about stuff that hardly matters compared to what she's suffering?"

The onslaught battered them into temporary silence. Jan could feel her own face beginning to burn. She *hadn't* thought about that, not even once. She searched her mind for the exact words she had said, there over tea and scones, tried to remember what Micky's reaction had been.

"That's not fair," Mary said irritably. "We were not 'bitch-ing,' as you put it, and Micky was joining in on the conversa-tion just like the rest of us. She was scolding Jan for saying that she didn't do enough, just like she would have in the old days. She was more like herself at that tea than she's been the whole week. And she made that cute joke about Bobby Seale's recipes."

"Well, what about that stuff when you started rationalizing your comforts by reviewing the vital things you're doing in your lives?" Sharon flared. Jan could see that her knuckles were white from clenching her hands so tightly onto the sofa cushion. "God, you'd think you were claiming victory in the I'm-just-like-Mother-Teresa contest. And the only thing you have to boohoo about is that you haven't saved the whole damned world yet. Sometimes I just want to run screaming."

So that was what the trip to the bathroom had been about, Jan thought. "Okay, Sharon Lee," she said quietly. "This isn't about Micky at all. You're pissed at us for you, not for her."

Sharon stared at her for a moment, dull red patches under her eyes, her mouth working; but she didn't cry. She drew a ragged breath and then plunged ahead.

"All right," she said. "Maybe that's true. You guys do it all the time, and you don't even know you're doing it. You go on and on about your kids—and now, Mary, your grandkid. Yesterday on Sea Gull Lake, you were complaining about not having more kids, Peg. And the rest of you were grousing half the time about when your kids come to see you and half the time about having them gone from your houses. Do you ever think how that sounds to women like Linda and me who don't have any kids?"

"Don't put me into the middle of this," Linda said mildly. She was still lounging back in her chair, apparently unflapped by the direction in which the conversation had turned. "I rather enjoy hearing about everybody's kids."

"Okay, then," Sharon cried. "Me! Just me. Don't you think about how it sounds to me?" And she let go of the love-seat cushion with her right hand, made a fist, and pounded it against her chest, so hard that Jan wondered if she'd hurt herself. But still, she wasn't weeping.

"Oh, Sharon," Peg said, her low, sweet voice full of sympathy. "How could we know that you were taking it so hard? You've never talked to any of us about your not having children. We've remarked on it to each other—that you don't discuss it, I mean. For all we knew, you and Kaz had *chosen* not to have kids. We said maybe you were so involved in the business that you didn't think you'd have the time."

Sharon was staring at Peg, her jaw gone slack with amazement. Clearly she had never imagined that such theories were circulated among them. At the same time, they heard footsteps coming from the stairwell. Every head turned to watch Micky, barefoot and clad only in her thin nightgown, come into the room. She looked groggy, confused, her blue eyes searching the room as if she couldn't spot a wholly familiar face there.

"Oh, you woke up," Jan said. "I hope we weren't making too much noise."

Mary sprang up from one of the upholstered chairs. "Come and sit here, Mick," she said, patting the seat. "I was just getting ready to sit on the floor, anyway."

Without a word, Micky crossed to the chair and sat down. Peg reached behind herself to pull an afghan off the back of the love seat where it was normally draped, and handed it to Mary. Mary tucked the blanket around Micky. "There," she murmured. "You need to stay warm. The rest of us have our robes." Mary herself was wearing fleecy pajamas and slipper socks that came up to her knees.

Now a long and embarrassed silence fell. Apparently no one knew how to begin a conversation that would act as a "cover" for what had been going on before Micky came downstairs. But it was Micky who finally spoke first. "What's up?" she said. "What are you guys talking about?"

The other women turned to look at Jan. As usual, she was expected to bail everybody out, to find a solution. She was fed up with it. Besides, she didn't believe that Micky always had to be protected from serious conversations, surrounded with puffery, as if she were a child—or a stranger.

"Sharon was saying that the rest of us are thoughtless," Jan said calmly, "because we talk about our children in front of her when she doesn't have any. And Peggy was pointing out that we had no way of knowing that this was a sore subject for Sharon."

She looked at Sharon, whose whole face was flushed now and whose eyes were snapping with anger, but she felt no remorse. Sharon had accused her of being indifferent to Micky's feelings, and she was plenty sore at her.

"I never talk about it," Sharon said, her voice almost a whisper, a hiss, "because I don't want people pitying me."

Jan was struck by the similarity between this sentiment and the position Micky had taken about her Alzheimer's. It was an insight that made Jan give up her personal sense of grievance at once and substitute for it the stance of the therapist.

"But you can't have it both ways, my dear," she said kindly. "You can't keep secrets in order to avoid sympathy and then lose your temper when people aren't sympathetic."

Sharon lifted her hands up to her face and then thrust them out in front of herself in a gesture of rejection. "You are so goddamned clinical," she said, and now her voice was shaking. "But you don't listen very well. I didn't say *sympathy*. I said *pity*. I don't want pity. But I hoped my friends might feel sympathy without my having to whine to get it. That they'd be sensitive enough to see, even if I don't always act deprived. But you guys don't think of me as a friend much, do you? I'm the clown, the court jester. You expect me to be funny all the time, to entertain you."

"That's just not true, Sharon," Peg said softly. "I can't believe you feel that way. You're the one who always turns a serious subject into a joke. You know you do. Sometimes, I'd like to have a serious conversation with you, to find out what you're thinking about something, but you always avoid it by turning it into a joke."

"Yes, you do," Mary said. She was sitting cross-legged on the braided rug now, looking up at Sharon. "I've felt the same way as Peg, that I'd like to be more intimate, emotionally, but you fight it off by cracking wise."

Sharon had buried her face in her hands while they were speaking; her lean shoulders were heaving, but she was making no sound.

"I know," she moaned from behind her hands. "I know that's what I do. I've been doing it so long, I don't know how to stop."

"Why?" Jan asked. "Why do you hide behind jokes? What are you scared of?"

Sharon dropped her hands into her lap, lifted her head, and stared at Jan. She was considering the question. Her eyes were damp, wounded, but also wondering, alert, as if she were listening to something inside herself that was trying to find voice. "I'm afraid," she said and then drew a ragged breath, "I'm afraid I have nothing to offer you guys. You talk about books and theater and concerts, and I go to Packer games and see Jim Carrey movies with Kaz. You have higher degrees and careers, and I help my husband sell tractors. I've always been like the 'poor relation' in this crowd. I don't even know why you keep on socializing with me. I didn't know why when we were at Auggies. I always feel I should be grateful that you include me. And it really sucks to feel that way. It feels like hell."

And now she began to sob in earnest—a choking, strangled sound. Tears coursed down her lean face. Jan realized that she'd never seen or heard Sharon cry, not once in all the years they'd known each other. She realized, too, how painful it was for this woman to cry, to let her feelings out in a way that made her vulnerable. Mike was like that too. Bottled up, buttoned down. So that when he *did* let loose, the resulting upheaval struck fear into people who knew him well. When someone so controlled lost control, it could seem as if he or she would never get it back again. Maybe Sharon felt that, too, was afraid to cry for fear that she might never be able to stop.

Peg slid over to Sharon at once, put her arms around the trembling shoulders. "Oh, honey," she crooned. "Have you really been feeling that way all these years? How did you ever get such ideas? We always wanted you for a friend. You're just the same as the rest of us, as far as I'm concerned."

"Of course," Mary said, reaching up to put her hand on Sharon's knee. "I can't even think about our group without you in it. That's not possible for any of us. Why do you think we care what you do for a living? I sell knickknacks, for God's sake. At least tractors are useful."

"And I've always admired your success," Peg said, giving her an extra squeeze. "If you want to know the truth, I'm often envious of how well you're doing. And I'd love to go to a Packer game, if I could get tickets. When you talk about your box, I'm green with jealousy."

Sharon struggled upright from Peg's embrace and stilled for a second. "Jealous of me?" she asked and her voice was genuinely incredulous. "You're kidding. You're only saying that to make me feel better."

"The hell I am," Peg cried, and everybody burst into laughter as they always did when Peg came even mildly close to profanity. Even Sharon made a snorting sound that ended with a hiccup. "I could have passed out when you bought that ring the other day."

"Look here," Linda said, sitting forward in her chair. She was looking hard at Sharon, and her usual detachment seemed gone. "Everybody in this room has always known that you have more common sense than the rest of us put to-gether—everybody but you, apparently. I don't know how you got those tapes in your head that keep playing 'I'm not as good as everybody else,' but I don't think we put them there."

Sharon sank back against the love seat and lifted her face toward the ceiling. "Oh, shit," she moaned. "You're right. I've done this to myself, all my life. And I'm turning myself into a drunk. But it's not your fault. I'm sorry. I'm sorry." And she began to sob again.

Finally, Jan lost her composure. She had no idea how to label the emotions surging through her; she only knew they were powerful and personal—she was no objective therapist now.

"Just stop that," she cried. "Stop apologizing. If you can't yell at your friends from time to time, then what the hell are friends for anyway? What makes you think any of us give a flying fuck what movies you go to see? Or whether you can make smart conversation about plays? Or whether you sell tractors or knickknacks or advice? Do you think you need to be ashamed, somehow, of taking a failing business and transforming it single-handedly into a success? Yes, you don't have to look at me with those big eyes. We all know about that. Kaz told Mike, who told me and—well, you know how everybody else found out, I guess."

She paused, feeling herself blush—this sort of outburst was not typical of her, and she could see from the startled expressions opposite her that these women were feeling the shock of it.

"I don't know what you want me to say," Jan went on in a more subdued voice, reaching out both her hands in Sharon's direction. "That we think of you as brainy and tough, that we admire your pizzazz? But that's no explanation either. There's no way to *explain* why you love the people you love, or why you want them around. You just do."

"That's right." They turned to where Micky was sitting swathed in the blue-and-white striped afghan. When she'd come into the room, Jan had assumed that she was "out of it," that the question "What's up?" had been just a formula phrase. When the conversation got under way again, Jan suspected that they had pretty much forgotten Micky was there. But at the sound of her voice, Jan looked at her face, saw tears sliding down her cheeks, falling onto the afghan under her chin.

"That's right," Micky said. "You belong to us. You're our Sharon."

Sharon gave a roaring sob now, a release of crying that sounded nothing like the choked noises she'd been making earlier. She sank against Peg's side and let herself be comforted. Mary patted her and patted her. Jan sat forward in the rocker and reached over to brush the tears off Micky's face. She used only her hands, no tissue, feeling the wet against her fingers and palms. Micky looked at her, the blue eyes focused and clear, and then she smiled—a slow, sweet smile.

After a few minutes, Sharon's crying began to subside. She sniffled for a while longer and then sat upright, fumbling for the box of tissues on the low table. Mary pushed the box closer to her and took a few tissues herself.

"I feel better," Sharon said, her voice still shaky. "Lots better." And she grinned at them before mopping her face.

"Good," Jan said. "Feel free to bawl on us—and at us—any time you like."

"Double ditto," Peg said, producing a phrase from their college days that Jan hadn't heard in years.

"I'm just wiped out," Sharon said. "What a hell of a day."

"We should turn in," Linda said, standing up in one of those fluid motions they admired. "It seems like last week when I had my massage instead of just this morning."

The others began stirring now too. Jan wrapped the afghan around Micky's shoulders when she noticed the shiver produced by Micky's coming out from under it. "We'll bring this back down in the morning," she murmured to Micky as she pointed her toward the stairs.

"Listen, you guys," Sharon said behind her. They turned to look at her again. She'd risen but was standing awkwardly in front of the love seat. "I don't want you to be worried about talking in front of me about your kids and your jobs and stuff. I really love those kids, and I want to hear about them, honest I do. It really wasn't about that, you know?"

"We know," Jan said softly. "What makes you think we could shut up about them, anyway? And we're pretty much incurable blatherers about work. So don't fret about it."

"Okay," Sharon answered, and she smiled a little. "Thanks. Thanks, you guys."

Later, lying awake in the dark, Jan could hear the distant rumble of thunder. One more storm, she thought, to finish off the day. The noise made it hard to tell whether Micky was asleep or not. She was turned away from Jan, and her side was rising and falling in a regular rhythm, but that didn't necessarily mean she was sleeping. After all, Jan herself was pretending to sleep. She realized with a profound sadness that she was afraid Micky would speak to her, would renew the subject of the suicide.

She could see that part of what she was feeling when she was talking to Sharon had more to do with Micky than with Sharon. She had wanted to shout, "I don't care that you can't talk about plays. I don't care that you don't remember what happened yesterday." And then Micky had said those words: "You belong to us. You're our Sharon." And she had almost screamed at her: "And you belong to us! You're our Micky. How can you talk about leaving us? How can you ask me to help you leave us?"

But the objective side of her mind knew it wasn't the same thing. Micky *was* leaving them. Little by little, she was going away. A time was coming when she wouldn't know them anymore. When she wouldn't recognize Peter or her own children. And after that, she would descend into labyrinths of terror and paranoia—she would howl in fear at the same nurse who had been spoon-feeding her five minutes earlier. And after that, she would become silent, unable to walk, strapped into a bed at night. This would go on for years. Because Micky was otherwise healthy, she wouldn't be carried off by pneumonia or cancer or kidney failure the way really old Alzheimer's patients were. No, she would eventually die of Alzheimer's disease—her brain would be eaten away in layers until one day she would forget to breathe; her heart would forget to beat. But long, long before that day, Micky herself, the Micky they loved, would be dead. Only a zombie who looked like her would be left behind. Jan knew. She had read the books and the articles.

And Micky was asking her to help stop that descent, to help her find the moment when the real Micky was about to die and see to it that her body died at the same time. Shouldn't a real friend answer such a plea? Tonight, she'd found Micky's nightgown for her, had helped her to take her pills, but she'd kept hunting for distractions from Micky's real cry of the heart, from the final "Help me." At the Angry Trout, she'd noticed how Micky kept lifting her face into the breeze, kept staring at the gulls. What was she searching for in that moving air, in those beating wings?

It reminded Jan of the geese, the ones she saw every fall on the St. Croix. Having already abandoned their Canadian summer retreat, they paused for a few days on the choppy waters, feeding off the late berries and seeds. Sometimes alone, sometimes in small groups, they would cross her line of vision, angling against the sky in seemingly random flights, as if their very bodies were trying to read the signs: the subtle changes in the slant of light, the hints of coming frost on the early morning air, perhaps some faint aroma in the wind, taking in the readings through those glistening feathers, mixing them inside the frail cage of bones, playing them over the intricate network of veins and arteries, until some moment of final recognition was reached and all their singing blood said, "Now!" And then the random birds formed themselves into one purposeful wedge, one arrowhead of southbound certainty, higher and higher, unwavering toward the unseen goal, far, far away where she could not follow. Gone.

When Micky lifted her face into the air like that, as if listening for something or trying to catch some faint perfume, was she hunting for the signs, nervous that some coming storm would ground her forever, strand her in a winter where all choices were gone? Here in midsummer, too soon for the friends of her youth even to begin to think of going away, was she already absorbing the signals that her high and solo flight was ready to begin?

18 / Micky

She knew the second she opened her eyes that it was going to be a good day. Her head felt clear, fresh, as if cool air was blowing straight through her skull. She knew at once where she was and why Jan was sleeping next to her instead of Peter. Through the open window, she could smell the aftereffects of rain, and she felt as if it had washed her, too, as if torrents of water had swept away cobwebs. And then there was a sound—a high, sweet musical note, held a long time and followed by a falling note. It was like a call, a summons. There it was again and then again, saying, "Come and see. Look what's here." There was light in the windows—no sunshine, but a soft, silvery light.

She looked over at Jan, sleeping on her back with her mouth open. Poor Jan. She must be feeling the strain. If she could have spared her, she would. And she hoped Jan knew that. But for now, let her sleep, let her forget what had been asked of her. Sleep was so sweet that way—it could let you float free of knowledge and pain. Sometimes. And sometimes it could patch your wounds and knit up the old connections in your brain. Not all of them. But some.

The birdsong came again, tantalizing, insistent. She swung her legs out from under the blankets, lifted the bedclothes with her arms so her movements wouldn't make any disturbance on the other side of the big bed. In the half light she

found her suitcase, selected jeans and a long-sleeved turtle-
neck. When she was dressed, she carried her tennis shoes and
her socks into the hallway, remembering to turn the door-
knob slowly on both opening and closing the door. She sat
at the top of the stairs to put on her socks and shoes, doing it
quickly and smoothly without any need to think about the
process. All around her, closed doors let her know that the
others were still asleep. She had no idea what time it was.

She stood for a moment in the little graveled parking lot,
breathing in the cool air, feeling it pass through her hair to
make her scalp chilly. She yawned, a big openmouthed yawn,
which she didn't bother to cover with her hand. On her
tongue, the air tasted of pine. The call of the unseen bird
came again, from high up and far away, but this time she
could tell the direction, and she turned her whole body
toward the song. It was there, in the woods behind the cars.
And, sure enough, there was an opening in the trees, a path,
almost as if someone had planned to have her go there to
find the singer. She set out, hearing the difference in the
sound when her feet left the gravel and fell onto the beaten
grass of the path.

   The trail was wide enough for a small car, she thought,
or one of those little dealies Matt used to drive at the fair-
grounds—what were they called? They had a name. Never
mind, it wasn't a narrow path; that's all she meant to think. It
curved to the left, and in just a few seconds, she was so completely surrounded by the forest that the breeze had gone
away. The smells were stronger here, heavier. The air felt wet
in her nose and lungs, rich with the odor of trees and rotting
vegetation. There were flowers along the sides of the path,
bright dots of color close to the ground and some purplish
red blooms on high, skinny stalks. And raspberries. Yes, those

were raspberries ahead of her; she recognized the bushes, the shapes of the leaves. She trotted forward, came to a stop. Clusters of small, bright berries drooped close to her knees. She stooped to pull them off into her hands, smelled at once the sweet aroma of the juice. Then she popped them into her mouth and crushed them up against her palate. The rush of flavor was instantaneous, flooding like joy over her senses. No garden berries were this sweet—the wild ones always made up in flavor what they lacked in size. Maybe there were more up ahead. She would have to keep a lookout.

Funny that animals hadn't eaten those ripe berries, had left them hanging here for her to find. Bears ate all sorts of berries, didn't they? Were there bears in this woods? She remembered something about a bear, had a clear picture in her mind for a second of a black bear, hunched down, with a row of white birch behind him. She stopped to listen, strained to catch any sounds of movement in the trees. But the woods on either side of her were quiet, except for the tiny, rustling noises you always heard when you were near trees and underbrush. Nothing to worry about. She smiled to herself and kept on walking. Then, softly, under her breath, she began to chant, "Lions and tigers and bears, oh my! Lions and tigers and bears, oh my!"

Samantha had always insisted that her mom watch *The Wizard of Oz* with her when it was shown annually on TV. Sam wasn't afraid of the witch, but the "flying monkeys," as she called them, always sent her ducking under throw pillows and cuddling up close to Micky's side. Before Sam was ten, she knew all the words to all the songs in the movie, would march around the kitchen bellowing, "We represent the Lollipop League" or "Dingdong, the witch is dead"—for weeks after the screening. Matthew joined the circle when he was old enough to stay up that late. Sam talked him through the movie for the first three years, echoing the phrases Micky had been using on her: "That's not really a talking tree. There are guys inside, dressed up like trees" and "The wizard isn't really scary. He's just a nice old man. Wait, you'll see at the end."

Peter hadn't been home much during the evenings in those days. When he wasn't tending to his patients directly, he was consulting with the research staff, attending meetings at the clinic, reading into the wee hours to keep up on the latest case studies and lab experiments. Oncology was a specialty, he would remind her, in which the stuff discovered in the morning was outmoded by late afternoon. There had been some rocky years there, when she had been working part-time and he had been working all the time. She felt herself turning into a shrew, heard the whine in her own voice when she said things like, "We never see you," saw him flinch at the sarcasm in speeches that began, "Stop off in your son's room before you leave the house and introduce yourself. I'm tired of showing him pictures of you."

She had unloaded all of her anger onto Jan one New Year's when the Werdens were in Rochester for a visit. "Look, Mick," Jan had said. "Who did you think you were marrying? Ozzie Nelson who was always home because he never had any job that I could see? You know damned well that if Peter slacked off at work in order to spend his time at home, he would despise himself and—more to the point—you would despise him." She had mulled that over in the winter months following and, by Easter, had admitted to herself that Jan was right. When the kids were both in school and she had gone back to work full time, things lightened up for Peter at the clinic—he could delegate more of the work, and committees got on without him.

But Peter Shaw was still an Important Man—with capital

letters. She knew it, had always known he would be. Even in college, she had realized that he was going to cut a swath. Not in any flashy or socially glittering way. She had very little respect for that anyway. But he was going to do great things. You could feel that about him. He was brilliant and serious and ferociously tenacious. He could enjoy parties and fun, sure, but even then, other people acted differently around him, deferred to him, called it a night when he said it was time to call it a night. He had purpose—yes, that was the right word: *purpose*. It was one of the things that had made her love him, right from the beginning. Oh, she was sometimes impatient with his unwavering drive, would have liked him to be more playful, less linear in his thinking. But those were little things compared with her need to love someone who could earn her respect.

The trail was beginning to go downhill now, at first gradually and then rather steeply. She found that she was almost trotting now. The sky overhead was brighter, the air less heavy. The noises of the forest were clearer—twitters, the harsh chattering of squirrels, the rustling of underbrush. And again the haunting call of that unseen bird, high in the trees, always seeming as far away as it had when she first heard it. She was no longer pursuing the bird. Not really. She would look up occasionally when she heard the high, sweet note, but mostly she was just enjoying the walk, relishing a sense of freedom made even more delicious by the feeling of having escaped, of having been rather naughty to go off alone.

She wanted more than anything to shake off the feeling of being caged. Her disease was the worst cage—a dungeon really, with dark passages and thick, black walls. She felt trapped inside her own body, a body that wouldn't let her say *psychologist* when she knew quite well what Jan was now.

But there were other cages too. People watched her all the time. She was hemmed in by eyes, vigilant eyes that would keep her from making blunders, that would prevent her wandering in a store. They were loving eyes, but they were cages too. Peter was the one who made her feel the most uncomfortable, because, of course, he was the one who loved her most. He had gone to part-time hours at the clinic so he could spend more time with her. And he was wonderful. Nobody could deny that. He did what he could to help her live in the moment, to enjoy the days he was with her, so she wouldn't have to think so much about what was coming. He listened intently to her when she spoke, supplied words when she began to grope, and most of the time, they were the right words too.

But—but. She felt ungenerous even to think a "but." Yet there was a constant strain in being with him. He hovered. He was protective and that was sweet—so sweet—but sometimes he jumped in and did things for her, said things for her, when she was just about to get it right. And he looked so scared all the time. She could see it in his eyes, even when he was making an effort to laugh and joke. He was afraid every minute that she was going to show signs that she was getting worse. And of course, there was nobody on earth that she wanted to be well *for* more than Peter; his pride in her and in her accomplishments had been so much a part of her well-being for so many years that she couldn't bear to see him disappointed. And no matter how hard she tried to think about it differently, this goddamned disease made her feel she was disappointing people, failing to live up to their expectations of her.

Being with her college friends like this was something of a relief from having Peter watching her. And of course, it must be a relief for *him* too. It made her heart sink to realize that such relief would become more and more necessary for him as time went on. A day was coming when he would dread spending time with her. But she couldn't let herself think about that, not today. What had she been thinking before that? Yes, yes, that was it—she'd been thinking about this vacation with Jan and Peg and Linda, with Mary and Sharon. They watched her too, of course, but not with the same terror in their eyes. Well, maybe Jan did, but her fear was about something else. And with these people, it was natural to talk about the old days at St. Augustine where they had so much history together. Now *that* was something she could talk about! Those were things she remembered, sometimes whole conversations. And the fun! They'd had so much fun, so little sadness, that it was pleasant to talk about it, to dwell on it.

Peter had come into the mix when they were juniors. Like Mike Werden, he was a transfer student, and everybody had gone bananas about how good-looking he was. Girls were panting over him, but he seemed not to notice it. Until then, she had thought that all handsome men were vain, that they had a constant awareness of the effect their looks created. But Peter Shaw moved and spoke with a genuine modesty. He dressed carelessly and sometimes came to class without even combing his thick, dark hair. They had met in an honors seminar on existentialism, a seminar in which he hardly ever spoke. She had been dating a senior at the time, a pre-law student, and she refused to get excited about the handsome newcomer. In fact, she had made fun of him to her girlfriends whenever they talked about him: "Oh, you mean the mute. What a sad case." But her heart would flutter wildly whenever he looked up from his folder and found her eyes with his dark gaze. She could recall that feeling even now, here in the woods, as if a bird were struggling, there inside her ribs, trying to fly free.

She came to a stop now, looking ahead at the trail. Some fifteen feet ahead of her, it branched, one path leading slightly to the right and the other turning sharply left. What should she do? Should she choose one way and go on? No, that was probably a mistake. She knew how she was feeling right this minute, knew that if this clarity lasted, she would be able to retrace her steps, would remember the fork when she came on it from the other direction. But clarity didn't always last very long. If she got confused, she would certainly get lost and then everybody would be thrown into a tizzy looking for her. It would spoil the whole day. She turned around and started back along the path, slowing her steps to make the journey last. It was such a lovely treat to be alone like this, to be remembering those early days with Peter.

In their senior year, when they'd been dating for about fifteen months, he had begun to speak of their future together as if it were a fait accompli: "We'll get married before my last year in med school. You'll be finished with your Ph.D. by then and we can live on what you earn for a while." He never proposed, never seemed to wonder if she wanted to get married. She had so many plans then, so much she wanted to try. But she didn't want to be married—not for a long time. She would flare at him: "Don't be so damned sure of yourself! Maybe I'll never get married. How can I know right this minute what I'm going to want three years from now?" In those days, three years had seemed like such a long time, like decades. Wasn't that a funny thing, how you thought about time at different points in your life? The three years from the time Samantha started senior high and the time she went off to college had seemed like a few months. But Peter had never got upset when she reacted that way to the things he said about their lives together: "Fine, fine," he would say, smiling at her. "Whenever you're ready, then. You'll pick the date."

She had gone off to Columbia without an engagement ring. Peter had bought one, had tried to give it to her at graduation. That was like him, trying to surprise her like that, without being aware at all that most girls went along to pick out a ring, that part of the fun was hiking from one jewelry store to another, looking at case after case of glittering stones in that hushed and elegant atmosphere that was almost like a church. She stopped walking now and held her left hand up before her face to look at the ring; a single, exquisite stone, marquise-cut and perched inside a delicate basket of white-gold prongs. The ring had been repaired five years ago—its shank had worn so thin that it had to be reinforced. But in May of 1968, she had handed it back to Peter, with a rush of irritation. "Not now," she had said. "I don't want to be engaged now." It made her heart squeeze a little, even now, to remember the hurt look in his eyes. But he had snapped the box shut, slipped it into his pocket, and said cheerfully, "Okay. You just let me know when you do want to be engaged. I won't let this get too far away from me till then." And he patted the pocket.

Peter had gone off to the University of Chicago med school, and she had packed her bags for Columbia. In the late sixties, Columbia had been a place seemingly tailor-made for her ideals and her ambitions. Its social work program was one of the oldest and most respected of its kind in the country. And New York City was a revelation in itself—a powerful contrast to Augsdale, Wisconsin. And then there was Kenneth. Tall, lean, always unkempt, his shaggy brown mane left to grow below his shoulders, Kenneth Billingsly was a charismatic leader of the antiwar movement on campus.

Once she'd got to know him better, she realized that he seemed never to be taking any classes, so it was hard to say if he was an undergraduate or a graduate student. He was twenty-four, he'd said, when she first met him at a rally.

There was nothing especially good-looking about Kenneth, no obvious physical appeal, but he was a mesmerizing talker, so passionate in his views that he swept others along with him. For six months, she had been one of those swept along. For Kenneth, having sex was not something to agonize over, not even a decision—he said, "You just do it." And she did. The affair had been intense and brief. It had ended when she realized that he was intent on "just doing it" with every young woman who caught his eye; he was bemused when she railed at him about it: "Your head is in a very old place," he'd said laconically. But she didn't regret the affair. In fact, she'd rather thought of it as a feather in her rebel cap. She wrote about it in her letters to her college friends, wondered if any of them would tell Peter; she was sometimes afraid someone would tell him, and sometimes rather hoping someone would.

But when she saw Peter that first summer, she could tell that he didn't know; the only expression on his face was an uncomplicated joy at seeing her again. She felt she had to tell him. Before she could get into a bed with him again, she would have to give him the chance to call it off, if that was what he wanted to do. After all this time, she knew that what was motivating her at the time was *not* a sense of fairness, but a sort of reckless curiosity. How would he react? Would he show himself to be a clichéd cuckold, losing his temper and raving? That would mean he was hopelessly square, and she would be justified in rejecting him permanently. But what he did was nothing like anything she'd been expecting. He buried his face in his hands, and he cried, sobbed like a hurt child.

And then she knew she would have to marry him. She accepted the ring that summer, and they were married just before his last year at Chicago—just as he'd suggested originally.

Thank God, she thought now, slowing even more as the path became steep; thank God she'd had the sense to marry Peter Shaw. They would celebrate their silver anniversary this fall—the date escaped her just now—and in all those years, she had never been out of love with him, had never felt contempt for anything he said or did, had never stopped caring whether or not he might feel contempt for her. There had been times when their sex life had been something less than thrilling, to be sure, but what couple didn't experience the same pattern? When the kids were small and Peter was "absent" so much of the time, they had quite a few dry spells. But always they would come back together, fall in love all over again: "You're more beautiful than you were in college," he would murmur against her neck when she was dressing for some party, and then they would forget to go.

Lately, she couldn't remember how long, she had been feeling more eager for sex than she ever had before. One of her doctors had said something about that. Which one? She couldn't call up the face or the name. But somebody had told her that one of the "symptoms" of early-stage Alzheimer's was "increased libido." It might be, he'd said, that old inhibitions were destroyed in the brain, or it might be some chemical reaction triggered by the death of cells. Maybe it was psychological, a desire to hold onto life in the face of approaching death. But whatever it was, she would wake up in the middle of the night with her nipples hard and a burning between her legs. Then she would reach for Peter, asleep beside her, cuddle up to him and nibble his ears, stroke his chest, take one of his legs between her own legs.

Sometimes, when he was slow to respond, remained groggy, she would become more aggressive, would reach inside his pajamas and take him in her hands, or sit over him and let her hair droop down onto his chest and face. When she still had hair. She put her hand up to her head now, rubbed it backward over the bristles. Sometimes when she looked into a mirror these days, the sight of her head made her want to cry. But Peter would stroke her hair, even now, would croon, "It's nice, kind of sexy. I like the way it feels when you rub your head against my back."

Yes, that was a better memory, Peter moaning in pleasure when she touched him, when she made her body move against his body in that rising tempo that meant release was almost here—almost. She was breathing hard right now, climbing the sharpest grade in the trail. Suddenly there was a sound ahead of her, around a curve in the path where she couldn't see—a noise of crackling underbrush, too loud and too big to be caused by any small animal. She came to a complete stop, looked around in all directions—where would she flee if she had to? But the sounds diminished, then stopped. She walked ahead, but slowly, putting her feet carefully into the soft grass at the edge of the trail, stooping in that posture of creeping that put the weight forward onto the balls of the feet.

When she peeked around some birch trees, she saw what had been making the noise, and the sight made her catch her breath. A moose, its hindquarters still in the woods, was kneeling at the edge of the path, nibbling delicately at the soft grasses and wildflowers that this ribbon of clearing had made possible on the forest floor. The enormous head reached forward to gather up the tiny blossoms, the pendulous lips almost delicate in their kissing care. The antlers swung gently from side to side as the head moved, the flattened blades cutting through the air at such a huge span that the movement must actually have caused a slight breeze. He was no more than twenty feet away from her.

She stayed absolutely still, watching, took air only in shallow and quiet breaths so as not to disturb the creature's breakfast. But finally, he lifted his head, swung the great rack of antlers in her direction, and looked straight at her, calmly, as if he'd known all along she was there. She didn't flinch or draw back behind the birches, but looked back steadily into the small eyes. High in the trees, very near, the unseen caller of the morning sent up the pure, summoning note—held almost impossibly long, before the trill came at the end. The moose lumbered upright, an awkward, but not hasty movement. He was an immense animal, at least six feet high at the shoulders, the massive head towering even higher. And then he simply backed up into the forest, turning at the neck at the last moment and withdrawing his antlers from her line of vision. The noise of his movements faded for a few more minutes and then there was only the answering call of another bird, like an echo of the one overhead, coming from somewhere behind her.

She laughed out loud, a ringing and joyous laugh that soared up into the forest canopy. What a beautiful world it was! What a magical and glorious place. Why couldn't everyone see this, breathe this air, hear this song? If they could, no one would ever want to leave here. No one would ever want to go to heaven.

19 / Linda

When Linda walked out into the hallway, she almost collided with Steve Olson. His appearance there startled her so badly that she made a sort of yelp and bounded backward into the doorway of her room. "Sorry, sorry," he mumbled. He looked worried, urgent. Linda knew it must be something serious to bring him up those stairs at this time of the day, risking encounters with partially clad women. She herself was fully clothed, and behind her in the room they shared, Mary was dressed except for her shoes.

"I thought somebody should know," Steve said, a deep red color under his tan. "Micky went for a walk along the hiking trail. Alone."

"Oh, God," Linda breathed. "Just now?"

"No," he answered, looking at a point on the wall just past her head. "More than half an hour ago. My assistant cook was just arriving when she went out of the parking lot—he saw her from the road. But he only just now mentioned it to me, and when he described her hair, I knew who it was."

"Should we wake Jan?" Linda asked, turning back to look at Mary who had come up close to the door to listen. "Should somebody go after her?"

"We'll go," Mary said decisively. "Let Jan sleep. It shouldn't always be Jan's job to look after Micky. We're dressed, and we can leave right away."

"Yes," Steve said, "It should be two of you. The trail divides after a bit. The branch on the left goes straight down Pincushion Mountain and then divides again. If she went that way, she could get really lost."

Linda could feel the dry taste of panic in her mouth as they followed Steve downstairs and out to the parking lot. Maybe they should call the police right now. Were there professional searchers for these woods? Somebody could get lost for weeks and weeks up here—even a mentally competent person. Would Micky stick to the path or wander off into the underbrush? How would they be able to tell? Surely it would be better to turn this over to people who knew what they were doing—not leave it to two city women like her and Mary.

"There's where she went in," Steve said, pointing. "Once you're in there a ways, you might want to try calling her—sound carries better if you call upward, at the sky. If you can't find her in half an hour, come back and let me know."

"Come on, Lindy," Mary said. "Don't just stand there. Let's run for a bit at first. Maybe if we hurry, we can catch up with her."

Linda drew a big breath and plunged in. The haste, the drama had a familiar feel, she thought as she trotted next to Mary, whose short legs couldn't set up much of a pace. Friendship with these women had always involved being dragged into "scrapes," as her own father had once put it. They were always cooking up risky endeavors, like that dinner dance thing they'd been reminiscing about yesterday, and sweeping her into them—against her better judgment, most of the time. And always it had been Micky who was the ringleader, the chief plotter. "Oh, what's the worst that can happen?" Micky would ask with a cheerful smile, if Linda or anyone else raised an objection to her scheme for painting the campus cannon with peace flowers in the middle of the night. Well, maybe the worst that can happen is that you fall down a mountain and your friends get hopelessly lost trying to rescue you.

"Let's stop a minute and call for her," Mary was saying now, panting between the words from the exertion of running. "We'll yell together after the count of three."

They cupped their hands next to their mouths, pointed their faces to the sky as Mary said, "One, two, three," and then both shouted, "Micky!"

Almost at once, they heard the reply, "Here." It wasn't even a shout. They looked at each other and then started forward again at a walk. Around the next gentle curve in the trail, they saw Micky strolling toward them, a big bunch of fireweed in her hands. Her cheeks were glowing with color, her eyes were bright and merry. A forest sprite, a fairy maiden with nature itself in her arms. "I saw a moose," she exclaimed excitedly. "A great big sucker of a moose as close to me as you are right now." She didn't seem to be curious about what they were doing on the trail, disheveled and shouting. "He was kneeling down," she went on as she came up to them. "It looked just like he was praying, I swear. But he was only having a little breakfast." And she handed them each a clump of the long-stemmed, purple flowers.

At their own breakfast a little later, Linda watched Jan across the table. The worry lines around her eyes seemed less pronounced, and her jaw was less rigid. Maybe the scene with Sharon last night had actually been good for her—a problem she could remedy, a hurt she could use her expertise to soothe. When she had got up this morning, they told her only that "We went for a little daybreak walk, and Micky saw a moose." And then she and Mary had simply let Micky retell the tale, complete with sweeping gestures. Everyone seemed cheered up by Micky's presence this morning—by her alertness and coherence.

Steve had brought news along with the French toast strata. Kim's friend, Denise, would indeed take them out to the Witch Tree tomorrow at 2 P.M. They were to meet her in the lobby of the casino. "Oh, she'll recognize *you*," he said with one of his lovely grins, when Jan asked how they would spot Denise. Linda couldn't help but wonder how Steve and Kim Olson described them to other friends and acquaintances, and she felt a stab of pain that she might be lumped together with the other "ladies"—a character, rather than a woman who might still excite interest by herself. On the inside, she was still Circe, the enchantress who might use a single glance, a single cooing sigh, to make this slim-hipped man forget there were any other women in the world.

"That leaves today to sort out," Peg said after draining her orange juice. "We know we're going to Pierre's for pizza tonight. But what about the rest of the day? Any adventures anybody hasn't had a chance to name so far?"

"I've got one," Linda offered. The others turned to her with expressions of mild surprise; they weren't used to having plans come from this source, Linda knew. "I've been seeing postcards of Cascade River and Cascade Falls around town. It looks like someplace I might want to photograph."

"Oh, it sure is," Mary said enthusiastically. "And there's a wonderful hiking trail that takes you upstream. Some of that river looks quite a bit like rainforest terrain."

"Well, is anybody up for a little hiking?" Linda asked. "We could take one of the cars down to the campgrounds and hike in from there. I seem to remember that it's not very far down the shore."

"It's just a few miles," Mary said. "I'd like to go again. It's uphill hiking, but it's not very tough, and there's a big payoff in natural beauty."

"I'll go too," Micky chimed in. "I love hiking, and the river sounds interesting. I'd like to see the falls."

Linda could tell by the way the others exchanged glances that Micky must already have seen the Cascade, perhaps even more than once. But no one spoke.

"I need to do some more shopping," Sharon said, breaking the embarrassed silence. "Kaz expects me to bring something for each of his nieces and nephews, and I hardly made a dent in my list the other day. Besides, you guys know how I feel about the great outdoors."

"I'll go into town with you," Peg offered. "I'd like to see what's new at the Johnson Heritage Post. Last year's exhibit was pretty impressive." To Linda's quizzical look, she answered, "It's an art gallery. There's a permanent collection of North Shore artists, but they have a section that's always showing new stuff. You guys can take my car down to Cascade Park."

Jan had been conspicuously silent. She was frowning slightly. "I'll go into town too," she said slowly. "I suppose the boys will be expecting some little token presents, and I've got my eye on a pair of hiking boots at the Trading Post."

"Super," Mary exclaimed. "We settled that in record time for this crowd. It'll be nice and even—three on one excursion and three on the other."

Linda could feel the crawl of nervous tension at the back of her neck. Jan was turning Micky over to her and Mary, was escaping from the watching and guiding role she'd taken ever since they'd left St. Paul. And for a whole day! With only Mary as backup, she would have to assume the caregiver's mantle. And it was too late to get out of it. If she changed her mind now, the reason would be too obvious. Especially since it had been her idea in the first place. She felt a flash of irritation at Jan. They had spared *her,* earlier in the day, by not waking her with the news that Micky had disappeared into the woods alone. And this was the thanks. But maybe it wouldn't be so bad. Micky really did seem just fine today, and Mary would be there too. It wasn't as if she'd be alone with Micky, wholly responsible for her well-being and safety.

When they told Steve about the day's plans after he came in with fresh coffee, he said, "You'd better wear clothes you don't care too much about—and good hiking shoes. Those trails are going to be wet. Maybe even standing water after last night's rain. But it looks as if you'll have some sun by afternoon." Oh, wonderful! Linda thought. Responsibility *and* mud.

There were a few other cars in the narrow parking lot off Highway 61 when they got to Cascade River State Park. Linda had driven Peg's Lumina with Mary and Micky in the backseat. On the passenger seat in the front, she'd placed her "kit": a folded tripod and a bag containing her best single-lens reflex Nikon, loaded with high-speed film, a polarizing filter, several lenses, and the cable-release mechanism that attached to the Nikon's electronic shutter. It was far more stuff than she'd taken up the Gunflint Trail on Wednesday, but then she'd been afraid to risk too much equipment to a canoe. She'd been thinking about that day on the drive down here, especially about the evening at Trail's End Lodge.

She had begun photographing Ada Thurley because the old woman's face was so interesting, almost like a landscape— those deep valleys around her mouth, the rifts and arroyos on her cheeks, the jutting brows and the rough plateau of her forehead. But as Linda watched through the viewfinder, the animation of that face was what finally captivated her.

She had imagined Ada's face as a still life, but it refused to be one, suddenly creasing into smiles or waggling from side to side, setting the ropy folds of her neck swinging. And the eyes—those sharp, birdlike eyes, dancing with light, so full of intelligence and humor. The challenge of trying to catch all that motion had reminded Linda of one of her earliest heroes, the French photographer Henri Cartier-Bresson, whose great gift was to capture the moment, the spontaneous flicker of life being lived, uncropped and *never* studied.

She had once stood for an hour in front of his photo of Giacometti crossing a rain-slicked Paris street. The picture was so clearly a work of genius. Bisected in the foreground by a narrow tree trunk, with a background of wet bricks and multipaned windows, the middle ground presented the great artist as an old man huddled inside the raincoat he'd hiked up to cover the back of his head. From his feet, a row of white dots—obviously the way crosswalks were indicated in Paris— seemed to flow diagonally in the lower right corner of the picture, gleaming like footlights on a stage. In that single second, in that particular space, Cartier-Bresson had caught Giacometti looking just like one of his own paintings: attenuated figures, a pervasive melancholy, an almost surreal detailing. It would be lovely to have such a talent.

As Mary and Micky climbed out of the car—they had been chattering on the drive—Linda began unloading her gear, hefting it in her hands and wondering if the hiking trail was too rough for this load. The bag alone was easy—it could be worn like a backpack, and she'd carried it through jungles— but the tripod was another matter. Well, maybe Mary could be pressed into service to help carry it. Or even Micky. She seemed so much better today, and really, she wasn't an invalid. Yes, the tripod could go along. Linda swung it over her shoulder and, slipping Peg's car keys into a zippered pouch on the camera bag, prepared to follow Mary's lead to the trail, which opened directly off the parking lot. They plunged into the woods and began to climb at a steep angle. The trail was covered in crushed rock, and there were steps, framed by rough-hewn tree branches, wherever the pitch was too extreme for average hikers. Linda paused several times to shift the tripod so she could keep her balance as they climbed.

"Here," Micky said finally, coming up to Linda. "Let me carry something. You look like a pack animal." And she grinned, her eyes glinting with her old sense of fun. Linda felt a squeezing sensation around her heart. She had been rationalizing her own desire to let somebody else carry part of her equipment, trying to justify using one or both of them as a "pack animal," and now Micky had so simply and good-naturedly volunteered, making it sound as if the photography part of the hike was a joint venture. Linda felt no impulse to cry over Micky when she seemed dazed or helpless—only when she behaved in ways that reminded Linda of what she had once been.

"That would be a real help," Linda said now, busying herself with lowering the tripod and handing it over, so that Micky would not get a direct look at her face, at her eyes. Micky slung the equipment over her right shoulder and started off again up the trail.

The falls itself was only a short distance above the highway; Linda could hear the sound of rushing water as soon as they got into the woods. Their first glimpse of it was from below as they rounded a curve in the trail: a twenty-two-foot column of boiling water, slashing down at them through the narrow gorge the river had cut between the scrub cedars and through the black rock that lay beneath the trees. Here Linda retrieved the tripod and set it up, adjusting the legs so they would have secure purchase, sighting through her lens to capture the best composition, the optimum light. She used the filter to bring out the contrast between the darker colors of the trees and the bright tumble of the water; chose first a fast shutter speed to freeze the water's motion, then a slower one to get the effect of blurring speed. Mary and Micky stood patiently by as she took shot after shot.

Once, when she was fiddling with a lens, she heard Micky say sharply, "Don't smoke here, Mimi!" When she looked up, she saw Mary sheepishly replacing her pack of cigarettes in the breast pocket of her knit shirt. Micky took a step toward Mary, put her hand on the shorter woman's plump shoulder, and said in a milder voice, "It feels wrong here, that's all. Can you wait till we get back to the car?" And Mary smiled up at her and said, "Sure, Mick. I should give it up altogether, I suppose."

After packing up the equipment, they climbed up to the top of the falls where a wooden platform had been built to jut out directly over the plunging water. A little crowd of people with cameras stood bunched up near the railing, clicking away at the falls and at each other.

"Maybe it will be quieter on our way back," Mary said, turning to look at Linda. "You'd like it better that way, wouldn't you?"

"Definitely," Linda answered.

"Then let's just go on up the river for now," Mary said. "There's plenty to look at farther inland. This river is interesting at every stage." She peeled off her denim outer shirt—the sun had indeed come out—and tied it around her waist.

The trail was wet, as Steve had warned them. Tiny rivulets of water spilled out of the trees on their left side, and there were pools of standing water on the packed dirt. Sometimes they had to detour into the trees to keep from getting soaked up to the ankles. And there was mud. Linda was glad she'd worn her hiking boots. Both Mary and Micky were wearing tennis shoes—"old ones," Mary had said about hers—and they would be in great need of the washing machine when this hike was over. But the scenery made the mess worthwhile, as Mary had said it would. At almost every turn, the rain-swollen river cascaded over mossy ledges, foaming and dancing toward them as they climbed. They stopped whenever Linda wanted to take a picture.

In a very short time, Linda no longer heard or saw her friends. She was swept into the familiar and absorbing world of her work, her eyes scanning up and down, back and forth, alert for the opportunity that might present itself at any moment. At one point, she actually got down on her stomach, oblivious of the damp moss, to shoot up at a drift of flowering bunchberry. With the camera against her face, she was composing, selecting, adjusting the focus so that the foreground would be sharp and the rest of the frame would reveal ascending layers of green and white, each slightly more blurred than the one below. There it was, the perfect balance of color and light and texture: to the right of center was the focal point, a single white blossom, its four petals cradled in a whorl of six pointed leaves. One more adjustment of the lens made the cluster of tiny red, berrylike dots at the center of the blossom pop into the near foreground; the dots were not much bigger than poppy seeds. Holding her breath and bracing her elbows, Linda squeezed the shutter.

Micky's voice came down at her as if from another world, like the voices that wake you from a dream: "They're in the dogwood family, you know. Pretty."

"No, I didn't know," Linda said, scrambling upright. She felt a mild embarrassment when Micky reached forward casually to brush the dirt and clinging moss from her shirt, backed off a bit and swiped at the shirt front herself. Sure enough, there was a stain.

"Are we going to hike the whole seventeen miles of this river?" Mary asked from behind Micky's shoulder. "I'm beginning to wear out."

"No, we can start back," Linda said. "I won't make us stop too many times on the way down, I promise."

"It's not the stopping I mind," Mary laughed. "It's the climbing."

They did stop once on the return walk, at a three-tiered cascade that presented a tantalizing prospect in the changed light. Linda set up the tripod and attached the camera. Mary and Micky were patient for three shots, and then Mary moved in front of the lens as Linda was focusing for the fourth.

"How about getting us into at least one picture?" Mary said playfully, dancing back and forth in front of the camera. "Then you can have prints made for us, and we can tell everybody we own an original Lindy Tourneau. Someday it could be worth millions and put my grandson through college."

"Okay," Linda laughed. "Come on, Micky. Get over there with Mary, right next to that cedar. And hold still while I check for the right light setting."

Micky moved quietly over to stand next to Mary. "A little more to the right," Linda said, stooping to look through the lens. "There, that's better. Now I can see those pines. Get ready to smile."

"You come over here with us," Micky called. "We should all be in the picture."

"Oh, no," Linda said, her usual horror at being photographed welling up. "I'm taking the picture, remember?" There it was again, the word *remember!* Would she never be able to edit her speech in front of Micky?

"That won't work this time, Linda," Micky said solemnly. "You've been using that cord dealie all day, so I know you don't have to be behind the camera. Hook it up and get over here."

Linda sighed and attached the cable release. Holding the end in her left hand, she made one last look through the lens and then walked over to stand next to Micky, turning her upper body so that most of the dirt stain on her shirt would be behind Micky's shoulder. "Lean in and forward a little," she said to both of them. "That way it won't look as if we have branches growing out of our heads." They obeyed, Micky's head centered between Mary's and Linda's. "Okay, now," Linda said, preparing a trick she had often used in studio photography when she wanted to surprise a subject into a true smile, "Say 'Communist party.'" The effect was instantaneous; both of the other women began to laugh, and Linda depressed the button at the end of the cable release, heard the shutter click.

When they'd packed up and started to move again, Linda thought about that picture. She knew exactly what it would look like; she was almost never surprised by what showed up in developed pictures, had already "seen" the finished product when she was composing the shot. Mary's round face with the ponytail hanging on its left side would be split by a grin so big that it would make her eyes into slits; her denim shirt, suspended from her waist, would form the downward line on that side of the frame. Micky, in the center, would have that surprised, natural smile that made her look sometimes like Jessica Lange. Her own face would have a more artificial smile; her eyes would not be looking directly at the lens. And the whole left half of the picture would be a three-tiered cascade of water, like a huge, frothy cake next to them.

What amazed her as she walked was that her feeling about

the shot was not wholly, or even predominantly, the cool, analytical calm she usually applied to a picture once she'd taken it. She felt a real eagerness to have it, to reproduce it for the others—not just Mary and Micky, either, but all her friends. A keepsake. That's how she thought of it—the very word *keepsake* was turning in her mind. For the sake of keeping, of holding on to this day, this trip, this everything. How odd it was that she had no pictures of Tom McDonald. She had met him when she was photographing his children, but in the fifteen years thereafter, she had never taken any pictures of him—not one.

Striding along behind the other two women—going downhill was so much easier than the other way—looking at the mud spatters on the backs of their jeans, she was realizing something that she'd never thought about before. She, who had made so few attachments in her life, who barely saw her own mother, who fell in love with safely married men so that there would be little risk of ever getting married herself, had attached to these friends. When the time had come to choose a professional name, she had almost automatically selected the nickname they had given her at St. Augustine. Her family called her "Linda," and Tom had always called her "Lin." She could not have explained why or even how an alliance formed at that point in her life, between the ages of eighteen and twenty-two, had continued to be important, almost necessary, in the thirty years since. Maybe it was precisely *because* they had dragged her into scrapes, forced her to have fun in spite of herself. And it *had* been fun, those days in college and other days since. Even in the times when there was less contact, she continued to hold her college chums in the lens of her mind, would actually imagine what they were up to. Their lives, so different from her own, had an enduring interest for her; the glimpses she had into their marriages had given her both a sense of relief that she hadn't married and some moments of acute regret over what she was missing.

One of the marriages, in particular, was a source of fascination because she felt she had played a role in bringing it about—an unwilling role, at that. After college graduation, she had moved immediately to Chicago, reluctant to return for even one more summer to the grim silences and projected demands she encountered in her parents' home. Late that August, Micky had stopped off to see her en route to New York by train. Linda had been living then in two cramped rooms in the basement of a shabby house. But she had welcomed Micky, and they sat up most of the night drinking cheap wine, talking breathlessly about the future. Around 3 A.M., Micky turned serious.

"You know, Peter is coming down to med school in a few weeks," she said, tracing the strings of the Chianti bottle with her fingertips. "I'm so afraid he's going to be miserable and lonesome."

"Well, he'll be lonesome for you, of course," Linda had replied. "But I imagine school will keep him plenty busy, and it'll be Christmas before we know it."

"I'm not coming back for Christmas," Micky said, glancing at her briefly. "Dad and I already talked about it—it's too expensive. I've got cousins in New Jersey, and that's where I'll go."

"Poor old Peter," Linda murmured. "That *will* be kind of hard on him. I don't suppose he'll be able to afford to go out there to see you either."

"No, he won't. We've both decided we have to try to be grown up about this. But I'm worried about him here in such a big city where he doesn't know anybody. You know how he is when he first meets people. It takes him three months just to start talking." And she took another gulp of the wine. Linda was trying to think of something reassuring to say when Micky turned her blue, intense gaze full on her. "I was hoping," she said, "that you could sort of keep an eye on him. You know, make him give up the books every now and then and go out for a beer. It's not so far from here to the campus, is it? Do you think you could do that for me?"

Linda took a few seconds to recover from her surprise, and in that time she saw in Micky's face what was being asked of her. Micky meant that she, Linda, must "keep an eye on" Peter Shaw so that he didn't get interested in any other girl, that she must keep him "on ice" until Micky could reclaim him.

"Yes, Micky," Linda had said after another, longer silence, "I think I could do that for you."

"Good. I'm glad," Micky had said, flashing one of those brilliant smiles and reaching out her slim hand to pat Linda's arm.

And Linda had seen Peter Shaw several times that year, had listened to him talk about med school and about Micky—his two controlling passions. By February, he was restless and depressed. "She's written only seven times," he said, brooding into his beer at a tiny, smoky bar where they'd met. "And when I call her on the phone, she's never there. Some roommate answers and then apparently never gives her the message." Linda watched the side of his neck where the dark hair curled out from behind his ear, looked down at the strong hands that rolled the beer mug from side to side while he talked. She had met no one interesting since leaving Green Bay, since leaving Lorenzo DiVitis behind. But, no, Peter Shaw was off limits.

When she received the round-robin letter in early March, she read Micky's account of her affair with a peace demonstrator and campus radical named Kenneth something. She was both stunned and outraged. Here she was supposed to be keeping Peter in cold storage for Micky, prevent his infidelity, but Micky was screwing old Ken and bragging about it to her girlfriends in an open letter. What appalling nerve!

She spent an entire weekend debating with herself about what, if anything, she should do. Telling Peter was out of the question. That was squealing, and nobody would ever forgive her for it, especially Peter. Especially herself. But she had already seen how easy it would be for her to seduce Peter Shaw—just a little more sympathy, a touch on his hand, a suggestion that a drink at her place was less expensive than meeting in a bar. She knew her own capacity to charm. And that would be an appropriate payback for Micky's treachery, something for Peter to have in reserve when they did get back together. Or she could seduce Peter Shaw and keep him. He was exactly the sort of honorable young man who could be convinced that a sexual liaison was tantamount to a commitment.

But in the end, Linda knew she wouldn't be able to do any of that. And, of course, Micky had known it too, known it right from the beginning. It was all there in that blue stare, the unspoken contract: "I'm turning Peter over to you because I know you won't betray me. You won't take him for yourself, even though you could, and you'll keep other females away from him until I decide whether or not I'm going to come back for him. And in return, I will be—I am—your friend." And so Linda had swallowed her anger, accepted the "use" Micky was making of her, and kept right on reassuring Peter Shaw that, of course, he and Micky were eventually going to be together; it was inevitable, like tides and the return of summer. At their wedding, Micky had said her thanks in the same way that she had asked the favor in the first place—one of those wordless looks while she held

Linda's elbows in her hands, one of those paragraphs from her speaking eyes.

They had arrived at the top of the falls again. The platform was empty now, its waist-high railing providing a convenient resting place for Linda's elbows. On the way in, she had seen that there would be very little advantage in using the tripod here to capture the falls itself. At this point the Cascade simply pitched straight down into a swirling plungehole far below. Any photos from here would have to be taken with a handheld camera. Mary and Micky walked straight to the guardrail where Micky lowered the tripod and leaned on it as they gazed down. Linda roamed up and down the rail, aiming, focusing, occasionally snapping off a shot. The angle was interesting, but problematic.

"I'm going over here to have my cig now," Mary called, pointing to a place at the far edge of the platform. "Where I trust I won't be violating either nature or other human lungs." She was already fishing the pack out of her pocket as she began to walk.

Linda went back to her work, trying to find a direction and angle that would eliminate from the frame all evidence of human construction and show only the plunging water with enough rock background to give perspective. As she swung the camera back to her own right, she found Micky in the frame, standing alone—very close to the railing now. As the camera paused, Linda saw Micky prop the tripod against the rail, lean forward and grasp the rail with her hands, her cropped head moving out and down. In a second of frozen horror, Linda saw the next frame in her mind's eye—saw the forward roll that would take Micky's lean body over the top.

Linda dropped the camera, just let it go from her hands. There was no strap and the camera fell away from her, crashed against the floor of the platform as she began to move forward, lunging across the space that divided her from her friend.

"Micky!" she cried, her voice high and wild. She caught Micky's left elbow, dragged her backward, saw the surprised, even frightened look as Micky's face swung toward her. Micky's right arm came free of the railing, sprang upward from the automatic impulse to regain balance. Linda caught that arm, too, folded Micky in a bear hug and shuffled backward with her until they were ten feet from the precipice.

"What the hell is happening?" Mary said, from somewhere behind them.

Linda released Micky from the hug, but hung on to one of her arms. "I thought you were going to fall," she murmured, looking up into Micky's face. Micky returned her look, a shrewd narrowing of her eyes showing that she was weighing the situation. Then a little smile turned up the corners of her mouth.

"You thought I was going to jump," she said quietly. "Don't worry about it, Lindy. Drowning is a bad way to go. I'd never choose that way. I promise."

Mary had come up to them now, carrying the camera. She was looking a little pale, and her brown eyes were wide with fright. Without a word she handed the camera over into Linda's free hand. A quick glance showed Linda that the lens was cracked, the metal around it dented and scratched.

"Could you get the tripod?" she said to Mary, her voice still high and breathless in her own ears. "I'll just stick this back in my bag before we go to the car. The pictures will be all right—the box isn't sprung. We'll still have our picture."

On the short hike down to the car, Linda held onto Micky's arm. It was not that she doubted what Micky had said—Micky didn't lie. But she had also said that she'd never choose *that* way, as if she meant she would choose some other way. And the thought of that made Linda feel reluctant to be out of physical contact with Micky—to lose touch with her living flesh. She remembered suddenly that just a few days ago on the trip up to Grand Marais, she had been talking about suicide, about how somebody with Micky's condition should just check out and even count on her friends to help her do it. Only now, after she had "seen" that death, did she recoil in horror from it. No, no. She couldn't imagine the world without Micky in it.

20 / Peg

A shop on Main Street had something new in the window—something they hadn't seen there on Tuesday—and it brought Peg to a standstill. She had rendezvoused earlier with Jan and Sharon for lunch at Sven and Ole's Pizza, where they each had soup and half a sandwich. The restaurant was one of Grand Marais's wry tributes to the Norwegian heritage of Minnesota; its facade featured a large cutout of two overall-clad farmers staring blankly onto the street. That *pizza* could be the mainstay on the menu of a place so named was part of the joke.

"Oh, look," Peg said, pointing. The other two, loaded down with shopping bags, dutifully paused. "Do you mind if we go inside to get a closer look?"

Jan and Sharon made the sounds that cooperative women usually make in such circumstances and followed Peg into the store. The new display was a quilt, a big one, draped over an old chair. Its predominant colors were forest green and wine, the very colors of Peg and Jerry's bedroom. Peg set down her one small bag—she had done more looking than shopping—and spread out the folds of the quilt so she could get a better look at its design.

"Oh, I just knew it," she exclaimed. "It's the tree, the Witch Tree." And indeed the center panel of the quilt was a recognizable representation of that local landmark. "Isn't it gorgeous? This would look fabulous on our bed."

"Why don't you get it, then?" Jan said. "It would make a nice souvenir of your trips up here."

"Oh, well," Peg said, feeling herself blush, "It's probably way too expensive. I don't even see a price tag. But I just love it."

"Let's ask somebody," Sharon said, shifting all her bags into one hand. And before Peg could stop her, she'd summoned the tiny woman who was sitting behind the counter just inside the shop's front door. The woman approached, lifting her brows inquisitively above her half glasses, which were held on each bow by a cord that disappeared under her gray curls. "How much is this quilt?" Sharon asked her, bending slightly to bring her face closer to the other woman's ear.

"That's four hundred and eighty-five dollars," the woman answered in a high, chirping voice. "It was made by a local woman who also does our original placemats."

"That's a good deal, Peggy," Sharon said, much more loudly than Peg would have liked her to. "A handmade quilt for under five hundred? Grab it. It'll go perfectly with those curtains in your bedroom."

"I don't know," Peg murmured. "We have a queen-size bed."

"This *is* queen size," the tiny woman said.

"It's so much to carry around," Peg offered now. "And it would practically fill up one of the cars on the way back to St. Paul." She was beginning to feel desperate as well as embarrassed—they simply could not afford a five-hundred-dollar quilt right now. It was out of the question.

"Oh, we can ship it anywhere you'd like," the saleswoman said, smiling up at her.

"Maybe you want to think it over," Jan said, and Peg could have hugged her. "We'll be seeing the tree itself tomorrow and maybe that will be enough for you. And, who knows? It could turn out to be a disappointment, and then you'll be stuck with the quilt."

"Oh," the saleswoman said, "No one is ever disappointed in the tree. There's something magical about that place. Are you renting a boat to sail past it? They aren't allowing land tours anymore, you know."

"Yes, we're taking a boat," Peg lied and could feel her face burning as she said it. Jan had apparently forgotten Kim Olson's warning about keeping secret the arrangement with Denise. "I will think it over—about the quilt, I mean. Thank you for talking to us about it."

The old face remained impassive, but the woman spent a few seconds rearranging the folds of the quilt on the chair, a subtle registering of her irritation at being taken from her post to satisfy idle curiosity.

"Are we ready to take our loot back up the hill?" Jan asked now. "Or should we check out that new coffee shop we were talking about earlier before we separated?"

"I'd like a coffee," Peg answered.

"Then we'll make it our last stop," Jan said.

"You guys go on ahead," Sharon said. "I'll join you in just a bit. I see some things in here I'd like to examine more closely."

"Oh, we'll wait for you," Peg said quickly. "After all, you were patient while I drooled over the quilt." She was feeling especially protective of Sharon's feelings since the confrontation of the night before, eager to include her in any and all activities.

"Honest to God, Peg," Sharon said with a good-natured laugh, "I would just make you both crazy if you had to hear me mumbling over every little thing I pick up. But you can help by toting some of these bags for me, if you would be willing. My poor knuckles are going to be dragging along the floor any minute now."

"Of course," Peg said eagerly. "Just hand them over." She felt relieved to be given an assignment. If only people knew what a kindness it was to your friends to *let* them do you favors. She always felt more warmth for people who asked her for help or who graciously accepted her offers of help than she felt for people who stoically soldiered on, refusing all aid. These latter types always seemed cold and distant to her, their self-sufficiency a species of pride.

As they were walking along together, just the two of them, Jan said, "My grandmother used to have quilting bees. I remember sitting on the floor under the frame and listening to the gossip when I was just a little girl. Sometimes, Grandma would let me push the needle back up from underneath after she'd positioned it."

"My grandmothers both died when I was so young that I hardly remember either of them," Peg said. "That's the trouble with being one of the youngest in your family, I guess."

"I saw my Grandma Farrell just recently," Jan said and then laughed a little as Peg stopped to stare sidelong at her. "On film, I mean. My Uncle Joe had his old sixteen-millimeter films put onto a videotape. He got that camera in 1947, after the war. This spring, he made copies of the tape for me and my sibs because there are quite a few scenes with our parents in them."

"That must be something," Peg breathed. "To see them young and moving around."

"Yes," Jan said softly. "And still hard for me, of course. It's been only two years since they died. But I started to tell you about my grandma. There she was, looking just the way I remember her. The film was at my Aunt Helen's wedding, when I was just a tot—my brother Jim and I are in the film, too, by the way. But I suddenly realized that the year was 1949. And in 1949, my Grandmother Farrell was only three years older than I am now. I was just stunned when I realized it. She looked like an old woman—black clothes and sensible shoes, hair pulled back into a bun under a black straw hat, breasts sagging down almost to her waist. And she'd been a widow for two years already."

"Those were such different times," Peg said. "Women thought of themselves as old when they were fifty, and so they dressed the part. And they had the sort of lives that aged them prematurely too, don't you think?"

"Hell, yes," Jan cried. "That woman had borne ten children, lost two of them, worked like a coolie both in her own house and cleaning the houses of rich women. And they ate a diet pretty heavy on pork and potatoes too, don't forget."

"We're lucky in lots of ways," Peg said softly, beginning to feel ashamed of having been embarrassed over the quilt.

"Amen," Jan said. And they walked the rest of the way in silence.

The coffee shop had attracted their attention because of its name—it was called Brew-Ha-Ha with the last *a* turned upside down, a conceit original enough to convince them that the coffee was probably wonderful too. Jan ordered a latté, and Peg decided on a vanilla cappuccino.

"That biscotti looks wonderful too," Peg murmured. "What do you think?"

"Sure, why not?" Jan replied. "We didn't have any dessert with lunch, after all."

As they were paying for their purchases, Peg was trying to put a label on the feeling she had been enjoying ever since they came into town, a feeling that hadn't been displaced even by the embarrassment over the quilt. She had been almost unaccountably cheerful and euphoric, poking around on her own in the art gallery, having lunch with Jan and Sharon, wandering aimlessly from shop to shop even when she had no real intention of buying anything. And now as they squeezed into the space behind one of the tables and sat down, she realized that what she was feeling was relief— the sheer relief of being apart from Micky for a few hours.

Until this moment, she would have answered "None at all," if someone had asked her, "How much stress is there in being around someone like that?" And she would not have been aware of telling an untruth. She had believed that Jan was bearing the full brunt of "taking care of Micky," that the rest of them had merely been enjoying Micky's company. But for five hours now, she had been either alone or with women whose movements she felt no need to check on, whose conversation was easy and familiar, whose sensibilities did not require an almost constant self-censoring of her own words, whose presence did not fill her with painful, heartbreaking pity. And now, of course, she felt guilty about being so relieved.

"You know," she said to Jan after taking a few thoughtful sips of her cappuccino, "on the first day after we got here, I was thinking that taking care of Micky as she gets worse wouldn't be so bad—that it would be kind of like taking care of a child you liked a lot. But it's nothing like taking care of a kid, is it? With kids, you just wade in and assert your adultness—if that's a word. And everything you do for them is instruction, a way to help them become more capable every day until they don't need you to do that anymore."

"What made you think about that just now?" Jan asked, looking at her intently.

"I was feeling so relieved all day today, just not being with her," Peg admitted, looking down into her coffee, feeling as if she might cry.

"I know," Jan said softly. "Me too."

"And if it's like that now," Peg said, almost whispering, "what's it going to feel like later, when she's worse?"

"That's the sixty-four-thousand-dollar question, isn't it?" Jan sighed.

"Does she know it, do you think?" Peg asked, searching Jan's face now. "That she causes such strain on people who love her?"

"Not all the time," Jan answered. "But sometimes, yes, she knows it. She's told me how much she dreads having that effect on Peter, on her kids."

"This damned disease is so awful," Peg said and now she could feel the tears welling up behind her lower lids. "For her, I mean."

"And for us, too, Peg," Jan said, closing her hand over one of Peg's. "It's all right to say that it's awful for us too."

"I can't help thinking," Peg said hesitantly, "that everything will be easier for us—even for her—when she doesn't know anything. But to wish that is to wish her not to be Micky anymore, and so I can't wish it. Whatever the pain now, it's better than for her not to be Micky anymore."

Jan was looking at her intently now, the hazel eyes wide, as if she were about to surprise herself by what she was going to say, but before she could speak, Sharon came bustling through the door, carrying even more packages.

"Oh, coffee and goodies," she cried. "Me too, me too." Then she looked more closely at their faces, seemed to notice for the first time that Peg was dabbing at her eyes with the paper napkin. "What's going on?" Sharon asked, sitting immediately and leaning in toward Peg. "When you left me, everybody was in a good mood."

"Oh, we were just talking about funerals," Jan said quickly, and Peg stared at her in amazement. Why did she feel the need to create a lie for Sharon's benefit? What was that about? "Our own, that is," Jan went on smoothly. "We were talking about how we've told people to handle things when we go— what kind of arrangements we'd like. That sort of thing."

"Oh," Sharon said blankly, and then she looked at Peg and a slow dawning came into her angular features. "And that made you think about Jerry and get all teary, I suppose," she said sympathetically. "Well, put it out of your mind. Jerry's fine now, and he'll probably outlive the rest of us."

"Yes, you're right," Peg said, smiling at her and then glancing quickly at Jan. "We shouldn't be so morbid, should we?"

"Kaz and I have all that stuff arranged," Sharon said in the same tone she would have used if she'd been discussing a banquet they'd planned together. "We even put our wishes in writing. Nobody's going to be hooked up to machines or have needles jabbed into every limb. And when we finally bow out, we're being cremated and having our ashes scattered in the woods around our lake cottage. Except those people who take care of that stuff don't say 'ashes.' They say 'cremains.' Can you stand it? Cremains! It sounds like a new brand of dessert topping. 'Here, let me put some cremains on your cake.'"

"Or maybe more like one of those coffee whiteners," Jan said. "You know, the powdered stuff, no part of which ever saw the inside of a cow."

"Please," Peg exclaimed, beginning to laugh now. "Not while I'm drinking cappuccino!" And they laughed together. As usual, Sharon had found a way to cheer them up.

When they got back to the B&B, they found the other three women already showered and relaxing after their excursion to the Cascade. Micky was looking apple-cheeked and cheerful, her damp hair clinging to her beautifully shaped head like a cap. She was sipping a scotch, sitting with her feet up against the stove. "Did you have a good hike?" Peg asked her. "Did you have to walk around a lot of water like Steve said?"

"Hell, Peg," Micky exclaimed, grinning up at her. "I walked *on* water."

The quickness of the response, the playful hyperbole, was so much like the exchanges they had shared in the old days that it took Peg's breath away. For that second, Michelle Marie Jaeger Shaw was as present to them in her best form as she had been thirty years ago. Peg bent down and took Micky's free hand in both of her own. "I always suspected that about you, Mick," she said. "That you could walk on water." What a relief to be glad to see her, to want to be with her again.

Micky's very pose was familiar and easy, that careless draping of herself in and on furniture that had always been one mark of her confidence. Thus she had looked in the women's lounge of Boyce Hall when they had studied together for the first big test in St. Augustine's required theology class junior year. Peg and Micky were in the same section, the one taught by the fabled Father George Conroy. He was a towering, muscular priest with a marine-style crew cut and a booming voice that made Mike Werden comment that if he were Cecil B. De Mille, he would cast Father Conroy as the voice of God. The man's arrogance was so over the top as to be almost comic, but his reputation for academic rigor was no laughing matter. When he told their section that the first test would be a true-false exam, no one made the mistake of thinking that it would be an easy one; they were expecting tricks.

On the morning of the exam, Peg met Micky in the lounge for one last run-through of their notes. When they finished, Peg sank back into the big chair she'd been sitting in and pulled its back cushion against her ears in nervous anxiety. Micky lounged on a sofa nearby, smoking a cigarette, dangling one shoe from the end of her bare toes.

"Try to relax, Peg," she said. "We're as ready as we can be for whatever the ogre is planning to throw at us."

"How can you be so calm?" Peg replied. "This stuff is beginning to blur together for me. The Pauline doctrine of justification by faith is countered by what? By who?"

"The test is true-false, Peggy," Micky said calmly, twisting a strand of her long, blond hair in her left hand. "You won't have to think of an answer on your own."

When Father Conroy slapped the exam onto the surface of her desk, Peg's heart lurched; the instructions took up most of the first page: "The items listed below are statements made up of two parts. If both halves of the statement are true and logically related to each other, label the item *A;* if the first half of the statement is true and the second half is false, but the parts are logically related anyway, label the item *B . . .*" It went on like that all the way through *G.* Peg's head was throbbing before she got to the first test item. When she read it, the words seemed like gibberish, not related in any way she could see to what they had been studying for four weeks. She left it blank and went on to the second item, then the third and the fourth. Murkier at each step. Then, near her left elbow, she heard a snuffling sound. She turned only her eyes—Conroy was a tyrant about the appearance of cheating—and saw Micky huddled over her desk, reading and then jotting something, looking at the ceiling, reading and then jotting. And all the while she was quietly laughing. Peg felt the taste of ashes in her mouth.

Fifteen minutes later, Micky rose languidly, walked to the

front of the room, and placed her exam paper on Conroy's desk. He looked up at her, his face impassive, and then looked down at his book again as Micky left the classroom. Peg labored on, going deeper and deeper into the dark waters of illogical-logical relationships. When the hour was up, she had four items left to read, had to hand in the exam that way. When she stumbled through the door of the lounge a few minutes later, she found Micky sitting sideways in one of the big, upholstered chairs, her skirt hiked up above her knees.

"What took you so long?" Micky said cheerfully.

"You shut your damned mouth," Peg shouted. "Just shut up."

"Why, Margaret Ann Ward," Micky said, all mock indignation. "How you do talk!"

"You were laughing," Peg cried, almost shrieking the last word. "The rest of us were in a daze, and you were finished in twenty minutes. How could you find that awful test so easy?"

"Oh, my dear," Micky crowed. "Of course I didn't find it easy. I was laughing because it was so absurd. The man is totally crackbrained. Even he couldn't pass that exam. I just made up patterns of letters, sometimes *B, C, E, D, A, G, F* and sometimes *A, F, C—* "

"You were guessing?" Peg didn't have enough breath behind the question to make it anything but a squeak.

"Oh, no," Micky replied, swinging her feet. "Guessing is something else. That would mean reading the stuff seriously and trying to make a match. I was just trying to use those letters to make up sentences after a while: *BAD DECAF GAG BEEF.* I could really have used an *S*, by the way."

When Conroy returned the test, he announced the highest score had been 57% and that he'd curved the grades accordingly. At 45%, Peg had a B-minus. When she glanced over at Micky's paper, she caught the numbers before Micky could turn it face down: 57%.

Was it any wonder, Peg thought now, that she had always thought Micky Jaeger could walk on water? Was it any wonder that she had always wanted to *be* Micky Jaeger?

21 / Mary

Pierre's was already crowded when they arrived at eight o'clock, its booths and tables filled with Friday night revelers. Weekends were always more hectic in Grand Marais because people from Duluth coming up for just two days were added to the summer vacationers who came for longer stays. Mary was beginning to feel self-conscious before they'd made it halfway across the place to the long table with the "reserved" sign. Kim Olson had confirmed the reservation for them and was to be their waitress. Normally, Mary would have enjoyed the crowded atmosphere, but this was the evening they had selected to wear their shirts, the matching shirts Angela and Elizabeth had sent up to the Sawtooth as their first-day surprise. Heads turned as they passed, six women in identical shirts emblazoned with the words *Camp Men-O-Pause*. She felt sure that her own ample bosom projected the logo more prominently than any of the other women's did, with the possible exception of Peg, and her own lower stature was surely bringing it almost into the faces of the seated patrons. She avoided all eye contact as they crossed to their table and sat down.

Almost the first thing she noticed was that they had all taken the same positions at the table that they had assumed at the B&B: Jan at one end and Linda at the other, with Micky and Sharon on one long side, Peg and herself on the other. What creatures of habit they were.

Kim flashed an appreciative grin as she approached them.

"Steve told me about these shirts," she said. "They look great. You all look great." She began passing out the big, stiff menus.

Mary thought it was Kim who looked great, her thick hair swept up into a beaded snood at the back of her head, her runner's body encased in a sleeveless white blouse and clinging black pants. Like all her jewelry, her earrings were conversation pieces: black and white enameled disks that came almost to her shoulders. Mary felt again the ache of envy—once she herself had turned heads the way Kim did now—and not because of a goofy shirt either.

"Can I start you ladies off with a beer?" Kim said, pulling a pencil from her hair the way she might have taken a stickpin from a cushion.

"You'd better bring a pitcher," Jan said. "Do you have Leinenkugel's Red on tap? Everybody likes that."

"We sure do," Kim replied. "The soup is wonderful tonight—fish, tomato base, very delicate."

"Oh, this is a pizza crowd," Sharon said. "Soup's not part of the plan."

Kim went off to get the beer, and they settled down to the business of selecting pizza: should it be one large or two medium? If there were two pizzas, they could have more variety—half vegetarian, half meat on one with more exotic combinations on the other. The hubbub was instantaneous and sustained. Mary remembered that it had always been this way when they went out to eat together: negotiations, argument, compromise. Good-natured, but spirited. You'd think the fate of the nation turned on whether or not pepperoni and black olives would be enhanced or ruined by the addition of anchovies. At a table behind Sharon and Micky, two couples were alternately staring and then whispering behind their hands. Mary wondered if they were commenting on the racket or on the shirts. Perhaps both. This, after all, could be a pretty rowdy group.

In college, Mary had worked part-time as a waitress at a small Greek restaurant in downtown Green Bay and sometimes had the dubious pleasure of waiting on groups of her classmates. The owner was a pig-eyed little man who treated his employees as if they were on work-release from prison and would certainly walk off with the furniture if he didn't keep them under constant surveillance. Whenever any of Mary's friends came in, he would sternly command her not to give them any extra attention—even if there were no other customers in her section. If they ordered only sundaes—as they sometimes did—the man would creep up quietly behind Mary as she was preparing them and say suddenly close to her ear, "Mary, Mary. Whipping cream is a garnish, not a meal." She would shiver to see the smug delight he took in "catching" her.

One Thursday evening, Peg and Jan and Micky came in about 9 P.M. and waited until they could be seated in her section. Peg had her father's car and had collected the other two from campus for an early movie. They were in a giddy mood, giggling and talking loud. All three ordered sundaes, and under the owner's disapproving scowl, Mary scurried to prepare them. When she came back to their table with the tray, Micky said rather loudly, "Is that him? The one who looks like Porky Pig in a bad toupee?" Mary had told many tales about her boss.

"Please, keep it down," Mary hissed at her. "You're going to get me in trouble."

"You're allowed to speak to us, aren't you?" Micky said, her eyes flashing.

"Only to take your orders and ask you whether you have

everything you want," she replied, setting each sundae down as deliberately as she could manage.

"Okay, then, we *don't* have everything we want," Micky said. "We want french fries too—a big bunch for all of us."

"Yuk!" Peg exclaimed. "Fries with a chocolate sundae. I don't think so."

"It's just something cheap, so Mimi can come over to talk to us again," Micky explained, using her patient voice. "We don't have to eat them—not all of them, anyway."

Out of the corner of her eye, Mary could see the owner, edging out from behind the cash register, moving in the direction of the table. Jan glanced up at her worried face and said quietly, "Put the order in, Mimi. We'll have the fries."

Mary scribbled *large fries* onto a kitchen order pad and hurried away without looking back in the direction of her boss. When she brought out the fries a few minutes later, she found her friends in the middle of a heated conversation. Micky was waving her spoon at Jan, who was trying to shush her.

"It's unjust, I tell you," Micky was exclaiming. "That other waitress over there has been twitching her little behind at those guys for at least five minutes now. And you don't see Porky getting on her case. It's because we're students, and we haven't ordered twenty bucks worth of greasy main dishes. He treats Mimi like some galley slave who has to jump when he scowls, and that's just because she's young."

Peg giggled, but Jan said quietly, "Climb down off the soapbox, why don't you? We can visit with Mimi at school or even after she gets off work. When do you get off tonight?" She was taking the platter of fries from Mary's hands as she spoke.

"Ten-thirty," Mary said. Then, louder, "Will there be anything else?"

"But it's so unfair," Micky insisted. "Our money is as good as anyone else's. Mimi brings business into this dump by having her friends come in to see her. He needs to have that pointed out to him."

And she sprang up from her chair, actually began to walk toward the cash register where the owner was ringing up the tab for a party of four. Mary looked down at Jan and Peg. "Oh, God," she breathed desperately. "I need this job."

Jan stood up immediately. "Come on, Peg," she said. "Here's a chance to practice your German."

"What?" Peg said, confusion drawing her round features into a frown.

"Just come on," Jan said, moving as she spoke.

Mary turned to see the earlier foursome collecting their change and Micky, twitching with impatience, standing right behind them. Helplessly, Mary moved back toward the counter, where her only other customer was sitting. There she would be close enough to hear without appearing to eavesdrop, and she could look busy by offering the man more coffee. The departing customers moved out of Micky's way just as Jan reached her.

"You're too fast for us, Elsa," Jan cried, catching Micky's elbow. Micky turned to look at her, the stubborn jaw dropping open in amazement. "Our friend is looking for the lady's room," Jan said to the boss, whose eyes were narrowed in suspicion. "But I'm afraid she doesn't speak much English. And I don't speak German, but our translator here can be of service. If you'll just tell me how to find the rest rooms—" And she paused, smiling ingratiatingly at the little man.

"There," he said, lifting one of his puffy hands to point. "Around the coatrack and to the left."

Micky had by this time managed to close her mouth, was tugging to get out of Jan's grip. Her eyes were like ice chips.

"Gertrude," Jan said, turning to Peg. "Would you tell Elsa what this man has said?"

Peg was at first too dumbfounded to speak, just stared at Jan. But the challenge had finally interested Micky, who stopped struggling and turned to look at Peg. "Ya, Gertrude," Micky said. *"Wo ist?"*

Peg was the color of the Christmas scarf around her neck. Mary could see her swallowing, taking a big breath. Then she leaned in toward Micky and said, *"Vater unser, der du bist in Himmel, geheiligt werde dein Name."* It was, of course, the opening line of the Lord's Prayer, which was recited at the beginning of every German class at St. Augustine. Mary glanced quickly at her boss, certain that he would recognize the line, but his porcine features were looking only perplexed, uncertain. Both Jan and Micky remained impassive, but Peg had a sudden coughing fit.

"Danke schöne, Fraulein Gertrude," Jan said solemnly. "Perhaps you could go with Fraulein Elsa to the powder room." And she handed off Micky's elbow to Peg's waiting hand. Peg hurried off, dragging Micky with her. And Micky had never uttered a single syllable of English in front of the owner.

Jan turned back to the man now, flashing a toothy smile. "She's an exchange student," she said confidentially. "Her father is a German industrialist. He will be so pleased to know that she's being treated kindly here in America." Then Jan leaned in toward him. "That little waitress," she said, nodding at Mary, "is just wonderful. You are to be commended for having a bilingual staff." And as Jan swept back to her table, Mary stole a glance at her boss. He was smiling vaguely, his confusion apparently beginning to give way to self-congratulation.

Watching Micky across the table now, Mary was thinking that her old friend's passion for justice in those days had sometimes made her rather dangerous. It was a lucky thing that Jan so often acted as a brake on that headlong rush of energetic certainty. Over the years, of course, Micky had mellowed somewhat, had begun to see that people might be more important than causes. But she never lost that potential for explosive outrage, a trait that made it both exciting and scary to spend time with her.

There had been times—not just while they were in college either—when Mary had seen Micky's beautiful face contorted in anger, saliva flying along with cutting words. Always sorry afterward, sincerely sorry, but full of confidence that her customary grace would command forgiveness, that her power to charm would always be able to pay the bill for her imperiousness, her occasional pettiness. Now there was fear in the wide eyes, a nervous eagerness to please: "Don't reject me. Don't turn away in disgust or indifference." Now she was more like the rest of them.

How many times, in those old days, had Micky seen that expression in the faces of her friends when they were looking at her? And had it inspired in her the same little spark of impatience that Mary felt now when she looked at Micky's face there across the table? Such neediness made a claim, imposed a responsibility, and could easily become an irritant for an already busy psyche. How quickly pity could tumble over into resentment. How seamlessly the impulse to stroke could become the impulse to strike. Maybe they had always forgiven Micky's bad behavior so easily because they secretly admired her ruthlessness, conceded that her tendency to bully them was the natural right of such a dazzling creature. To be chosen by Micky Jaeger, to be considered worthy of her energetic managing, to be swept up into her fierce causes had given them a sense of importance. They didn't want her to be like the rest of them. They might not be able to forgive her for it.

Tonight, Mary noticed, Micky was quiet, letting the chatter flow around her without even trying to join in. Sharon had asked her, "You always liked pepperoni, didn't you?" and Micky had nodded. But that was all. Maybe the alcohol was affecting her—scotch this afternoon and now beer. Should someone in her condition be drinking so much? Well, bad for her or not, who could grudge her any pleasure she could get now?

She was probably just tired—up before dawn to tramp around in the woods and then hiking up the Cascade. That incident at the falls had been very strange. Linda had offered no explanation, and Mary had not asked for one. But something serious had happened, she knew. Linda had dragged Micky away from the railing—that was the only part Mary had seen. Had she tried to jump? No, impossible. Probably Linda had only overreacted to her getting too close to the edge. A woman couldn't be laughing one minute and throwing herself into a plungehole the next. But still, who could know how the mind worked when a terrible disease was killing brain tissue every day?

Before they had eaten very much of the pizza, Linda excused herself to go to the bathroom. Mary watched her as she walked past some customers who were getting up to leave. One of the men looked down to read her shirt, colored, and looked away quickly. The two women in the party read the shirt, grinned at Linda and, when she had passed, leaned in toward each other to whisper their reactions. Mary guessed that the women were about forty or forty-five. A few moments later, when Linda was returning to the table, Mary again saw several men look at her—appreciatively, for Linda was a very good-looking woman—drop their eyes to her chest, and then look away in embarrassment. Apparently men of a certain age had more trouble dealing with public allusions to "The Change" than women did.

Just as Linda was about to resume her seat, Steve Olson came strolling up to their table. He was wearing his lovely grin and the same jeans and knit shirt they'd seen him in that morning.

"You ladies mind if I join you for a beer?" he asked.

To a chorus of "Not at all" and "Please do," Steve reached over to grab a chair from a neighboring table. Linda, who was still standing, pulled her own chair to the left and said, smiling at him, "Here. You can share this end with me. And feel free to share our pitcher of beer. I'm sure Kim will bring an extra glass."

Mary could feel the prickling of irritation at the back of her neck. How quick Linda was to grab him for a place next to her! The rest of them had chosen to wear their shirts over jeans, so the whole effect might suggest an actual camp uniform, but Linda had decided to wear hers over a swinging gauze skirt, whose rose and cream print was complemented by the chunky earrings and beads she must have packed to wear with that skirt. And she'd spent a half hour applying makeup and doing up her hair with combs, leaving a mess on the bathroom shelf after she'd finished. All to come into town for pizza and beer. Did she think she was going to find a new man in Grand Marais? And did she care whether that man was married or single?

Mary knew it was catty to think that way about one of her oldest friends. And probably unfair too. Just because the old marrieds like herself looked upon vacation as a reprieve from makeup and skirts didn't mean that every woman did. Linda's end of the table was closest to the entrance, to where Steve had stopped to speak, so it was natural to invite him to sit right there. And not everyone was as big a neat-freak as she herself was—Chris teased her about her compulsive tidiness. That bathroom shelf wasn't in her house, after all, and she didn't have to live with Linda on a permanent basis. Tolerance, tolerance. One of the symptoms of growing old was lowered tolerance for petty annoyances, so she'd better watch herself. And she had to admire Steve for coming up to them like this. It took a brave man to sit down so easily with a table full of middle-aged women sporting shirts that said *Camp Men-O-Pause.*

When Kim brought the extra glass for Steve, she stopped to chat for a few minutes.

"Did Micky tell you what she saw on her trail walk this morning?" Steve asked Kim as she was pouring his beer.

Hearing her name, Micky came to attention, lost some of her blankness and looked inquisitively at Steve.

"No," Kim said. "What was it?"

"What was what?" Micky asked, looking back and forth between the Olsons.

"The moose," Steve prompted. "You should tell Kim about the moose."

"Moose?" Micky echoed. "Did somebody see a moose?"

There was a stunned silence at the table.

"Who saw a moose?" Micky went on. "I've always wanted to see one. I'm sorry I missed that."

Kim recovered before the rest of them could. "I sometimes see them on my early runs," she said. "It's quite a sight, I can tell you. You guys need another pitcher of beer, I think." And she lifted the pitcher for them to get a look. They nodded at her in silence.

The conversation didn't begin again for several moments. Mary supposed that the others felt as she did: How could it be possible for Micky to have had such a good day, for her to have been so alert and full of her old sense of fun, and then simply to lose it all? And so fast! She had regaled Steve at the breakfast table with details about the moose, about how he was kneeling to eat flowers, about his retreat into the woods. And that had been less than twelve hours ago. Obviously her brain had not loaded any of that incident into her long-term memory, and her short-term memory couldn't hold onto it for even a whole day—not the scene itself and not her re-telling of the scene either. Images and words, just gone. Evaporated.

Mary was struck for the first time by what it meant to lose your memory: it meant the same thing as to lose your self. Because what was the self if it wasn't this intricate interplay between experience, the recall of experience, and the re-telling of experience; the immediate emotion of the moment refined and stored by recasting it into words; the moose and the story of the moose wedded into a new piece of the whole persona known as Micky Jaeger Shaw? But she didn't have that piece anymore, couldn't add new pieces at all. And worse—so much worse—she was losing the old material too. A day was coming when the four-year piece called college-at-St.-Augustine would be eroded away, and Mary-plus-the-stories-about-Mary would no longer be part of Micky's self. If she asked Micky now, "Do you remember when you made Peggy say the beginning of the Our Father in German to my boss?" Micky might still laugh and be able to supply details. But someday she wouldn't. Someday she would say, "Peggy? Who's that?"

They were the last group of customers to finish their meals. The second last was a threesome of women, all silver-haired, who approached Jan's end of the table before they went to pay their bill.

"We couldn't help but notice your shirts," one of them said. "They're really cute."

"Yes," the second woman said. "What is Camp Men-O-Pause anyway?"

"And how can we sign up?" the third one asked. It gave everyone a chance to laugh.

"It's sort of a private camp," Jan explained. "Our kids gave us the shirts because this is the second year of our reunion up here. Just the women. No men or kids or jobs. We went to college together."

"That's wonderful," the first woman said. "Good for you. Old friends are the best friends, I say. Look at us three. We've been close since we were kids. All of us widows now. Grown kids living all over the map. But we got each other. And we're still having ourselves a time."

"That's good," Jan said. "And it's hopeful."

When the threesome had left, Mary could see that the staff of Pierre's were getting restless, eager to close. They had stopped serving at ten, and it must be after eleven by now. Jan had noticed the same thing, apparently, because she said, "It's time to hit the road, isn't it? Let's make a big pile of money and get out of Kim's way. Big tip too. She's had a lot to put up with."

"She puts up with a lot from me all the time," Steve said, pushing his chair back from the table. Kim was, of course, close enough to hear both of these speeches, and both had been made for her benefit. She flashed one of her dazzling smiles at them. The ritual of pooling the money was a protracted one, fraught with the usual problems: "I only have a twenty." "Well, wait for a while, and there'll be change." Mary saw Sharon wait for the hubbub to create a distraction and then lean in toward Micky to help her select the correct bills from her open wallet. Micky let her do it without protest, but her cheeks colored, and she did not look up as she tucked her wallet back into her purse.

The PA system at Pierre's, which had been playing soft elevator music as background throughout the evening, suddenly got louder, starting right in the middle of a noisy rock-and-roll song.

"Oh, my," Kim said. "That's our chef. He must think all the customers are gone. He brings along his old sixties tapes and the cleanup crew listen to them while we're closing. I'll tell him to turn it down."

"Oh, no," Mary said, as the first song was ending. "That last bit sounds like our kind of music. We're from the 'old sixties,' too, remember?"

The next song began with tinkling piano music before breaking into full, four-chord rock.

"Listen," Sharon exclaimed, looking up from the pile of bills she'd been counting. "It's Sly and the Family Stone! How long has it been since you've heard that?"

Sure enough, the familiar lyrics resounded through the little restaurant: "End of the spring and here she comes back. Hi, hi, hi, hi, babe." Steve Olson walked up to Micky's chair, bowed at the waist, and said, "May I have this dance?" She looked up at him, startled, her eyes immense. His narrow face was only a few inches from hers, his ginger-colored eyebrows lifted, his nice-guy grin in place.

Micky looked to left and right at the rest of them, all of whom had stilled their check-paying chatter. Then she stood up slowly, took the hand Steve offered her, and walked with him to the space that opened between tables and coatracks near the front entrance. Without letting go of Micky's hand, Steve began to demonstrate that he could do a sixties-style jitterbug despite his youth. For just a few seconds, Micky watched his feet, and then she swung into the dance herself, her long legs flashing—one, two, one-two-three. Mary ran forward with Sharon, who had apparently formed the same thought at the same instant: together they dragged the tables backward, snatched chairs away, so that a sizable dance floor was formed.

"Those summer days, those summer days." And Steve pushed Micky away from him and swung her back into his body. "That's when I had most of my fun nights. Hi, hi, hi, hi, babe." The women made a circle of spectators, clapping along to the music as Micky whirled under Steve's arm, spun back into a facing position, lifted her free hand to wave in the air. "County fair in the summer sun and everything is cool. Hot fun in the summertime. Hot fun in the summertime."

What a miracle, Mary thought. The body remembers. And this, too, was part of the self, this rhythmic moving of muscle and bone, this joyous response to the hypnotic pounding of the beat, this stylized flirtation complete with sidelong glances and coquettish laughter. Micky had always been such a great dancer. Who could say how long this would last for her? Perhaps she would still be able to do this even when she was saying, "Peggy who?"

When the song ended, so did the dance, to wild applause. Still clinging to Micky's hand, Steve made an elaborate bow in their direction, and Micky dropped several curtsies.

"I'll stay to help Kim close," Steve said, as they began heading for the door. "You guys have a key, so I won't see you, probably, until breakfast."

Outside, they discovered that rain was falling, apparently for some time, for the pavement was gleaming brightly in the streetlights. The rain wasn't driving, just a steady drizzle. Their cars were parked in the next block; no spaces nearer were available when they'd arrived, but now the streets were almost deserted. In a resort area where canoeing and hiking used up a great deal of energy, people turned in early.

"Oh, come on," Sharon said good-naturedly as the others huddled under the overhang of Pierre's roof. "So we'll get a little wet. So what?"

"Remember the 'Stroll'?" Micky said suddenly. "That was such fun."

"God, yes," Peg said. "It was a way to dance even if you didn't have a partner. What were those songs?"

Nobody remembered any words, but Jan came up with a melody and—more crucially—the rhythm. "Da, da dum," she began, booming on the heavy downbeat. With Sharon in the lead, they formed a stroll line, arms thrown over the shoulders of the neighboring dancer: Peg next to Sharon and then Jan, Micky, Linda, and last, Mary. Dancing sideways down the empty street, calling out the beat in strident unison, they bowed their heads and lifted them again as the inside foot crossed over the outside foot, lifted their faces into the cool rain, catching drops in their mouths as they laughed and sang.

22 / Sharon

Sharon had counted on the chatter in the car on the way up to Grand Portage to give her a chance to think; because she was driving, she wouldn't be expected to join in. Mary and Linda had even taken the backseat together, leaving her alone up front. But their topic of conversation had made it almost impossible to tune them out.

"I've been meaning to ask you something," Mary said to Linda after one of those silences that fall on car trips. "For a long time. Ever since I moved back from Pennsylvania, really."

"This sounds serious," Linda replied. A quick glance in the rearview mirror showed Sharon that Linda had sat forward a little and turned toward Mary.

"Oh, well, it's under the heading of 'old business,' I suppose," Mary said. "Nothing that needs to worry us now. But I've been curious about it."

"Okay," Linda said. "Shoot."

There was a little silence now, and Sharon could tell that Mary must be deciding how to word her question.

"When we were at St. Augustine," Mary began, "how did you handle it when David came on to you?"

"David?" Linda asked, her voice registering confusion. "Your David?"

"Of course," Mary answered, and now she sounded a little

irritated. "What other David would I be asking such a thing about?"

"Whatever gave you the idea that David came on to me?" Linda sounded genuinely curious, not just stalling or pretending the way people did when they were embarrassed by a question.

"He told me," Mary answered. "He said he'd always had a thing for you, that if you'd given him a chance, he never would have kept on seeing me."

"That son of a bitch," Linda breathed. "When did he tell you this?"

"While we were negotiating the divorce settlement," Mary replied. "Oh, don't worry. He also told me you wouldn't go to bed with him. I'm not mad at you about it or anything. I'm just curious about what happened."

"You sound mad," Linda said, and Sharon thought she was right; Mary did sound pissed just a little. "Have you been chewing on this for all these years since your divorce?"

"I don't know what you mean by 'chewing on this,'" Mary answered. "I believed him about his not sleeping with you. He gave me a long list of the women he *had* slept with, so I had no reason to doubt it. Can't I just be curious about what you did?"

"Look, Mimi," Linda said quietly. "I have no idea why David told you that he propositioned me in college. Maybe he was just trying to find ways to hurt you, to make you think you were second-best right from the start. But what he told you happened never happened. He never made any moves on me, and he never even looked at me in that way."

There was a long silence now, and Sharon almost drove her Mazda onto the shoulder of the road from looking up into the mirror at the two faces—Mary's round, well-scrubbed one facing off against Linda's sleek, carefully decorated one.

"You wouldn't fib to me about this, would you, Lindy?" Mary said finally.

"No, I would not," Linda answered, her voice firm. "I can tell when a man is interested, even if he never says a word. And I'm telling you, David Schneider never had that look when he looked at me. If he'd made a pass at me, I would have decked him. And I would have told you about it."

"You would?" Mary sounded like a little girl now.

"A lot of women would keep it a secret, I suppose," Linda replied. "But you must know that I'm not like a lot of other women. I would have punched his lights out, and then I would have found you and said, 'He's a loser. A disgusting creep. You deserve a lot better than him.'"

The Mazda made at least a mile's progress toward Grand Portage before Mary spoke again. "It's funny, isn't it?" she said finally. "You'd think, wouldn't you, that after everything David put me through, it wouldn't matter to me anymore, that I wouldn't care whether or not he ever really loved me at all? But I guess it does. I have been chewing on it. It bothered me to think that he married me just because he couldn't have you."

"For what it's worth," Linda said, "I think he was crazy about you then. How could anybody mistake the way he doted on you?"

"That's absolutely true," Sharon put in, startling herself by the loudness of her own voice. "I used to watch him watching you, and he was just starry-eyed."

"Starry-eyed!?" Mary echoed, and then she began to giggle. "Oh, Sharon. I haven't heard that expression in twenty years."

"Well, it's what he was," Sharon cried. "Whatever happened to him after he got out to Pennsylvania, he didn't start out as a hound."

"Wouldn't it be pretty to think so?" Mary said, her voice quiet, the bitterness gone.

As Linda and Mary went on talking, Sharon considered her own response to hearing some of the details of the Schneider divorce over the years. She had felt keenly disappointed, almost as if she had been betrayed too, because she had idealized that couple, had really thought in expressions like "starry-eyed" about them. And poor Mimi had shared in that illusion, it seemed, had suffered about having to rethink the whole relationship right from its beginning. That must be the worst thing about infidelity, having to wonder if everything has been a lie, a pretense: If he could deceive me in this way, now, how can I believe that there was ever a truth in him? But nothing was ever all one way, was it? You could love somebody and want to murder them at the same time. You could, at any moment, be made sick with revulsion by the same people who stood so close to the core of your life that you couldn't imagine the world without them in it.

She had dreamed about her parents last night, one of those dreams in which she wound up screaming at her mother, spitting out an almost annihilating rage. When she woke from the dream, it was near dawn, and she was unable to fall asleep again, lay there tasting the horror of the emotion still clinging to the dream even after she'd forgotten its details. Her parents still lived on the farm, although her brother, Carl, was the real operator now. He lived in a flat, ugly ranch house across the road from the old, drafty house where she'd been raised. It was less than an hour's drive from her present home, and she made the trip frequently, always taking something she thought they would be able to use: fresh fruit, a pie, a cardholder for her mother whose arthritic fingers could barely close around the cards when they played sheephead or hearts.

Her parents were essentially unchanged from what they had been when she was a child; old age had only ingrained more deeply the mental and physical habits of a lifetime. Suspicious, querulous, rigidly puritanical. "If people are going to behave like pagans, they deserve the diseases that their filthy behavior makes them catch," her father would say. "Those new people who bought the Bredahl farm are non-Catholics," her mother had said in June. "Carl better see to the easement because we don't know what to expect from them." Yet whenever Sharon noticed how frail they were getting, how her father shuffled when he crossed a room, how her mother's voice shook on the phone, she felt a terrible dread: they were going to die and pretty soon too.

She had never told them that she'd stopped going to church. When she was there on a Sunday, or even a first Friday, she would go to Mass with them. They almost never visited the Kazmerinskis in Oconto—"Too fancy for us," her mother would say dismissively—and not at all on Sundays, so the issue never came up at that end. Her sister, Rosemary, knew, but she agreed with Sharon that it would serve no purpose to have their parents find out. Rosemary had married a neighboring farmer—not the father of the baby she'd given up for adoption—and was now the chief caretaker for the elder Gills. In a nice piece of irony, Rosemary had been recast in the family mind-set as the "good daughter." She, after all, had been suitably ashamed of her early disgrace, had conformed her conscience to their parents' standards, and had "settled down" to a life strikingly like theirs: five children, regular contributor to church bake sales, a yearly vacation at Wisconsin Dells, frequent winner of blue ribbons at the county fair.

It was Sharon who aroused in them both suspicion and resentment. "Where do you earn your money?" her father would ask. "In America, right? So how do you get off buying them foreign cars?" And her mother frequently began sentences with "If you had some children to keep you busy." These sentences had a variety of endings: "You wouldn't be getting in your husband's way at work" or "You wouldn't be running off to Chicago and Lord knows where else" or "You wouldn't have time to lay around reading all the time." Yet these were the people who had made it possible for her to go to St. Augustine, who had bragged to neighbors when she was valedictorian of her high school class.

Jan was right. There was no explaining why you loved the people who belonged to you, no explaining why you couldn't be objective about them, or indifferent to their disapproval. They were woven into your soul with millions of threads, and cutting them out would make you bleed to death. So there it was. David Schneider was always going to be stitched into Mimi's soul, was always going to be fifty percent of the blood and brain of her daughters, twenty-five percent of her precious little grandson. And their group of friends, these women in her Mazda and in the Lumina behind her, were stitched into each other's souls, too, no matter what. There would be some jealousy, some envy, even wounded feelings sometimes. So what? What else was new?

When the two cars pulled up next to each other in the parking lot at the casino and Sharon caught sight of Peg Brunner's smiling face in the Lumina, she remembered what she had meant to think over on the way up here. She had to find a way to get that quilt into Peg's house without making it seem like charity. Yesterday, when she'd finally persuaded Peg and Jan to go on to Brew-Ha-Ha ahead of her, she had bought the quilt and arranged to have it sent to her own house in Oconto. Maybe, after a few weeks had passed, she could tell Peg that she'd been thinking about the quilt since they got home and called the shop to have it sent and that now she didn't like it for her own house at all—wrong colors. So Peg would be doing her a favor taking it off her hands. No refund was possible because this was a consignment item.

Did that sound plausible? Or would Peg see through that and resent the manipulation? Maybe she should offer to let Peg buy it from her for a hundred dollars. People were less likely to smell a rat if they thought they were getting a good deal. But, hell, why shouldn't Peg have the thing when she was so clearly gone on it, so hot for this whole Witch Tree business? Just because the Brunners might be having a little money problem right now, that didn't mean Peg should miss out on a one-of-a-kind thing like this. The old woman in the shop said she expected the quilt wouldn't stay in there long at that price, and Sharon believed her. And the quilt maker never made the same design twice. So, of course, she had to snap it up for Peg. Too bad that you had to finesse these things, couldn't just say the truth: "I can afford it, and I want you to have it. So take it and shut up about it." But she had to admit that, if it were the other way around and Peg was buying stuff for her, she would have to be finessed too. Well, she would have to keep working on the problem.

The casino, which had been under renovation last summer when they'd been here, was now finished: a huge, sprawling facility, with acres of cars around it, many with Canadian license plates. Sharon was tickled that the Indians, who had been robbed of a continent and shoved onto the most unappealing tracts of land that the white government could find for them, were now getting rich by taking advantage of the "sovereignty" the treaties had offered them as a pathetic compensation for their indignities. In states where casino gambling was illegal, the government found that these sovereignty clauses allowed the Indians to build casinos on their reservations. And in a lovely irony, white people flocked there in droves to hand over millions of dollars into the obliging hands of their former victims. Almost enough to make you believe in a just and provident God.

"Oh, oh," Peg was saying as she stepped from her car. "Look back there." They turned to look at the direction Peg was indicating, back along the road they had just passed over. Behind them, the Sawtooth Range loomed up against the horizon and over it, a bank of black clouds was boiling up into the heavens. They had driven through patchy sunshine here along the shore, but that sunshine was apparently not going to last long.

"Well, maybe it'll be a fast-moving storm," Jan said soothingly, "Like the one last night. Our appointment to see the Tree isn't until two, and that's still hours away."

"Oh, I hope you're right," Peg said, a worried frown between her gray eyes. "It would be a shame to miss it again this year."

"We'll hold a good thought," Linda said. "Maybe if we have bad luck in the casino, we'll have good luck with the weather."

"We're bound to have bad luck in the casino," Sharon said. "Don't you know that it's set up that way?"

Micky had climbed out of the Lumina last and was now standing next to Jan, but she hadn't even looked back at the clouds when Peg pointed. At breakfast, she had said no more than a few words, had left most of her food on the plate. How could twenty-four hours make such a difference? Sharon wondered. Yesterday, she had seemed almost normal, except for a few hours there at Pierre's, and even then, she'd recovered enough of herself to dance and make the rest of them dance. Maybe she had bouts of depression, and who could

wonder at that? If Alzheimer's wasn't enough to depress the
hell out of you, what was? Maybe it was just *because* she was
sometimes so much like her old self that she got depressed to
think it couldn't last.

When they got inside the casino, the noise and the smell
of burning tobacco surrounded them immediately. They
threaded their way through the crowds to a cashier's window.

"Micky and I are going to pool our money and play the
poker slots together," Jan said, raising her voice to be heard
above the hubbub. "Let's plan to meet in the lobby at about
five to two. Okay?"

When that was agreed on, they separated to find the
games that would appeal to each of them. Sharon bought
forty dollars worth of quarters and headed for the poker slots
that used wild cards to make a hand; they had lower payoffs
for wins, but allowed for more small victories that would keep
you inside your budget longer. On the way, she became distracted by the blackjack tables. Not that she would ever
play—the minimum bet was five dollars!—but she liked to
watch. At the nearest table to her, she paused to watch a man
in a Hawaiian-print shirt pushing stacks of chips onto the
table. He kept one chip in his right hand to tap against his
cards when he wanted the dealer to hit him again. In the five
minutes she watched him, he lost ninety dollars, fished out
his wallet, and handed the dealer a hundred-dollar bill—one
of those new ones with the enormous head of Franklin on
them—for more chips. Blackjack was the only casino game
where you didn't even have to leave your chair to convert
more of your money into the chips or coins you were about
to lose. Not that the trip to the cashier's cage seemed to
induce many people to change their minds. The latest addi-
tions to the casino, she noticed, were the strategically placed
ATM machines that allowed people to bankrupt themselves

even if they had originally come in with only a certain amount of money they thought they could afford to lose.

Sharon moved on, found an empty stool in front of a poker machine, and gave her plastic cup full of quarters a shake for luck before beginning. She had lost twenty dollars by the time the man at the machine next to her lit a cigar and that was enough to make her decide on a move. She went first in search of something to eat; maybe the others could make do with only two meals a day, but she got too hungry to wait for the late dinners they'd been having. A small, counter-style grill offered sandwiches, sodas, and even liquor. Sharon decided on a ham and swiss on rye and a diet Coke. Since Thursday night when she'd unloaded on her friends, she'd felt less thirsty for booze; at Pierre's last night, she'd had only two glasses of beer. And this morning, she'd wakened early with a burst of energy, had volunteered to take Steve's Airedale for a walk before breakfast. As the big dog pulled her along the shaded road, she began to consider what connection there might be between crying your guts out and a diminished need for alcohol. When she got back home again, she was going to have to think about that some more.

When her stomach felt nicely satisfied, she went looking for her friends; gambling alone didn't seem like very much fun. On her way back across the crowded casino, she noticed for the first time how many people were just hanging around—not gambling at all. Some of them looked lost and forlorn, as if they might have already gambled away this month's rent but couldn't muster up the energy to leave. Others just looked drunk—in the middle of the day. Boy, that was not a good look. Bad enough to look drunk in some bar or club at midnight. But boozing for breakfast was clearly the fast way to perdition.

Finally, after a brief search through the slot machines, Sharon found Jan and Micky sitting close to each other in front of one of the poker slots. As she came up behind them, she heard Jan saying, "If we get rid of the jack and the eight, we have a chance at a straight." Micky said only, "Okay," and then Jan marked the two cards and punched the "draw" button. The straight didn't materialize.

"Hi," Sharon said. "How's it goin' here?"

"We're down a few bucks," Jan said, "But we had a ten-dollar win a few minutes ago."

"Good for you," Sharon said, noticing that a woman to the left of them was getting up from her stool. "Are you coming back, or can I have this machine?" Sharon asked her.

"Help yourself, honey," the woman said, pulling her mouth into a wry expression. "It's eating quarters like a starved hyena and not giving many of them back."

Sharon perched on the stool and began feeding the machine more quarters. She glanced occasionally at Micky, who would say, "Sure" or "Fine" to whatever Jan was saying about the choices they might make, but was not even looking at the brightly lit screen displaying the cards in each hand.

"Holy shit!" Jan breathed. "Look at this!"

Sharon leaned over to look at their screen. It was displaying the queen and jack of hearts, the ace of hearts, and two wild cards.

"Is that the first hand or the draw hand?" Sharon asked her, her own heart beginning to beat a little faster.

"The first one," Jan answered. "Am I going blind, or is this a royal flush?"

"That's the genuine article," Sharon cackled. "You've hit the second biggest one in the machine—fifty bucks. Better punch 'cash out' before something happens."

Jan pushed the button, and they all listened to the music

of two hundred quarters raining down into the bin beneath the screen. Such a sound always made neighboring players pause in their own gambling to listen and to glance over at the lucky winner. Jan was making small noises that sounded like "woo-woo-woo," and Micky's expression had changed to a look of confused delight. She and Jan were scooping up quarters by the handfuls and jamming them into the big plastic cups that were conveniently placed on top of the machines.

A shabby little man who had been standing near them began coming closer all the while the coins were falling, and by the time they had scooped up all the quarters, he was at Micky's elbow.

"I'll take a cup of those if you're feeling generous," he said, his voice low and wheedling.

Micky turned slowly to look at him, a little frown of concentration forming between her eyebrows.

"Do I know you?" she asked. "Am I supposed to give some of this to you?"

"Of course you know me," the little man said. "I've been bringing you luck over here. I saw you win the ten a little while ago, so I got even closer and now you've hit a big one. I'm just looking for a little justice."

"Don't pay any attention to him," Jan said caustically. "We do not know him. He's just looking for a handout."

Micky had already started to extend one of the plastic cups toward the man and now she stopped, her slim arm held out in front of her, a dazed look beginning to creep over her features.

"You stay out of this, lady," the little man said to Jan in a vicious whisper. He looked as if he hadn't shaved or changed his clothes in days, and his eyes had a red-rimmed, wild look. "If this generous and beautiful angel wants to let me share her luck, what's it to you?"

Jan put her hand onto Micky's arm and tried to pull it down. "Don't even look at him," she said, glaring at the man herself. "He's a complete stranger and a con artist of some sort. He's trying to fool you."

Micky wrenched her arm out of Jan's grasp and whirled to look at her. "Let me go!" she cried in a voice so loud that people turned to look from as many as five slot machines away. "I know it's a stranger. I want to give her some money."

"Her?" the man crowed. "Better look a little closer, pretty lady."

Jan backed off from Micky and rushed at the man, making him back up in a hurry. "You'd better get far away from us," she hissed at him, "or I'm going to call the security people to have you thrown out."

"What's the matter with your friend?" he said, not bothering to lower his voice. "Is she mental or what? Can't she tell a man from a woman?"

Sharon saw Micky's face go dead white—even her lips seemed drained of blood. Then she simply dropped the plastic cup, opened her hand and let it go; it hit the floor with a sharp bang. Quarters rolled in all directions as Micky turned and ran. People scattered to get out of her way, but some of them—including the dreadful little man—dropped to their knees and began scooping up the scattered coins.

"Grab those other cups and come on," Sharon said to Jan who was seemingly frozen in place, her mouth opened slightly. They collected their belongings—Micky's jacket was still draped on the stool she'd been occupying—and threaded their way through the crowd into which Micky had disappeared.

"I see her," Jan gasped after a few seconds. "There at the doors. She's going outside."

When they'd crossed the lobby to the big doors, they

could see that it was raining, a steady drizzle that was streaking the glass with tiny rivulets. Micky was already halfway across the parking lot when they got outside—not heading in the direction of their cars, but just walking, head bowed against the rain. Sharon and Jan trotted to catch up with her.

"Where're you going?" Jan asked quietly when she'd run around in front of Micky.

"I don't know," she said, her voice muffled, "But not there, not back to that place."

"He's a stupid jerk, Micky," Sharon said, putting her hand onto Micky's arm because she was still plodding forward. "He doesn't matter. If you want, I'll go back in there right now and slap him around for you."

Micky came to a stop and looked up at her. Rain was trickling down out of her cropped hair, dripping from her nose. "It's this whole thing," she said, and she spread her arms wide to take in the parking lot and the casino. Maybe the whole world. It was hard to say what the gesture meant. "Why am I here at all? I can't do any numbers anymore, and you know that, Jan. You know I can't play any games. So why did you drag me here? Do you think this is fun for me?"

"Oh, God, Mick," Jan said, and her voice broke. "I thought it would be fun to just all be together."

"But you can *see,*" Micky cried, lifting her hands next to her face as if she meant to convey that her own eyes didn't work anymore. "I try to say something, and it's another— another thing comes out. All those people. Laughing."

"Nobody was laughing, Micky," Sharon said softly. "Honest to God."

But Micky didn't turn to look at her; she just kept staring at Jan, her eyes wide and desperate. "You can see now, can't you?" she whispered, and the words were aimed straight at Jan. "You can see why I asked you. Why I need you to answer."

Jan didn't speak. Rain was soaking her hair, making it sag around her face, but she didn't move either, just stood there with her gaze locked onto Micky's eyes. Whatever it was that Micky meant by those words, Jan seemed to understand her. The whole exchange scared Sharon a little. The other women looked like fighters who might suddenly start hitting each other.

"We can go back if you want to," Sharon said to Micky; she still had hold of her arm, which was shaking now. "We'll just get in the cars and go to Grand Marais." She was beginning to feel almost desperate to break the strange spell that seemed to be locking Jan and Micky into this face-off.

"No," Micky said quietly. "Peg wants to see that tree thing. We came here for that, didn't we?"

"We probably won't even go if it keeps on raining like this," Sharon said. "And we don't all have to stay. We have two cars. I'll take you back, and everybody else can stay to see the tree."

"No," Micky said fiercely, dragging her arm out of Sharon's grip. "I said we'll all stay." Her shirt was sticking to her torso now, and rain was streaming down her shivering arms.

Sharon remembered suddenly that she was carrying Micky's jacket, and she reached out to drape it around Micky's shoulders. All she could think was that she had to make Micky look at her, to distract both these friends from the fierce contest which she didn't understand, a contest that was starting to seem positively dangerous. But Micky did not turn toward her, did not even pull the jacket around her shivering body. Jan, too, held the fierce stare she had been directing at Micky ever since they'd stopped walking; her narrow frame was quivering as if she had been seized with a sudden palsy. When she finally spoke, her voice was just an angry hiss.

"Stop goddamn bossing everybody all the time! Why the hell do you have to *mind* everything so much? What difference can it possibly make to you what a pathetic old bum in a casino says about you?"

"You'd mind it just as much wouldn't you, Jan?" Micky said to her. "Look me in the face and try to tell me you wouldn't."

Sharon watched Jan struggling to find an answer, saw her intelligent eyes considering a lie. But finally she said, "I can't tell you that. I don't know how I'd feel." And all the while, the rain was battering her narrow face.

"Yes, you do," Micky said simply. "You'd feel like me."

Jan stood for a moment longer, her hands clenched into fists at her sides, her eyes locked onto Micky's face. "Yes, Mick," she said finally. "I *would* feel like you."

Sharon felt more frightened than ever. It was as if these women were speaking in a code. But somehow she guessed— she could feel it crackling in the space between them—that the coded message was a matter of life and death.

"Well, I'll tell you what I think," Sharon said, lifting her hand to wipe the rain away from her eyes. The other women both turned now to look at her, their expressions dazed, almost as if they'd forgotten until this moment that she was there. Sharon spoke on into their blank stares, her voice getting louder and louder with each sentence. "I think you *both* mind stuff way more than people should. All your lives, you've had to be the smartest and the best at everything. You measure yourselves in IQ points, as if that's the only value people can have. If you can't be on top of the fucking dean's list every single minute of your lives, you think life isn't worth living. Well, I've got news for both of you. Lots of people get laughed at and taken advantage of and even kicked in the groin, but they're too busy getting on with their lives to stand around in the rain gabbing about how goddamned much they *mind* it all."

The other two women were gaping at her, their eyes wide.

"Well, what about you?" Jan said finally. "The other night you were moaning and groaning about how inferior you feel because you aren't applying *your* impressive IQ to stuff you think is valuable. You seemed to mind all of that quite a lot."

Sharon drew a ragged breath, swiped at her face again. "All right," she shouted, "Me too, then. All of us. The whole damned Sextet from Mensa. We all know the *others* of us are wonderful, but we can't seem to include ourselves in that opinion. But we're all damned fine women in lots of ways, not just because we're smart. Well, isn't that true? Isn't that what you both were saying to me the other night?" She looked back and forth between them, wondering if she herself looked as soggy and uncomfortable as they did. Crisis should have some dignity, shouldn't it? Not just this half-comic, drowned-rat discomfort. "So, come on, then," she said, more quietly now. "Why is it so hard to tolerate imperfection in yourselves, when you're so ready to tolerate imperfection in other people you love? Why can't we give ourselves a break once in a while?"

Micky took two quick steps toward her, so sudden that Sharon felt a little alarmed, almost flinched away. But all Micky did was reach out and take her arm, easing her slim hand into the damp crook of Sharon's elbow.

"Let's give ourselves the break of getting in out of the rain," Micky said softly. "I dragged you both out here, so now I can drag you back inside where we can get dry."

Sharon stood her ground, tried to search Micky's expression. "Did you hear what I said to you, Mick?" she asked.

"Yes, Sharon, I heard you," Micky said, lifting her gaze to

look directly into Sharon's eyes. "It's something to consider. I promise you I'll think about it." She said it in her old voice, the one that soothed terror, the one that didn't lie.

Then she turned to reach out for Jan. Huddled together, arm in arm, the three women walked back toward the dazzling light of the casino, their heads bent under the slicing rain.

23 / Micky

S he rubbed the towel over her hair, let the scratchy folds of
terry cloth hide her face as she sank into the lobby chair.
Somebody had handed her the towel after they got back inside the casino; she hadn't looked at the person, only at the
towel, at her own hand as she reached out for it. Anything to
escape the pitiless stares, the blank indifference of idle curiosity, as if a circus elephant had strolled into the lobby, streaming with rain. Now in the jerry-rigged cave, her coconut-
scented shampoo blended with the smell of wet hair, and
through the darkness where she hid, she could see Samantha's
hair glistening in the rain. Cross-country races weren't can-
celed because of the rain. Sam had said that was one of the
reasons she loved the sport—not for sissies, she said.

Micky could remember the very texture of the air at that
meet—damp and heavy against her arms as she stood near
the finish line, pressing against her eyes as she strained to
catch a glimpse of the approaching runners. Samantha was
running second, her dark ponytail swinging in that lazy
rhythm that made her stride seem effortless, almost as if she
were out for a casual jog in the park. But that rhythm was the
secret to distance running, Micky knew—conserve energy for
the long haul, none of the flashy heroics of the sprint. Sam
always found another gear as she neared the end of a race,
lifting her knees higher and surging forward. On that wet

day, it wasn't enough—the lanky blonde who was ahead of Sam when Micky first saw them found another gear, too, and ran past Micky some ten feet ahead of her daughter.

But Sam flashed her a grin anyway, jogged in circles for a few minutes to cool down, yelled encouragement at her teammates struggling toward the finish. Of course, she didn't speak to her mother, didn't approach her. No sixteen-year-old would ever do anything so uncool. It had been only a year since Sam had got over being embarrassed at having parents at all. But Micky knew it was important to Sam to have her there, to know that her mother had left ungraded papers behind to stand patiently in the rain, quietly exulting in a second-place finish.

Micky was always amazed at how easily Samantha accepted what she herself would have regarded as a defeat. "For Pete's sake, Mom," she'd say. "It's not about always coming in first. It's a team thing and a personal-best thing. I'm running against the clock, not those other kids." That Sam was competing in a varsity sport at all filled Micky with a kind of wonder. In her own high school days, that had never been an option. Augsdale High in the early sixties had only one role for girls where sport was concerned—cheerleaders—and it was a role Micky fiercely refused to play. "You're so beautiful," her mother would say in her soft, wheedling voice. "I'm sure that if Beth Miller can make the squad, you could too." Crackling with outrage, Micky would respond, "Beth Miller is as dumb as a post, Mother. Is that the kind of company you want me to keep?"

Bob was the athlete in the family. He was cocaptain of the varsity basketball team when he was only a sophomore, won state track medals every year he competed. She used to tell her friends that the only way she ever got to see her father was when she attended the sports events in which her younger brother starred. She would sit among those friends and watch her father, always close to the action, his angular face bunched into tense excitement, then springing open in a shout when Bob made a score. He never even looked at the other players. And she knew early on that there was nothing she could ever do that would make him focus on her the same passionate pride. She could top the honor roll every semester, and he would murmur, "Good for you," without even looking up from his newspaper. Bob never got a grade higher than B, but he had the privileged status of the son, the golden boy who could be flaunted on fishing trips, whose picture on the sports page of the local paper would be mentioned wherever her father went around town, so he could say, "Yeah, the boy is doing all right, I guess." She'd heard him make this speech, seen his face compose itself into the lines of a false modesty that made her seethe.

"My father," she would say to her friends, "is such a cop. It's not just his job; it's the whole key to his personality. He's conventional in every way, rigid, judgmental, controlling." But all the while she was listening to her own angry voice, there was a little girl huddled down at the bottom of her soul, aghast at the words, terrified that he might hear, no matter how far away he was at the time, horrified lest he should hate her instead of just ignore her.

Whenever she thought about her father, even now, she saw his boots—the black, laced-up boots that were part of his policeman's uniform. The soles of those boots were over an inch thick, stiff and unyielding when he walked so that his gait was awkward, stubbed like the monster in the Frankenstein movies. In her childhood, she had gone barefoot whenever she could get away with it, running all over town in the summers until even a sprint across gravel didn't cause her any discomfort. "Put something on your feet," her father would say on those few occasions when he noticed her at all. "People will think you're being raised by wolves." But she'd already accepted that defiance was the only tool she had for chiseling cracks in his indifference. By high school, that defiance had found its focus in ideas, in political positions she knew were anathema to him.

She'd been almost finished with college before an old friend of her father's, the Augsdale newspaper editor, had told her outside of church one Easter break, "When you got that scholarship to St. Augustine, your dad was just busting his buttons about it. Came into the print shop special to tell me it should be in the paper, should be on the front page." She had almost started to cry, right there in the parking lot; the little girl at the bottom of her soul was shouting, "Why didn't he tell *me?*" but out loud, she said only, "Really? That's nice."

And he didn't change. His thick-soled boots walked over the sixties and the seventies and even part of the eighties before he retired. In a St. Augustine English class, Micky found the words to help her know what she thought about her father's relationship to the world. The words were in a poem by Gerard Manley Hopkins; she had committed the poem to memory, could still have recited it now, at least the parts that had first made her gasp with the shock of recognition: "The world is charged with the grandeur of God. . . . Generations have trod, have trod, have trod . . . nor can foot feel, being shod." She had immediately thought of her father, his inch-thick soles keeping him from any intimate contact with the planet whose destiny he was so sure he had a right to control.

He wasn't the only one of course. He was just one of that juggernaut she saw as rolling over the earth, causing their inventions to separate their flesh from other living things.

Their boots, their cars, their tanks made it possible for them to move over the surface of the world without touching it, without making contact. People should be made to walk barefoot on the ground at least once a month, she took to telling her friends; they should let mud squish between their toes, let the cool grass or the rough, spongy texture of moss press up against the tender arch. Surely a man who did that, and did it often, could not invent napalm, would not be able to sit in those laboratories made of cold stainless steel and glittering porcelain and contrive there, on purpose, a substance whose sole function was to burn the flesh off the trees and the backs of children. And surely a barefoot man could not shrug off the execution of four young people at Kent State with "The little punks should have expected it."

"I don't know why you're always so twitchy around Grandpa," Samantha would say with that teenage certainty that her view of people was always correct. "He's just a regular old guy, and he's always so sweet to me."

And, indeed, he was sweet to Sam, asking her about her schoolwork, her running, even her friends. Micky would just cook with free-floating irritation whenever she saw her father's leathery face soften at the sight of his grandchildren. But it was no wonder, really. Sam was such an easy, sunny child, dimpling with good cheer whenever anyone spoke to her. God, how she missed Sam! There was a hollow ache low in her stomach, in her womb, when she thought about her daughter—little more than a voice on the phone these days, grumbling a bit about Dallas traffic, speaking cheerfully of the hot sun she loved so much. And Micky knew she was going to lose Sam permanently, literally forget who she was, stare into those dark, thick-lashed eyes someday and find there only a stranger.

She pushed the corner of the towel into her mouth, bit

down on it, tasting the bleach and detergent. You were supposed to bite down on something to keep from crying out in pain. That was in all the movies. She had yelled a lot when she was in labor with Sam—Matthew too—just gave herself up to the waves of pain, the clamping agony of the contractions. It was a help somehow to gather the energy of her diaphragm and launch that bloodcurdling sound into the antiseptic air, into the faces of those cooing nurses. But primal screaming wouldn't help this pain, wouldn't have any effect except to make the staring faces harden into horror: Somebody dial 911 and have this crazy woman taken away from us! If you were having a baby, you were allowed to scream.

She missed her work, missed the seasonal renewal of young faces, so eager to do good in the world, so ready to believe that her classroom instruction could fortify them against the squalor and drift they would find when they actually became social workers. She even missed the committee meetings, the tussles with the dean and the academic vice president who regarded her program as "soft" in comparison to chemistry or composites engineering. Every day, she would put on her suit and wade in to do battle against materialism, social indifference, and the profit motive as the only justification for pursuing an education. And it was fun, exhilarating.

Her love for her work was another thing she'd never been able to make her father understand. "I don't get it," he'd growl whenever she talked about school in his presence. "Peter must be raking in big bucks at Mayo. Can't you guys afford whatever you need or want without you having to go out and work too? You could take care of your own kids, instead of telling other people how to take care of theirs."

"I do take care of my kids, Dad," she would tell him, struggling to keep her voice calm, dispassionate, the way she did when Dean Lundquist talked about budget cuts. "I'm not working just for the money. I'm the director of a whole graduate program." As soon as she realized that her voice was rising, that she was losing it, she would clamp her mouth shut, change the subject, even leave the room. No sir! She wasn't going to play that old game: Look at me, Daddy! See how well I'm doing!

When the time came, when she decided to leave the road before it plunged into complete darkness, would her father be able to respect that? Would he admire it as a courageous gesture, or would he be angry, ashamed of her for quitting? She would never be able to know—like the secret of his talk with the newspaper editor after she won the scholarship, only this time she wouldn't be around for someone to clue her in years after the fact. She no longer believed that she would be able to look back from beyond death, to watch the living or to hear their thoughts. There would be only nothingness, a blank, with her consciousness shut off, disappeared. People might cry, but she wouldn't know it.

Her father had cried after he'd learned of her diagnosis. She hadn't witnessed these tears, but her mother told her about it afterward. She and Peter had gone to Augsdale to tell her parents in person what the neurologist had said. Peter did most of the talking, and she watched their faces— all three faces. Her father scowled and blustered: "That's ridiculous!" he said, waving his hand in that dismissive way of his. "There's nothing like that anywhere in the family." Peter closed his eyes, waited for the storm of denial to pass, and then explained in his calm, professional doctor's voice. Her mother wept, sobbing softly into her apron. Her father fell silent, his face setting into grim lines that looked to her like disapproval. She had disappointed him again.

"He cried and cried," her mother said—When? Not on

that visit. More recently. But it was too much work to think about when something had happened. "He cried like a baby," her mother said, producing the cliché that seemed to Micky the most unlikely description of her father that anyone could conjure up. "He's sure it must be his fault somehow—'genetics,' he says."

Despite the cliché, her mother had surprised her in that talk. Micky had never given much thought to her relationship with her mother; it just *was,* like tides, like seasons—predictable, steady. Not always fun, but reassuring and natural. She had always believed that she had her mother figured out: beautiful, feminine in an old-fashioned way, passive; maddeningly complaisant to her husband's authority, but emotionally warm; devising little ways of smoothing ruffled feelings, murmuring conventional wisdom in a voice that never seemed to make strong demands. Yet on the day of their talk—it had been in Rochester, in her own house, she remembered now—Joanna Jaeger had surprised her.

"Your father and I can come here," she'd said in a firm voice. "We've talked it over, and we're agreed. When you need more help, we can be right here in the house. Peter can't just give up his work, and you won't want strangers around you. You know how you are."

Micky had stared at her mother for a moment. "Absolutely not," she said finally. "You have your own life in Augsdale. Your friends, your sisters, your church. You're—" and here she groped for the exact age, couldn't find it—"you're not young anymore, and I won't let you give up what's left of your life for me."

"We're your parents," her mother said, her usually mild eyes flashing. "We're retired now, and there aren't so many things for us to do. We have the time, and we want to do this."

"I don't hear Dad saying this," Micky replied. "And I can't picture him wiping the slobber off my blouse when I can't remember anymore how to chew and swallow."

Her mother sat back in the chair, her face draining of color. "I already told you that we both want to do this," she said quietly. "Why do you have to turn it into one of your old fights with your dad?"

"Okay, Mother," Micky said, her voice rising. "Then let's just stay on the original subject. Should *you* give up what you had every reason to believe would be a peaceful retirement and go back to diapering a baby? Because that's what it would be, eventually, you know. And Dad won't be much help to you in that department—he never was. All of the work will be on you. I won't have it. If I'm still around at that stage, I won't know or care who's changing my diapers, so your sacrifice will be for nothing."

Her mother's big eyes had filled with tears, but her voice when she finally spoke was strong, even angry. "I had one daughter and one son," she said, "and neither one of you would ever let me do a thing for you after you were babies. Both of you cared only about your father's attention. You didn't have to prove anything to me, so I might just as well not have been there."

Micky was shocked into silence for a long moment. "That's not true, Mom," she said at last. "Bob and I both depended on you to—to—" This time the groping wasn't a symptom of her Alzheimer's; she was struggling to discover what she felt about this, because she'd never before turned her consciousness toward it.

"You can't even think of anything," her mother said sadly, starting to rise from the chair.

"Wait a minute," Micky said desperately, and she reached out to take her mother's hands, to push her back down. "Bob and I counted on you to be *not Dad.*" It was all she could say, but her mother seemed blessedly to understand, smiled at her and patted her wrist.

"Then I can be 'not Dad' for you again when you need me, can't I?" she said.

"It's too soon to talk about this, Mom," Micky said, squeezing her mother's hands. "I won't need daily help for years yet. We'll come back to this another time."

"But you'll think about it?"

"Yes, Mother," she'd lied. "I'll think about it."

"Micky?" The voice penetrated into her terry-cloth cave. "Mick? Are you all right?"

She pulled the towel off her head to find Sharon's frowning face hovering above her. Dear, loving Sharon who everyone else thought was so tough.

"Yes, I'm fine," she said. "I'm just trying to get dry."

Sharon smiled a little, but her eyes kept the worried look.

"It's okay, Kiddo," Micky said, standing up. "Really, I'm fine."

Why did she have to keep telling that lie? Why couldn't she just give herself up to the wrenching agony, contract her diaphragm, and shove a scream out into this glittering palace of failed hope? Why couldn't she give up the notion that everybody would stop loving her if she weren't at the top of the fucking dean's list?

24 / Jan

"**H**at Point was the launching place for the canoes when my people set out for Isle Royale," Denise was saying. "That can be a rough passage because storms are sudden and that's twenty-two miles of open water."

Jan was trying to listen, to attend, but she was distracted by her own heavy thoughts. They were trudging two abreast along a woodland path, paved only with leaves and pine needles, flanked on both sides by wire fencing. The air was heavy with the smell of wet vegetation coming from thick underbrush covered in moss. The pungent odor reminded Jan of the root cellar where her mother had stored potatoes and onions. Bearded lichen hung like bedraggled hair from the branches overhead. It had stopped raining, briefly, but the streak of sky visible above them was dark gray, still so full of moisture that it seemed to sag against the forest canopy from the weight of that water.

They had met Denise in the lobby of the casino as arranged. She was not what Jan had been expecting, although she couldn't have said why she had been picturing something else—something more exotic. Denise, who never offered her last name, was young, about twenty-five, and no one seeing her in town would have guessed her Native American heritage. She was of medium height, slim; she had fair skin, long brown curls, hazel eyes behind stylish glasses, a straight nose, and beautiful, even teeth. Dressed in jeans and a flannel shirt, she gave no evidence even in her jewelry that she belonged to the Chippewa tribe. There *was* something in the cheekbones, high and acutely angled, that might suggest her heritage to someone who had been told it.

"Isle Royale was the summer residence of the band," she was saying now, in her high, breathy voice. "The fishing was better, and there were strawberries, blueberries, cranberries. The Anishinabe called the island Minong, the good place."

Jan was not in the mood for a tourist trek, not geared to absorb new knowledge. The day had become a sort of nightmare, ever since Micky had run out of the casino into the rain. Once back inside, they had dried off as best they could with towels provided by the management. Their clothes were damp for a longer time, of course. But now Jan had begun to see the casino for what it was—a dreary and sad monument to human folly: people huddled over slot machines, hollow-eyed robots hoping to buy a little luck, desperately pursuing the chance that experience had taught them was elusive and mocking. The air, thick with smoke and despair, had a sickening effect after a while. She had stayed close to Micky's side, partly to offer comfort if that were needed and partly to prevent Sharon from asking the question that was in her eyes: "What did Micky mean by 'You can see why I asked you. Why I need you to answer'?"

They had made no other attempt at gambling. Sharon said she'd already lost enough money and would just "hang" with them. They tracked down Peg and Linda and Mary and watched them lose money for a while. Micky spoke only in monosyllables once they got back inside, seemed absorbed and far away.

Jan couldn't shake a feeling of doom. Even though Micky had calmed down after Sharon's speech in the parking lot, there was no guarantee that she would even remember that speech; she had forgotten about seeing the moose yesterday morning, forgotten even before the day was over. And the danger was always present that a relatively small outrage like the odious little man's remark could push her over the edge—perhaps long before she might otherwise have meant to kill herself. How could they count on always having loved ones close at hand to reassure and soothe her?

Of course, it had occurred to Jan that she might agree to help Micky with an eventual suicide even if she had no intention of following through, just say, "All right, I'll get the drugs, and I'll help you take them when you tell me you're ready." That might have a calming effect on Micky, might help her be more at ease living in the moment, not having to fret and plan for a future she was becoming steadily less able to control. If she relaxed, her quality of life would improve for the short-term and, in the long-term, she might reach a point where she no longer remembered her suicidal intention. Then she, Jan, would be off the hook. She might even go so far as to secure some drugs and show them to Micky as reassurance.

That course had two big problems though. While Micky was having trouble finding words and had no concept of numbers anymore, her emotional radar was still fully functional. She would spot the insincerity, would see in Jan's face that she was only trying to put off the decision. They had known each other so well for so long that they couldn't put things over on each other. And the second problem was that Jan hadn't yet convinced herself that Micky's decision was the wrong one. Perhaps the greatest kindness she could offer her friend was to feed her a lethal dose of barbiturates and then hold her hand while the pills did their work. Walking along this forest path, she was struck by the thought that it might be immoral to just stand by watching the prolonged agony of Micky's disintegration, like watching an animal writhing on a hot grill to which it was tied, when you had a gun in your hands and could put it out of its misery with a single shot.

Micky was plodding along beside her, just to her left. Despite Jan's objections, she had taken her sandals off as soon as they got into the forest, and now she was regarding her bare feet with an intense stare, as if they might suddenly go off in a wrong direction if she didn't keep them under a strict watch. How much of Denise's presentation she was hearing was impossible to guess. This part of the forest seemed primeval, as if they were walking backward in time, as if every step away from the blaring casino and the acres of cars was taking them a hundred years into the past. And Micky seemed to be attending to that journey with particular care.

"It was white people who gave the name Witch Tree," Denise was saying, "because they thought the exposed roots on the rocks looked like gnarled fingers. But it's not a good name. *Witch* suggests that there's something evil about the tree, and that certainly isn't part of our tradition." She laid only a little stress on *our*, as if she did not mean to emphasize too strongly that she differed culturally from her guests. "The Anishinabe people called the tree *Ma-Ni-Do Gee-Zhi-Gance,*" she went on, panting slightly from the effort of walking and talking at the same time. "*Ma-Ni-Do* means 'spirit' or, more accurately, 'mystery.' *Gee-Zhi-Gance* means 'little cedar.' So the Chippewa name means Mystery Little Cedar. But the tree does look like a bent old woman, and the people sometimes call it, affectionately, Nokomis. That means 'grandmother.' A long way from witch, though, wouldn't you say?"

"Absolutely," Mary said. She was hurrying along with her short stride, right behind Denise, and Peg was beside her.

Sharon and Linda were behind them, with Micky and Jan bringing up the rear. Jan had noticed that Linda didn't have a camera with her on this trip. She had cracked the lens on one camera yesterday at Cascade, Mary said, but she had several others. Jan had seen them. So why, when this tree was supposed to be so fascinating to artists, had she left her tools behind? Odd.

"Here we are," Denise said and came to a halt where the path cut between two large boulders, rocks of the unmistakable black diabase so characteristic of the North Shore. Almost as if at a signal, a fine drizzle began to fall, hissing softly against the trees that surrounded them.

"Shall we go ahead?" Denise asked. "Or start back? The shore and the tree are right past these rocks."

"Of course, we'll go ahead," Peg said. "We've come this far. What's a little rain?"

The others murmured agreement, and Denise turned to lead them forward. When they passed between the rocks, the forest ended at once and the shore was before them, steeply pitched boulders shaped into platforms and precipices. Black, black rock already slick with rain. And there was the tree. Straight ahead of them across the treacherous rock where no other tree or shrub had found a foothold was an upthrust rock whose far edge fell straight to the water of Lake Superior. At the very edge of that platform was a dwarfed cedar tree, its sparse canopy lifted up against the black and gray of rock, sky, and water.

"You can see it better from over here," Denise said, pointing. "But you'll have to be very careful on the rock."

Emerging from the shelter of the forest, they could feel the winds of the lake, blowing the rain against their faces with a stinging chill. They formed a line now to follow Denise, picking their way over the boulders, placing their feet with elaborate care. Jan saw to it that Micky went directly in front of her. But she soon realized that she needn't have worried. Just as Micky could still dance with her old grace and ease, she could hike and climb as she had always done— like a mountain goat. Her bare toes curled to fit the surface of the stone and her arms lifted easily to find a balance whenever she shifted her weight. She had laced her fingers through the straps of her sandals and didn't even seem to notice that she was carrying them. Finally Denise brought them to a halt on an outcropping of rock parallel to the tree, but slightly lower than the narrow escarpment from which the tree sprang. For a long time, no one spoke.

The roots of the tree were almost on a level with their heads: exposed roots gripping the black rocks, hugging the stone with fierce closeness and then disappearing into unseen fissures, plunging through and beneath the hard-surface to gain nourishment from—from what? No one could call this unyielding, adamantine crust "soil" or "dirt." There was nothing like nourishing earth anywhere near this upthrust cliff to which the little tree was clinging. If it had not been for the green of the stunted canopy, anyone look-ing would have guessed that the tree was dead, its pewter gray bark fossilized, as solid and impenetrable as the stone. The trunk was twisted like a bonsai tree, tortured into a grotesque spiral by the constant battering of wind and wave. Even the limbs that supported the canopy were warped and spiraled like deformed arms.

Denise, her glasses misted with the rain, looked up at the tree for a moment longer before she spoke. "Botanists from the university estimate that the tree is four hundred years old," she said. And then there was another long silence while they imagined the fifty-degrees-below-zero temperatures of four hundred winters, the raging storms that must have encrusted the whole shore in thick ice.

The rock below the tree was covered in orange lichen, the only other vegetation capable of sustaining any life along the shoreline. Beyond the point, far out, the immense lake churned under the wet sky. The surface looked like boiling lead—just that color and that thick, sluggish consistency: plop, plop, plop; the waves had no rhythm, just a seemingly random eruption of water to expel trapped energy. Closer to them at the foot of the little cliff, the water swirled and eddied. A few hopeful gulls skimmed in and out over the surface of the water, listless, their normally raucous voices stilled.

The women huddled together, their shoulders touching, their faces lifted into the rain as they looked up to the cedar tree's sparse hair, a deep green proof of vitality in the face of deadening gloom. Denise stepped a little apart from them, turned to face them. And as she did, the rain stopped as suddenly as it had begun, just as if a sprinkler had been turned off.

"Well, that's better," Denise said with a little smile. She removed her glasses briefly, used the tail of her shirt to wipe them dry, and then put them back on. "The people would bring their canoes here," she said, gesturing down at the swirling water of the bay. "Before they went out on the lake. They would bring offerings to the tree, usually tobacco to scatter on the rocks and the water. The Anishinabe word for tobacco is 'ah-say-ma.' They would ask the Ma-Ni-Do for the power of her protection—for a safe journey. The underwater spirits might erupt, might reach up suddenly and overturn the canoes. The wind spirit might come up all at once and blow them into death."

Jan could see that Micky had roused herself from her

earlier torpor; the dazed and sullen look was gone. She was focusing intently on Denise, watching her face and following her gestures to look wherever she pointed.

"The people would ask the tree to lend some of her power to them," Denise went on. "So they could pass unhurt over the lake spirits and slip unnoticed under the dangerous gaze of the wind spirits."

"It seems like a lot to ask of a little tree," Mary said, and they turned to look at her, so little herself among the rest of them. "They thought this tree had more power than the lake?"

"Oh, Mary," Peg murmured, mild disapproval clouding her voice. "It's not *our* tradition."

"I'm not criticizing," Mary said peevishly. "I'm just curious. I find it admirable, really, that people would reverence something despite its being stunted like this."

Denise turned her cool, level gaze onto Mary for a moment, her dark eyebrows arching slightly. "Oh," she said softly, "the people didn't reverence the tree *despite* its being twisted and small. They reverenced it *because* it was twisted and small. Because the spirits of the lake and the wind had battered it and punished it, but they couldn't kill it. The spirit of the tree must be great indeed if it could withstand the power of the wind and the water. It was exactly that spirit they asked for themselves every time they went out in those fragile canoes."

"Oh," Mary said in a small voice. "I see."

"This is a sacred place," Denise went on calmly, "because here the elements of earth and water and wind are all present. But the earth is the mother, the womb from which the people are born. Birds are born of the wind and fish of the water, but we come from the earth. The mother spirit protects us when we go into the places of water and wind. She stands there, the Nokomis, the grandmother, facing the lake, watching over the people who go from the land. The water and wind hurt her, but they cannot kill her. She is old. She has great power."

The whispery voice was like a chant, like a prayer. And it was suddenly easy to believe that the blood of the forest people was flowing in the veins of this girl who otherwise looked so much like the European conquerors whose bloodlines had masked her original heritage. Jan looked from her to Micky who was gazing up at the tree, her face expectant, wondering, as if she were waiting for the ancient cedar to speak. Her arms were close to her sides, the sandals dangling unnoticed from her right hand. Behind her head, low against the sky, Jan saw a shape approaching from the north and east. It was a black shape, a shadow darker than the water, sailing nearer and nearer.

"Look," Jan breathed, and Micky turned her cropped head to face the boiling water. The gliding form was a bird, and as it came in toward Hat Point, Jan could see that it was a big bird—not just some grackle. With a last dipping swoop, reaching ahead of itself with its talons to grasp the rock, the bird landed below them some fifty feet away.

"Raven," Denise said quietly. It could have been an announcement; it could have been a greeting. No one moved for a few seconds. The bird took a few steps toward them—the awkward, jerky movements of birds on land. It tipped its glistening head from side to side, the black, piercing eyes watching them, boring into them. And then Micky dropped her sandals and began to walk toward the raven, to feel her way across the rocks with her slim white feet. The bird did not startle, but came to a stop, focused now on Micky and on Micky alone.

"Don't," Jan said, reaching her hand after Micky but too

late to touch her shoulder. She felt a wave of dread, a sudden chilling certainty that the bird had come to seal Micky's fate, an evil omen that Micky herself recognized. "Give me some small stones," Jan said under her breath to no one in particular. "I'll scare him off."

"Why?" Linda asked, but she wasn't looking at Jan when she said it. Like the others she was watching Micky's progress toward the raven, a deliberate pace, but not a cautious or sneaking one. The bird held its ground, the sleek head stilled now with the intensity of its focus.

"Why?" Jan echoed irritably. "Because it's ugly. And probably dirty too. Who knows what diseases it might be carrying. Why isn't it flying away? It must be sick or something." And all the while she was speaking, trying to offer reasonable explanations, her throat was closing with panic, with an ancient atavistic horror: this was a bird of ill omen, and its message was death.

"These birds haven't known any danger from humans out here," Denise said softly. "White people are afraid of ravens because they think they're bad luck, so they try to kill them. But Indian people don't have the same view, so the birds aren't afraid of us."

Micky had come to a stop now, had straightened up with her back to them. She and the raven were locked in some face-off, neither moving.

"What *is* the Indian view of ravens?" Sharon asked in a whisper. For the whole of the walk out here and since their arrival on the shore, she had said almost nothing. Her characteristic wisecracking had disappeared, almost as if she had some sense that this was a place that would not welcome foolishness.

"The Anishinabe revere the raven for his cleverness," Denise answered, her voice intended for everyone because they were not looking at each other now; all were focused on the strange confrontation below them at the water's edge. "The raven can be a trickster, so he must be listened to carefully. He is a messenger with important things to say, but the message can be either good or bad. The listener must decide, not let himself be fooled."

The bird was looking up at Micky; only its feet were moving now, doing a tiny, plucking dance against the black rock. Micky lifted her right hand and extended it, palm upward toward the bird, which danced backward a few steps but did not open its wings. Above them both, the ancient tree spread its misshapen arms, enclosing the woman and the bird in a wide embrace.

"Some of the Northwest tribes have a very high place for the raven." Denise was whispering now, a hypnotic, hissing sound that seemed to reach no further than the small band of women on the stone platform. "They revere him as a creator. They say he is the spirit who brings the sun back every day."

In the tableau below them, there was no movement for a few more seconds, and then the raven simply opened its wings, unfurled those powerful arms, and just lifted up off the shore, silent and black against the gray of sky and water. It swooped out over the lake, dipped to the right and then, with a few beats of the massive wings, soared back toward them, circling as it rose over Hat Point, over the twisted cedar tree. Micky raised her arm above her head in a salute, turned her body to follow the flight of the raven. Her face was lifted skyward. When she turned far enough for the other women to see her expression, Jan caught her breath in surprise. Micky's face was luminous, glowing, a dreamy smile turning her pale lips up like wings.

Jan began to move toward her, walking quickly without

even looking at her own feet as she followed the course Micky had taken to get to the shore. Micky was still looking up, her slim arm thrust like a mast against the sky. When Jan reached her, she lowered her face, offered the joyous smile to her oldest friend. She brought her arm down slowly to her side and stood quietly. Jan reached out her right hand, placing her fingers lightly against Micky's elbow. One by one the other women joined them, first Sharon and Linda, then Peg and Mary. They surrounded Micky, but nobody seemed disposed to break the silence. One by one, they reached out to touch her—Peg took her right hand; Linda put a hand on her left shoulder; Mary slipped an arm around her waist; and Sharon put one palm against the middle of her back.

"Thank you," Micky said, her voice ringing in the stillness. "Thank you all." And the whole time, her face was shining, transfigured, beautiful.

Finally they remembered Denise, looked up to where she was standing above them. She didn't look alarmed or even puzzled about what was happening below her on the shore; she was just waiting, self-possessed, serene. The women separated now, began climbing back up over the boulders. Peg kept hold of Micky's hand, and Jan closed her fingers more tightly on her elbow. Jan looked once behind herself, meaning to stop for Micky's shoes, but she saw that Linda had already retrieved them, was holding them tightly against her chest. When they had reassembled near Denise, Jan finally let go of Micky's arm.

Micky turned now to Mary. "Give me a cigarette, Mimi," she said, and even she must have heard how peremptory it sounded because she rephrased it. "Could I please have a cigarette?"

"Oh, Mick," Mary said reprovingly. "This isn't the time to start smoking again, is it?"

Micky stared at her blankly for a second, and then she put her head back and laughed. "Oh, Mimi," she gasped at last. "I don't want to smoke it. Just give me one of your cigs."

Mary fumbled around for a few seconds in her purse and then produced the crumpled packet, fished out a cigarette, and handed it to Micky. She took it, broke it in half, and rolled the pieces in her right hand so that the tobacco fell into her left palm. Then she carefully crushed and handed the empty papers and filter back to Mary. Turning to Denise, Micky lifted her left fist toward the tree and said softly, "May I?" Denise nodded, a slow movement of her chin toward her chest, her expression impassive.

Micky clambered up from the platform where they were all gathered, scrambling over a huge boulder. She couldn't reach the tree—the sheer face of its escarpment prevented that—but she got close. Then she put her hands out in front of herself, in a gesture that looked for a second like prayer, and rubbed her palms together so that the tobacco fluttered down in a slow shower. The wind caught some of it, lifted it so that a little came to rest on the twisted root that was nearest to Micky; some of it blew further, cascading over the cliff onto the swirling water below the tree.

Micky turned to look down at them, her pale face luminous still against the blackened silver of the rain-soaked tree trunk.

"For good sailing," she said. "For protection against the storm."

The rain had started again—a slow, cold drizzle. But none of them noticed it.

25 / Jan

They were finishing up the packing now, Jan scanning the big bedroom to see if she could spot anything they might be in danger of leaving behind. This Sunday morning had brought the sun back while they were eating breakfast, spreading a bright parallelogram onto the dining-room table. The light was bathing the room now, and the air coming through the screens felt light and dry. Down the hallway, Jan could hear voices, laughter. Micky was bent over her suitcase, stuffing things into corners, separating a pair of sandals so she could slip them along the back edge of the case. Her smaller tote bag was already zipped shut after Jan had made a check of the bathroom to make sure the shampoos and conditioners had been cleared out of there.

No one had spoken about the experience of yesterday afternoon, not on the way back to Grand Marais and not since. They seemed to know instinctively that whatever had happened at Hat Point was literally a wordless experience, that talking about the mystery would spoil it somehow— diminish it. Jan felt sure that the one person who had most fully experienced that series of encounters was Micky, and *she* certainly was past being able to formulate in words what had gone on as she stood a few short feet from that great black bird. The message, the omen, was locked in her heart and in her dying brain. Whatever she had made of it, whatever she had intended her ritual of the tobacco to mean, it had changed her mood, had made her seem peaceful—even joyous.

But Jan was certain of one effect the day had had on her. In some wholly inexplicable way, she had found the resolution to her dilemma, the answer to Micky's request. She had felt certain about it from the moment the raven lifted off from the shore and circled the twisted cedar tree. Whatever messages had come to Micky from the bird and the tree, an extra message had been delivered to Jan—a bonus. And now she was ready to tell Micky what she'd decided—here while they were still alone, before the noise and distraction of the leave-taking could intervene.

When Micky set her closed suitcase on the floor next to her tote bag, Jan caught her hand before she could straighten up again.

"I need to talk to you, Micky," she said, "before we take this stuff downstairs." She was looking straight into the blue eyes while she spoke, saw there a quick flicker of understanding.

"Okay," Micky said. "Let's sit down then."

They walked the few steps to the edge of the unmade bed and sat down. Jan hadn't let go of Micky's hand, and now she folded it between both of her own hands.

"This is about what you asked me to do," Jan said, pausing now to draw a ragged breath, thinking, "Help me find the right words, please," without any clear idea of where or to whom she was addressing the plea. "You gave me until the end of this trip to decide, and now I have decided. I can't do it, Mick. I can't do what you asked, and I'm going to expend all the energy I can to keep you from doing it, to help you not *want* to do it."

Micky's facial expression did not change during this

speech—alert, attentive, unsmiling. After a few seconds, Jan could feel inside her own hands a small answering squeeze.

"I don't know what you mean," Micky said calmly, in the tone she might have used to say, "I don't know who is the premier of China." She leaned forward a little, bringing her face closer to Jan's. "I don't remember asking you to do anything," she said softly. "You know what my memory is getting to be these days. I'd forget my ears if they weren't holding my head together."

Jan stared for a few moments into Micky's eyes. She could see that Micky did remember, knew exactly what she, Jan, was talking about. But Micky had changed her mind. And she clearly did not wish to talk about it directly, did not want to explain why. Jan leaned toward her, put her own forehead against Micky's.

"Never mind, Toots," she whispered. "Some things aren't worth remembering."

Micky sat upright, gave Jan's hands a little shake to get her full attention.

"My memory is a funny thing, as you know," she said. "Maybe next year or the year after that, I'll remember what you're talking about." And here she paused, watchful, to make sure Jan was clear about her meaning. Jan gave a little nod, and then Micky went on. "But just now I can't recall. Do you understand? Whatever you're talking about, it's not in my mind right now. But I can't say for sure that it will never be in my mind."

"I understand," Jan said quietly. "Who can say what might be in any of our minds a year or two from now? The big thing is to find out ways to love the day we're in."

"Or at least to respect it," Micky said, and a little smile began to play around her mouth. "At a minimum, we can try to respect it in the morning."

"Oh, Micky," Jan laughed. "Bad. You are so bad." Then she slid closer and gave Micky a quick hug.

"So," Micky said against her ear. "Let's get this stuff downstairs. What do you say?"

They lugged the bags into the hallway, to the top of the stairs. Sharon came out of her room now, dragging her large suitcase.

"Jesus!" she breathed. "How can clothes weigh more when you take them home than they did when you first packed them?"

"Well," Jan laughed. "Maybe it has something to do with all the stuff you bought while you were up here."

"No, I swear," Sharon replied, groaning as she hefted the case to put it next to theirs. "The stuff I bought is in the trunk of the car. It must be the dirt. That's it! I'm ready to formulate this as a principle: dirty clothes weigh a bunch more than clean clothes."

"And how are you defining 'a bunch'?" Peg asked from the doorway of her room. "More than a pound?"

"Yes," Sharon answered, turning to grin at her. "And bigger than a bread box."

"Where's Lindy?" Micky asked, peering down toward the end of the hall. "And Mary?"

"Oh, you know Mimi," Sharon cackled. "She was packed before we had breakfast, and she obsessed at poor Lindy for the rest of the morning, just willing her to be second in the who-can-get-organized-fastest contest."

"That's the melodramatic way of saying that they're both downstairs," Peg chimed in, "with their suitcases poised in front of the outside door."

"I wish mine was there too," Micky said ruefully, looking down at the bulging suitcases near her feet.

"Do you think we could just throw them over the railing?" Sharon asked, draping one long arm over Micky's shoulders.

Micky looked at her for a few seconds before her face broke into a grin.

"Probably not," they said in unison.

"Oh, don't be such babies," Jan cried. "Gravity is on our side." She lifted her own suitcases and started down the stairs. She felt such a rush of giddy energy that the cases might have weighed twice as much without daunting her. Now that Micky had lifted that most terrible burden from her shoulders, she felt almost light-headed with joy. She wanted to rush at the others, swamp them in hugs, laugh out loud with relief.

Downstairs in the dining room, the table was cleared and the door to the deck was standing open. Linda was sitting sideways on the love seat, and Mary, twitchy with anticipation, was pacing from the table to the door and back again.

"I heard that bird of yours this morning, Mimi," Sharon said, after dropping her suitcases with a resounding thump.

"The one that sounds like a flute?" Mary asked, pausing at the buffet.

"Yeah, I guess," Sharon shrugged. "A lovely sound, anyway. High and far away."

"Like someone calling," Micky said, her face dreamy. She wasn't looking at any of them, but at the east windows as if she saw something there, in the birches.

"Well," Mary said, "This morning it was probably calling, 'Good-bye, but come back. Come back again.'"

They were quiet for a moment, looking at Micky, who stood with her shoulders squared, her face lifted toward the morning light. A little smile played across her delicate features.

"I love this place," Peg said softly, and the others nodded.

The door to the kitchen swung toward them, and Steve Olson came into the dining room carrying a book that looked like a ledger of some sort. He seemed a little surprised to find them so quiet. Jan thought he looked a bit sheepish, even shy.

"I've got my reservation book here," he said. "I thought maybe you'd like to reserve your spot for next summer. Beat the rush." And he gave them a wry smile. "This way you get your pick of any week in the summer."

The women exchanged glances. Jan could see in the other faces her own uncertainty. What would a year bring? What changes in Micky could happen in that time? Would she be able to make a trip like this next summer?

Micky turned from the windows now and offered one of her dazzling smiles to Steve, who reddened slightly with pleasure.

"Of course, we should sign up now," she said, walking toward him. "Can we have this same week next year?"

"Yes," Steve said, smiling at her. "July is wide open after the fourth."

"Would that work for everybody?" Micky said, turning to them.

The silence that followed her question was due, Jan suspected, to the fact that every throat in the room was closed. Linda stood up quickly and moved toward Micky.

"Of course, it'll work," she said. "We'll just clear the decks so that we're free that week. Other business can wait until August, can't it?"

The others were quick to agree, stepping up to the table to write deposit checks. Jan listened as the level of chatter began to rise, a soothing sound, signaling a return to ease and comfort.

"Jan," Micky said, as she fished her checkbook out of her

purse. "Could you help me fill out a check for Steve? I can sign it all right, but I might need some help with the rest of it."

She hadn't lowered her voice, hadn't tried to take Jan aside. There was a sudden stilling of the talk around them, so Jan knew that the others had heard, that they understood what was happening.

"Sure," Jan said, and now she felt no need to force the cheerfulness into her voice. "You just sign it, and I'll do the rest. If you find out in a month or so that I've taken a trip to the south of France, you'll know that I made it out to myself and cashed it for a million."

"Oh, I'm not worried," Micky said, ripping the signed check out of its pack. "I trust you." And as she handed over the check, she winked at Jan. "After all, I know where you live."

In the parking lot, they stood together near the picnic table, looking around in silence. The cars were loaded. Steve had volunteered to carry the larger cases, shrugging good-naturedly when Sharon drawled, "It's so-o-o nice to have a man around the house." He had taken last snapshots of them with the cameras that still had unexposed frames at the end of films. And then he took leave of them with hugs all around and left for a run with Duncan, the Airedale, dancing around him and then speeding ahead of him up the driveway.

"I wish you guys were all on e-mail," Mary said suddenly. "I'm telling you, it's wonderful. I can e-mail Carol in the Philippines, and she gets it on the same day I sent it. If you got hooked up, we could write whenever we felt like it."

"We can do that now," Peg reminded her mildly. "It just takes a stamp and a trip to the post office."

"That's snail-mail, though," Mary answered. "It's easier to stay in touch if you can do it right from your desk."

They began to move toward the cars, dragging their feet a little now that the moment of parting was so near.

"But the key thing is to stay in touch," Linda said. "By whatever means. Alexander Graham Bell gave us that wonderful invention, and we should resolve right here and now to use it more often. Okay?"

Everyone murmured agreement.

"We can't lose each other," Sharon said, her voice shaking a little. "Not like we did for a while there in the late seventies." Then she began rummaging in her purse for her car keys, as if she needed some activity to keep herself from saying any more, or to keep the others from seeing how close to tears she was.

"Well, that's not going to happen," Peg said firmly. "So there's no need dwelling on the past." She already had the driver's side door of her Lumina opened.

"That's right," Jan said. "We start over every day, anyway, don't we? The place to look is straight ahead, and just forget the stuff we can't undo."

"Of course," Micky said, coming up next to Jan and touching her elbow lightly. "After all, some things aren't worth remembering."

They took a last look around at the clearing, at the house nestled in its circle of birches, at the wildflowers that splashed color across the slope of lawn. Then they stepped silently into the cars and began the journey that would take them south along the rim of Lake Superior. The water would be calm today, Jan thought. Calm and bright under the summer sun.

A Reading Group Guide to
Seasons of Sun and Rain

Questions for Discussion

1. Having read *Seasons of Sun and Rain*, do you feel that the main audience for this book is female? If so, why? Because the characters are women? What about books in which most of the primary characters are men, such as *Moby Dick*? Are they primarily for men? What makes a book more of a women's or a men's book?

2. With which woman in the book did you most closely identify? Which of them did you like? How would you characterize the women in the book? Is Peg the most maternal? Is Jan, the psychologist, the perennial caregiver? Mary is the only grandmother among the six—does she seem grandmotherly? Linda, the photographer, likes to frame the world through her viewfinder. What does this say about her? Is Sharon's brassy exterior a mask for inner turmoil? And what about Micky?

3. At times, the women speak of the round-robin letters they have sent over the years to keep in touch. How does this help explain the way the book is organized, with the chapters moving from one to another of the six women?

4. Do you have an opinion about the ethics and morality of assisted suicide? Does Micky have a right to make that choice? Or to ask Jan to help? Why is it easier to accept putting animals, such as a horse with a broken leg or a dog mangled by a trap, out of their misery? What do you think of Micky's ultimate choice, in the scene at the Witch Tree?

5. Every eight seconds someone in America turns fifty. All of the women in this book have recently turned fifty. As Jan says at one point, "I don't *feel* any different than I did at thirty." How do the other women deal with getting older? Is there a freedom that comes at this age?

6. Have you known someone with Alzheimer's disease? Can you imagine, as Marjorie Dorner did in writing this book, what it would feel like on the inside if you suffered from this disease? How would it be different to have early-onset Alzheimer's? Note: Research shows that younger Alzheimer's disease sufferers do tend to react differently. They also tend to be physically fit and active, and they may be more aware that something is wrong because they have high expectations of their abilities and capacities. (Source: www.alzheimer-europe/young.html)

7. Do you think that women tend to have groups of friends more than men do? Do you think that people who are connected to groups of friends or have strong family bonds are happier because of that interconnectedness?

8. There is a great deal of bird imagery in *Seasons of Sun and Rain*. For instance, there are winter sparrows in the scene

when Micky first asks Jan to agree to assist her in committing suicide. What might those winter sparrows mean? Can you think of other instances of bird imagery in the book? (Hint: there are gulls, geese, hummingbirds, and a raven.) Do you think the author intends these birds to have significance?

9. The women in this book all went to college together in the 1960s. Do you think that decade of activism and of the blossoming of the women's movement uniquely shaped their generation? Are the issues for women the same today as they were then?

Other Readings and Resources

In creating the character of Micky, Marjorie Dorner researched Alzheimer's disease, drawing on organizations and books, including the following:

Living in the Labyrinth: A Personal Journey through the Maze of Alzheimer's by Diana Friel McGowin

Alzheimer's Association, 919 North Michigan Avenue, Suite 1000, Chicago, IL 60611. www.alz.org

Alzheimer's Disease Education and Referral Center (ADEAR), P.O. Box 8250, Silver Spring, MD 20907. www.alzheimers.org

National Institute on Aging, National Institutes of Health, U.S. Department of Health and Human Services

About the Author

Born in eastern Wisconsin on a dairy farm homesteaded by her great grandparents in the 1880s, MARJORIE DORNER published her first short story in a national magazine at the age of fourteen. In addition to *Seasons of Sun and Rain,* she is the author of a collection of short stories, *Winter Roads, Summer Fields* (available from Milkweed Editions) and four mysteries (all now out of print): *Nightmare, Family Closets, Freeze Frame,* and *Blood Kin. Nightmare* was the basis for an NBC movie in 1991 starring Victoria Principal. Dorner teaches literature and writing at Winona State University in Winona, Minnesota.

Praise for Marjorie Dorner's *Winter Roads, Summer Fields*

"In these dozen interlocking stories, Dorner evokes the reticence and austerity of a Wisconsin community. . . . Each story is accompanied by a date, like an epitaph on a tombstone, from the Depression to the present day. . . . In the best of the stories, Dorner achieves a pathos reminiscent of John Steinbeck."—*Newsday*

"Like leafing through an old photograph album, we catch glimpses of America. The Depression, wars, national holidays—all are recorded, discussed, and then put aside to deal with the everyday problems of rural living. The writing, like the characters themselves, is straightforward and emphatic, resisting the sentimental in favor of the genuine. . . . Dorner's skillful narrative makes these farm families come alive."—*Bloomsbury Review*

"Her sure hand matches her near-perfect vision in characterization, plot, style, and structure." — *Minneapolis Star Tribune*

"Perceptive and rich. . . . Her attention to even the smallest details makes every story ring with the clarity and power of a hammer against an anvil." — *Saint Paul Pioneer Press*

Interior design by Donna Burch
Typeset in New Baskerville
by Stanton Publication Services, Inc.
Printed on acid-free 55# Sebago Antique Cream paper
by Maple-Vail Book Manufacturing